AT
GENERAL HOWE'S SIDE
1776 - 1778

The diary of General William Howe's aide de camp, Captain Friedrich von Muenchhausen. Translated by Ernst Kipping and annotated by Samuel Smith.

ERNST KIPPING

SAMUEL STELLE SMITH

PHILIP FRENEAU PRESS

Monmouth Beach, N.J.
1974

Other titles in the Philip Freneau Press
Bicentennial Series on The American Revolution.

BRITISH MAPS OF THE AMERICAN
REVOLUTION
Peter J. Guthorn
LC No. 72-79889/ISBN 0-912480-07-6

AMERICAN MAPS AND MAP MAKERS OF
THE REVOLUTION
Peter J. Guthorn
LC No. 66-30330/ISBN 0-912480-02-5

THE HESSIAN VIEW OF AMERICA 1776-1783
Ernst Kipping
LC No. 72-161384/ISBN 0-912480-06-8

VALLEY FORGE CRUCIBLE OF VICTORY
John F. Reed
LC No. 70-76769/ISBN 0-912480-04-1

THE BATTLE OF TRENTON
Samuel S. Smith
LC No. 65-28860/ISBN 0-912480-01-7

THE BATTLE OF PRINCETON
Samuel S. Smith
LC No. 67-31149/ISBN 0-912480-03-3

FIGHT FOR THE DELAWARE 1777
Samuel S. Smith
LC No. 74-130878/ISBN 0-912480-05-X

THE BATTLE OF MONMOUTH
Samuel S. Smith
LC No. 64-56379/ISBN 0-912480-00-9

This Bicentennial Series
on the American Revolution
has been designed throughout by Paul R. Smith

Photography by Daniel I. Hennessey

Copyright 1974 by Philip Freneau Press
Library of Congress No. 73-94002
International Standard Book No. 0-912480-09-2

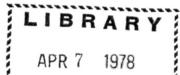

INTRODUCTION

The papers of the commanding generals of wars are frequently rich sources of war study information. It is fortunate, therefore, that many of the papers of three of four American and British commanders in chief during the period of the American Revolution have survived these nearly 200 years.

Letters written by General George Washington, the United States commander in chief throughout the war, are housed in the Library of Congress. Some of these letters were published in the early 1800s and also again in the late 1800s, but the most significant publication includes all known correspondence written by him that is held in public or private hands. The latter work was published by the Library of Congress in 39 volumes, from 1931 through 1944, titled *The Writings of George Washington from Original Manuscript Sources 1745-1799,* edited by John C. Fitzpatrick.

Other papers of George Washington, mostly letters written to him from 1745 through 1799, form another body of source material held by the Library of Congress. These papers, although not yet in published form, are arranged chronologically on microfilm. The use of this material was made more effective in the publication, *Index to the George Washington Papers,* by the Library of Congress, in 1964.

On the British side, many papers of two of their commanders in chief have survived. Those of the first, General Thomas Gage, who commanded from 1763 through 1775, and those of the third, General Henry Clinton, who commanded from 1778 through 1782, are housed in the William L. Clements Library at Ann Arbor, Michigan. These papers were acquired by purchase from British sources in the 1920s and early 1930s.

Unfortunately there is no similar body of surviving papers for the second British commander in chief, General William Howe, whose command extended from October 10, 1775 through May 23, 1778. This attests to our interest in this work. After the war, in 1799, following the death of his brother, Admiral Richard Howe, William Howe succeeded to an Irish title, as 5th Viscount Howe. It is said that in Ireland his papers were consumed by fire. General Howe's Order Books for 1776-1778 survived, as has the journal of Howe's deputy adjutant general, Lieutenant Colonel Stephen Kemble. These two collections were published in two volumes in 1884-1885, by The New York Historical Society, under the title *The Kemble Papers.* With this background in mind, we come to the present publication, a diary of an aide to General Howe, which should fill another gap in our knowledge of the Howe command.

The aide, Captain Levin Friedrich Ernst von Muenchhausen of the Hessian Leib regiment, was appointed wing adjutant to all German auxiliary forces, and aide de camp to General Howe, on November 18, 1776. From the day of his appointment until the General's departure from America, on May 23, 1778, Captain von Muenchhausen not only spent much of his time at General Howe's side, but kept an accurate day-to-day account of his headquarters activities.

The principal reason why this young officer was chosen for such a responsible assignment was that he could speak and write German, French and English. General Leopold von Heister, commanding general of the German forces, which made up more than one third of General Howe's entire army in America, understood German and French, while General Howe's only accomplished language was English. Prior to von Muenchhausen's appointment, orders from Howe to von Heister were much delayed in making translations. Upon von Muenchhausen's appointment, Howe's orders were passed on to von Heister and other German commanders without delay. In filling such a vital command link, von Muenchhausen was almost constantly at the pulse of the British-German war effort.

Captain Levin Friedrich Ernst von Muenchhausen, who signed his name Friedrich, and was called "Fritz" by his family and friends, was trained for such an assignment. His tutor had been his older brother, Wilhelm August Friedrich von Muenchhausen who held a similar position as aide to British Lieutenant General John Manners Granby, commander of British Troops on the continent during the Seven Years' War. It was to his brother, now war councellor at the Royal Court of Hannover, that von Muenchhausen addressed his diary. It was sent from America back to Hannover in eleven parts, the end of each transmittal being determined by the departure of a packet bound for Europe.

One of the remarkable facts concerning this diary is that it was actually kept on a daily basis. Von Muenchhausen aimed for truthfulness as witness this entry of July 7, 1777, "Be assured that, to the best of my knowledge, I do not write anything that is not the truth, and, since I am at English headquarters, I think one can certainly put as much faith in my diary as in anyone else's." Von Muenchhausen also tried to be as accurate as possible. If he found that something happened that was not quite as he had written it down the day before, he provided a revised appraisal. Further, Muenchhausen was the source of information for other Hessian diarists serving in America. He noted that he sent from British headquarters "information to Capt. Baurmeister and also to others who keep diaries, in spite of the fact that I am sometimes reluctant to do so, so that I will have something in my diary, which they do not mention."

It appears that the von Muenchhausen diary was circulated among numerous high ranking officials in Europe as well as in Britain. Certainly the diary was read by the Elector of Hannover, whose war councellor was Captain von Muenchhausen's brother, Wilhelm. Captain von Muenchhausen also noted that his diary was being forwarded to Brunswick where "the reigning Duke and His Highness, the Prince Hereditary, give me the honor to read my diary." Captain von Muenchhausen's uncle, Friedrich Ernst von Muenchhausen, was the personal councellor of the Duke. As to additional important readers of the diary, von Muenchhausen mentions on January 1, 1778, that he has learned from his brother that "a copy of my humble diary has passed through several hands and finally into the very high-placed hands in London."

The von Muenchhausen diary is housed in the Main Archives of the State of Lower Saxony in Hannover, Germany. The diary and other von Muenchhausen papers came to the State of Lower Saxony Archives in 1932 from the family Hammerstein-Equord on the estate of Equord near Peine in the vicinity of Hannover. It is not clear how the diary came into the possession of this family, perhaps it was through an aunt, Friedrich Ernst von Muenchhausen's sister Amalia Gertrud, who married a George Gottlieb Maximilian von Hammerstein-Gesmold. Additional papers were added to the collection in the 1950s, some of the material coming from the library of the estate of Apelern near Hannover, where a member of the family, Baroness Marie Louise von Muenchhausen, presently lives.

The manuscript division of the New York Public Library has a hand written copy of the diary, in German. It probably was made about 1870 in Germany under the sponsorship of William Bancroft who was U. S. Minister to Berlin from 1867-1874. The Bancroft copy is complete except for the dates February 15 through May 23, 1777. The Hannover diary is missing the section from February 15 through a part of March 3, 1777. No part of the diary heretofore, appears to have been published, either in German or English, other than a small section covering one day's entry describing the battle of Germantown, October 4, 1777. This entry was translated by the American scholar, Joseph G. Rosengarten. His translation was published in 1892, in *The Pennsylvania Magazine of History and Biography*.

Levin Friedrich Ernst von Muenchhausen was born May 11, 1753, presumably at Moringen, Kingdom of Hannover, Germany, where his parents lived, and where most of his thirteen brothers and sisters were born. He was the eighth child. After he became adult, he dropped the name, Levin. Friedrich Ernst's known paternal ancestors were Borries, Borries, Ernst and Ludolf von Muenchhausen. His corresponding maternal ancestors were Sophie Magdalene Christiane aus dem Winkel, Sophie Catharina von Voss, Catharina Sophie von Ditfurth and Anna von Bismarck. The early line of this von Muenchhausen family had been bailiffs of the districts of Remeringhausen, Moringen and Oberdorf in the Dukedom, later Kingdom, of Hannover, since 1594. In 1748, Friedrich Ernst's father, Borries von Muenchhausen, was appointed bailiff of these districts by the King of Hannover, with the rank of major general.

After a basic education in the house of his family, Friedrich Ernst, in 1768, at age fifteen, began his studies at the Collegium Carolinum in Brunswick as noted in his diary entry of December 6, 1776. After a year and one half of study there, he entered the military service of the Duchy of Brunswick, and was promoted to lieutenant in the Brunswick regiment de Corps on April 30, 1770. At age 20, in September 1773, he was promoted to first lieutenant, and was given the court title of chamberlain (Hofjunker).

On March 3, 1776, after severing his service with his Brunswick regiment, von Muenchhausen was given a captaincy in the Leib, or de Corps, regiment of the Landgrave of Hesse-Cassel. One month earlier, on February 12, 1776, Landgrave Friedrich II and George III of Great Britain had signed a subsidiary treaty to furnish Hessian troops for the American colonial war. The signing of this treaty undoubtedly was the motivation for von Muenchhausen's entry into the military service of Hesse-Cassel.

Captain von Muenchhausen left Germany for America at the head of a grenadier company of his regiment. Along with other German auxiliary troops, von Muenchhausen's regiment was landed on Staten Island, August 12, 1776. Three months later, on November 17, Captain von Muenchhausen was appointed aide to General Howe. While with Howe, von Muenchhausen was repeatedly urged to leave Hesse-Cassel service and to join British service in which Howe could assure him steady and deserved promotion. Von Muenchhausen declined these offers, but he did wear a British uniform throughout the year and a half he served under Howe.

In the spring of 1778, knowing he was going to leave his command soon, General Howe planned to do something for Captain von Muenchhausen in appreciation for his valuable service. Howe asked Lieutenant General Wilhelm von Knyphausen, then commander of German forces in America, to organize a new grenadier regiment from those already existing, and to make Captain von Muenchhausen colonel of that regiment. Von Knyphausen agreed, and von Muenchhausen was so informed. Von Muenchhausen was at first elated, but when he learned, a few days later, that General Howe was about to leave his command, he declined the offer on the basis that he too might now wish to leave America. When General Howe turned over his command to General Henry Clinton, Captain von Muenchhausen was asked by Clinton to remain as his aide, and wing adjutant for German forces. Von Muenchhausen agreed to stay, but less than a month later, he asked for his release so that he could return home.

There is no indication that von Muenchhausen was dissatisfied with conditions under Clinton. His reason for wanting to return to Germany was that the War of Bavarian Succession was imminent. It was his plan to see the Landgrave of Hesse-Cassel "begging and getting from the Landgrave permission to go and serve as a Volunteer with the prinz heredit. [ary] of Brunswick," in which service he had been prior to coming to Hesse-Cassel.

Captain von Muenchhausen sailed for home on June 14, 1778, according to Major Baurmeister in a letter to Baron von Jungkenn, Hesse-Cassel Minister of State. He wrote, "On the 14th of June I sent your Lordship by Captain von Muenchhausen another part of my journal so that the continuity would not be interrupted, though I am well aware that the said Captain von Muenchhausen can furnish a better account in person." Undoubtedly this was Baurmeister's letter covering May 18 to June 11, 1778, printed in the *Revolution in America,* edited by Bernhard A. Uhlendorf, 1957. (Dr. Uhlendorf also has been helpful in the preparation of this diary for publication).

It would appear that in his conversations with the war minister, and possibly with the Landgrave himself, Captain von Muenchhausen was persuaded to remain, at least temporarily, in Cassel, in the service of the Landgrave. Here, in April 1779, Friedrich Ernst von Muenchhausen married Charlotte Eleonore von Bardeleben, daughter of Ernst Christoph Wilhelm von Bardeleben, colonel of the Guards and later lieutenant general and commander of Cassel. Friedrich Ernst and Charlotte Eleonore had five sons and one daughter.

On January 6, 1784, Captain von Muenchhausen left Hessian service to return to Brunswick. Here he became chamberlain and Premier Captain of the administrative district of Gebhardshagen, where he died on January 25, 1795, at the early age of 42.

Ernst Kipping

Samuel Stelle Smith

TABLE OF CONTENTS

FIRST TRANSMITTAL
November 17, 1776-December 26, 1776

November 17, 1776. Our Leib regiment received orders to prepare for embarkation the next day.[1] On the 18th at seven o'clock in the morning we marched to New York [City] via Kings Bridge and the presently designated Fort Knyphausen, formerly Fort Washington, so named by order of General Howe, as I believe I reported in my last letter.[2] We arrived in the afternoon at three o'clock, after a march of 22 English miles.[3]

When we were about to make camp on the outskirts of New York, an aide of General Howe arrived, and asked for me. He told me that General Howe wanted to see me, whereupon I rode back immediately. I arrived at English headquarters in the evening and was presented to the General who appointed me his aide.[4]

In spite of the fact that my horses were very tired, I immediately left, and rode back to General Heister to whom I reported the news.[5] General Heister was very pleased with the appointment because he had often received oral and written English orders, which he did not understand.[6] Leaving General Heister, I again rode to my regiment, settled my account with Major von Wurmb whose company I had commanded, and then returned to English headquarters on the 22nd.[7] In the meantime the following events took place:

November 19. In the evening at ten o'clock, the Hessian grenadiers, jaegers, and the English reserves, a total of 5,000 men under the command of Lord Cornwallis, broke camp quietly.[8]

November 20. At dawn this force was ferried across the Hudson River on large flatboats at two spots and was disembarked approximately six miles from Fort Lee. Both Fort Lee and Fort Constitution were defensible.[9] On the morning that our troops were taken over, both Generals Washington and Putnam were in the fort. When the news of the advance of our troops reached the fort, Washington departed, after giving Putnam the command. Putnam, half an hour later, handed the command over to the senior colonel. Shortly thereafter the colonel took flight with all his men, without waiting for a single shot.[10] The rebels left behind 7 mortars, 32 cannon, 432 tents, 400,000 rounds of ammunition, provisions for three months for 5,000 men, and 73 invalids.

November 21. Beginning this day, Lord Cornwallis started to deploy his corps in the area toward Hackensack, and left only a small guard at the two forts taken the day before.

November 22. I had just arrived at the headquarters in New York when my General departed for the Hudson River by a big detour, and from there crossed to Jersey with two of his aides.[11] The others, among them myself, he sent back to New York with orders to keep dinner waiting for him because he intended to be back in New York late in the evening.[12] In the evening about ten o'clock our General arrived at New York, and all of us had dinner at that time.[13]

November 23. In the morning, Admiral Howe, Lord Hotham, Commodore Parker, Generals Clinton, Lord Percy, Governor Tryon, and some others arrived at General Howe's where they held a council of war.[14] Two of my horses have already perished in the short time that I have been an aide.

November 27. A brigade of English crossed over to Jersey.[15]

November 28. Three regiments of Hessians under the command of Colonel Rall crossed to Jersey.[16] Last night two couriers of Lord Cornwallis arrived at New York headquarters.

November 29. The two forts, Lee and Constitution, situated on the other side of the Hudson in Jersey, were razed.

November 30. Lord Cornwallis advances without opposition to the left toward the Delaware River.[17]

December 1 and 2, [1776.] Lord Cornwallis advances still farther, Colonel Rall follows up with his brigade, but he always stays to the right to cover the right flank of Cornwallis. Lord Cornwallis has arrived at Brunswick, after having covered the areas of Hackensack, Bootbridge, Bergen, Elizabeth Point, Elizabethtown, and Amboy.[18] There have been no important engagements up to this time, only small skirmishes. While taking possession of Brunswick, a Hessian grenadier, Captain von Weitershausen, and several grenadiers were killed.

December 3 and 4. Lord Cornwallis is standing quietly at Brunswick; he has orders not to advance, but to rebuild the dismantled bridge over the Raritan River, near Brunswick.[19]

December 5. In the morning, unexpectedly, General Howe went to Jersey in a sloop, taking us [his aides] with him. We landed at Elizabethtown Point and inspected the fortifications that the rebels had constructed between Elizabethtown Point and Elizabethtown. Then we went to Amboy, where General Howe and his suite lodged with General Grant, who with his 4th brigade of English, had been left behind at Amboy by Lord Cornwallis, with instructions to cover the rear. This was most necessary since all the information we received regarding the corps of General Lee indicated that he intended to cross the Hudson River and get into the rear and on the right flank of our corps.[20]

December 6. Early in the morning, and with great enjoyment, I saw from a distance my long-held post on Staten Island. My small redoubt, which we built, looked very large from a distance.[21] At nine o'clock we were off to Brunswick. General Grant was ordered to advance with us, leaving behind the 46th regiment. With the 46th was Lieutenant Blondel, who attended the carolinum at Brunswick [Germany] for a year and a half during my stay there, and whom I knew very well.[22] We were both delighted at meeting here in America so unexpectedly.

At four o'clock in the afternoon we arrived at [New] Brunswick where we met Lord Cornwallis with his corps. Immediately upon our arrival, the Hessian grenadiers received orders from General Howe to move out to the right one hour's march.[23] We dined at Cornwallis' headquarters, where I met two rebel officers. They were Pennsylvanians by birth and spoke better German than English. They were both upright and well-behaved gentlemen. They had been on an exchange-of-prisoner mission.[24]

December 7. In the morning the whole corps marched in two columns to Princeton.[25] The Hessian grenadiers and jaegers, who had advanced yesterday, made up the second column, marching one hour's distance to the right. Our column of only Englishmen accompanied General Howe. We marched in trains except for two battalions of light infantry, two battalions of grenadiers, 150 mounted light dragoons with eight 3-pounders, all of whom marched in battle order ahead of us.

The rebels were always barely ahead of us. Since General Howe was with the vanguard, we advanced very slowly, and the rebels had time to withdraw step by step without being engaged.[26] Jersey is a beautiful, though mostly flat country, but there are numerous small woods and dense thickets. In one of these woods several of our scouts were killed. They were supposed to have scouted to the front and sides, but they had not done so efficiently enough. They were suddenly surrounded, and so were lost. Following this incident, the troop of 150 rebels hastily retired, without our being able to chastise them.

In the evening we arrived at Princeton, which is 14 English miles from Brunswick. Princeton is a nice little town and has a fine college. Its main building has 36 windows on its length and 24 on its width, and is four stories high.[27] A remarkably excellent library

has till now been spared by the war.

December 8. After a dismantled bridge had been repaired, the march continued toward Trenton in a single column, the Hessian grenadiers having joined us last night after having marched as a second column yesterday.[28] Again today, we had in front of us a vanguard in battle order, which followed closely on the heels of the retreating enemy.

Trenton is 12 miles from Princeton. Beyond Trenton is a plain more than 200 paces wide with the Delaware to the right and a wooded valley to the left.[29] At two o'clock in the afternoon we reached Trenton outskirts. Some inhabitants came running toward us, urging us to march through the town in a hurry so we could capture many of the enemy who were just embarking in boats and were about to cross [the Delaware].[30] General Howe, who probably knew that the rebels had strong batteries on the other side of the Delaware, surmised that they hoped we would follow the straggling parties and become exposed to enemy fire as we reached the plain.[31] The General therefore ordered a halt of all troops except some light infantry and jaegers.

With these troops, General Howe, Lord Cornwallis, and three of us aides, went through Trenton and down to the plain. Just as we arrived, the rebels opened a terrific fire upon us with all their batteries, containing 37 cannon. The light infantry and jaegers were forced to retreat in the greatest hurry to the valley at the left. On their way, in the blink of an eye, they lost 13 men.

General Howe rode with us all around, stopping from time to time; he stayed there with the greatest of coolness and calm for at least an hour, while the rebels kept their strongest fire going. Wherever we turned the cannon balls hit the ground, and I can hardly understand, even now, why all five of us were not crushed by the many balls. Then, just as General Howe was about to move back into the town, a ball landed so close to him in soft ground that dirt splattered his body and face.

A little earlier I had the honor to receive a small contusion on my knee. We were just standing still when a ball took away the hind leg of my horse, and hit some stones on the ground, one of which hit me in the knee, and caused my leg to swell up. I was lucky, for my horse fell to the ground with me, with great force, and feeling the blow on my knee just then, I believed that I was really seriously wounded. Afterwards General Howe gave me a superb English horse to replace mine.

When General Howe returned, he ordered the troops to march into town. Lord Cornwallis was detached in the evening, with four regiments, to move to the right beyond Pennington, 22 miles away. It was hoped that he would find boats or perhaps a good ferry so that he could cross over [the Delaware].

December 9. News was received from Lord Cornwallis that a crossing was impossible, because he could find neither boats nor a ferry.[32] Besides, the rebels had been informed of his intentions.[33] He therefore returned to Pennington, eight miles from here.

Since my General has been in Jersey, I have received daily orders in English for all the Hessians with us, which had to be translated into German for them. It is said for certain that General Lee has crossed the Hudson with 10,000 rebels and that most of his troops are in our rear.

General Howe's First Adjutant General Colonel Paterson received orders today to reconnoiter along the Delaware.[34] He asked me to accompany him; we returned unhurt, even though the rebels shot many cannon and even more muskets at us. The rebels must know the house where our General is staying, for they have thrown several shells at our house. But so far none have come very close.

December 10. General Lee who is in our rear, makes our support line very unsafe. He often sends out raiding parties.[35] Last night one of them captured a small escort with eight baggage wagons. Six of Philadelphia's first and most prominent citizens, who are not in rebel service, have crept through the lines and arrived at my General's headquarters. They brought much information, I suppose. It is a great pity that we cannot get across the Delaware River. If we could, nothing would stand in the way of our getting to Philadelphia before the year is out. There is no broken terrain, but, rather, nice flat country leading to it. Philadelphia is poorly fortified, more explicitly, not at all.

December 11. Last evening and last night the enemy opposite us marched off. They left behind to oppose us 11 cannon, and according to two deserters, 4,000 men. The balance of the army has been spread along the river by corps.[36] The support lines behind us become more and more unsafe because of General Lee, who is very audacious. He has captured several patrols and individual dragoons with letters, and has also taken 700 oxen and nearly 1,000 sheep and hogs from our commissariat. Tonight 400 Hessian grenadiers and jaegers under the command of Colonel von Donop were detached to the left along the Delaware River toward Philadelphia to look for boats or to find any other means of crossing this cursed river.[37]

December 12. The rebels brought up from Philadelphia about 13 row galleys mounted with heavy cannon, some as large as 36-pounders. These craft are propelled by many oars, so that they do not need favorable winds to advance. With these galleys they alarm our riverside very much. We do not have heavy artillery with us, and if we did, we could not get them in place to fire before we would be attacked by the galleys, unless we did so at night.

The detachment under Colonel von Donop, which left yesterday, advanced as far as Burlington, 21 miles from here, and 18 miles from Philadelphia. They failed to find a way of crossing the Delaware River.

Most of the Gentlemen of Congress, or rather the States, as they call themselves, have moved from Philadelphia back to Carolina.[38] They realize that once we have crossed the Delaware we should soon capture them, and then elevate them a bit. It seems that they are not content to be quiet on this earth, so we might accommodate them by suspending them between heaven and earth.[39]

December 13. Victoria! We have captured General Lee, the only rebel general whom we had cause to fear. Because General Lee made things unsafe behind us, we often detached strong commandos to the rear. Colonel Harcourt, commander of the mounted light dragoons here, took 30 dragoons with him yesterday to make a patrol to the rear. He proceeded farther than usually, upon orders from my General.[40]

Early this morning he chanced upon a light dragoon of the rebels who was on sentry duty. The sentry was about to shoot but was cut down before he could fire. Colonel Harcourt reasoned that, judging from the presence of this mounted guard, the enemy could not be far away. He thereupon carefully pushed ahead and seized a second light dragoon on sentry duty before he could sound the alarm.

Under emphatic threats of being hanged, the prisoner confessed that General Lee with a corps of 900 men was not far behind. Colonel Harcourt was about to force this fellow to lead him and his party to the house where General Lee was staying, but the sentry said he did not know the exact location of the house.

While Colonel Harcourt argued with this fellow, he saw, some distance away, a rebel dragoon officer riding toward him. The officer was captured in spite of his efforts to escape. Upon being questioned, the officer at first would not admit that General Lee

was nearby. But when preparations were made to hang him, he not only confessed, but promised to lead Colonel Harcourt to General Lee's house.

Two dragoons, one on each side, rode with the officer, under orders given in his presence, to cut him into pieces if he attempted to lead the Colonel and his dragoons to the wrong house, or into a trap. A cornet with six dragoons, mounted on our best horses, were then detached with orders to guard the doors of the house. Harcourt followed some hundred paces behind the detached cornet.

The whole Harcourt party, including the advance detail, proceeded very slowly as long as they were not discovered. When they were close enough for the captured officer to show them the house where General Lee had his quarters, they dashed in all possible haste toward the house and surrounded it. Then, Harcourt shouted that he would set the house on fire if Lee did not come out instantly.

Meanwhile an 18-man guard detail of General Lee, which had been in the nearest barn, came out, and they and the dragoons began shooting at one another. Then an aide of Lee came out of the house, defended himself desperately, and, refusing a pardon, was cut down. General Lee and his adjutant general, a French Colonel, fired from the house with pistols, but Lee shortly came out of the house for fear that he might perish in the burning building.

Lee gave himself up as a prisoner and asked that his life be spared. The French colonel also came out and asked for his life while upon his knees.[41] Colonel Harcourt took them both as captives and rode off. Surrounding the house, firing, taking prisoners, and getting away, took only about four minutes. It all happened at 10 o'clock in the morning.

Lee's corps, which had been only about 200 paces away, closed in, in force, but arrived at the house too late to save their general, but soon enough to see us taking him away. Lee had to mount a dragoon horse. But since there was no horse for the French colonel, a servant of Harcourt who rode next to him, was about to take him on his horse with him. The Frenchman protested that riding the same horse with a servant was below his dignity. But after the servant had given him some good nudges in the ribs, probably also an insult to his dignity, he finally gave in and mounted, although he later complained regarding the indignity, in a pompous memorial to my General.

December 14. Since there is no possibility of crossing the Delaware, we were constrained to give orders to go into winter quarters. It was also ordered that inhabitants who ventured, in mobs or individually, to fire at our passing men, would be hanged at the next tree without trial. It is now very unsafe for us to travel in Jersey. The rascal peasants meet our men alone or in small unarmed groups. They have their rifles hidden in the bushes, or ditches, and the like. When they believe they are sure of success and they see one or several men belonging to our army, they shoot them in the head, then quickly hide their rifles and pretend they know nothing.

At eleven o'clock this morning General Howe started to ride back to New York, taking us with him. We rode to Princeton, where I saw Lee who has behaved very impudently until now, but has suddenly lost heart. The reasons are as follows: (1) He has repeatedly asked to see General Howe, but Howe will not see him nor speak to him. (2) He has begged to be paroled and vouches that he would not attempt to escape, so that it would not be necessary to keep a strong guard over him. The answer to all this was that a man such as he, whose life was in danger because he could be considered a British deserter as well as a rebel, could not possibly be trusted to keep his parole.

As a result, he is not allowed to write letters, and one officer and two sentries are continuously in the room with him, in addition to many other sentries being posted around the house in which he is kept. This is very annoying to Lee.

Lee is a man about 40 years old. He was a captain in British service, and a few years ago he was put on half-pay, as the English call it, with the rank of major. Then, he left England without taking his leave, and went to America to join the rebels where be became the second ranking general, with only Washington his senior. As to his ability and knowledge of the art of warfare, he is undoubtedly the first general.

December 15. Got as far as Brunswick.

December 16. Left Brunswick early in the morning and arrived in New York at two o'clock the next night. We met Major Cuyler, adjutant to our General. He had gone from here to England on September 6 to bring the King news of the first successful feat of our campaign, the affaire at Flatbush, etc. He brought back with him the Baronet or Sir William title and the Order of Bath for our General.

December 17. Received information today that the fleet and troops that left some time ago under the command of General Clinton have taken Rhode Island. The rebels had left it shortly before their arrival.

December 21. On orders of my General (note how important a man Fr. Muenchhausen now is, but he nevertheless wishes that he were still in Brunswick [Germany]) I am to take the Hessian grenadier battalion Koehler and an English artillery train, among them four 24-pounders and six 18-pounders, over to Jersey. The Hessian colonel of grenadiers has orders to follow my directions, and I have in hand a written order to all commissariats to give me needed horses etc. At 3 o'clock in the afternoon I embarked with my army and cannon, as well as 300 rebels, who were to be exchanged. As commander of the fleet of seven ships, I gave orders to depart by firing three cannon shots.

December 22. Early in the morning of the 22nd we dropped anchor at Amboy. I immediately disembarked and began to round up the 280 horses and ammunition wagons that we needed.

December 23. Disembarked the grenadiers and artillery early in the morning, and led them nine miles on the way to Burlington.[42] They were properly handed over to General Erskine, whereupon I returned to New York that night.[43]

December 24. Arrived at New York in the afternoon and was glad that General Howe was satisfied with the way I accomplished my assignment.

December 25. Two more English regiments left from here today to go to Jersey.[44]

December 26. I will now close my diary because today is the 26th, and letters will be sent tomorrow to the 64 gun ship of the line *Bristol,* which will return to England to be extensively repaired. It suffered dreadfully during the expeditions of Sir Peter Parker and General Clinton to South Carolina. General Cornwallis will go to England aboard this ship but will return next spring, that is, if there is to be another campaign, which we doubt.[45] And there certainly would not be another one if Congress or the free states would stop practicing the fine art of keeping the common man under rebellious arms by making pleasing promises, such as the coming of a French auxiliary fleet and 50,000 auxiliary troops, partly French and partly Spanish. Were it not for these promises we would surely have peace now. The short but successful campaign and capture of their best general whom they counted on most, depresses the rebels considerably.

I forgot to tell you that while my General was returning here today, I played the role of a dragoon.[46] I took 20 light dragoons and deployed them all around the General, about a quarter of an hour's march from him, to search out any harm that might befall him. I came upon five peasants with rifles who were lying behind a ditch. At that moment I had but one dragoon with me. They fired without hitting us, and then ran away. But we caught up with them. Two other dragoons, hearing the shots, rushed to our assistance. Two of the rebels were wounded, which must not be interpreted as cruelty, for a person is naturally hostile to anyone who has just endangered his life. Had I not intervened, all five of them would have been cut down by the dragoons.

Here [at New York] we have balls, concerts, and meetings, which I am already weary of. I do not like this frivolous life, and would much prefer that a campaign would begin again, or that there would be peace so that I could return to Brunswick and be a captain. I could certainly have a company of Englishmen, should I want one (they offered one to me), but I thanked them and refused, although British soldiers do exceedingly well, and most of the English troops will probably stay here for some time after peace comes. A large volume of letters written to and by many prisoners must be read by us [aides] which keeps us busy many an annoying night.

In New York are stationed: Generals Howe, Heister, Stirn, Mirbach, three Hessian regiments, and one English brigade, which consists of four regiments, and half a regiment of mounted light dragoons.

In Jersey are stationed: Generals Grant and Erskine, with posts at Amboy, Elizabethtown, Bergen, Powles Hook, Princeton, Trenton, Pennington, Burlington, Maidenhead and Bordentown. At Bordentown are four Hessian grenadier battalions and Hessian jaegers. In Jersey there are also the English reserves, consisting of two battalions of English grenadiers, 1,000 English guards, 800 Scots, and the 33rd regiment, altogether 2,800 men. Additional Jersey troops are one regiment of light dragoons, the English light infantry, consisting of two battalions, the Hessian Rall brigade, and two English brigades, plus the Waldeckers.

In Rhode Island are: Generals Clinton and Lord Percy, with a battalion of English grenadiers, one battalion English light infantry, plus half a regiment of dragoons and seven Hessian regiments.

On Long Island are: two English regiments.

The Delaware River does not freeze-up every year. If it should this year, I think we will push over it so as to have made the crossing before spring.[47]

December 26th, 1776.
F. v. Muenchhausen

P.S. I have reopened this letter to report an unhappy affair. Colonel Rall, who was at Trenton with the Knyphausen, Lossberg, and Rall regiments and 50 jaegers, was compelled to surrender at dawn on the 26th, after a fight of one hour, owing partly to the suddenness of the enemy surprise, and partly to their superior power. Two officers and 17 men the only ones that saved themselves, brought the news to us. We know no further details at the moment.[48]

SECOND TRANSMITTAL
December 27, 1776-February 14, 1777

[*December 27, 1776-December 31, 1776.*] To maintain the continuity of this journal, I will relate what has happened since my last letter. I believe that I mentioned the unhappy event at Trenton. Nine hundred and some seventy men were captured, together with six cannon and all the flags of the brigade, as well as the baggage.

To his good fortune, Colonel Rall died the same day from his wounds. I say this because he would have lost his head if he had lived. This unhappy occurrence has caused us to leave the whole of Jersey except for posts at Brunswick and Amboy.

January 1, [*1777.*] General Howe has sent Lord Cornwallis over to Jersey and has put him in command there.[1] Lord Cornwallis immediately marched foreward with his corps of about 7,000 men. To cover his rear, as he advanced toward Trenton, he left an English brigade at Princeton about half way between Brunswick and Trenton.[2] Prior to that, he recalled several regiments stationed between Princeton and Trenton.

January 2. In the afternoon Lord Cornwallis arrived at Trenton after several forced marches, which greatly fatigued his men. All of the time he was in sight of the retreating enemy army of General Washington, about 1,200 strong.[3] Since he could retreat no farther because of the Delaware River, which he would have had to cross, Washington quickly formed his lines into battle formation.

Lord Cornwallis did not dare to attack General Washington with his fatigued troops, which were further weakened by the troops he had left behind at Princeton, etc.[4] The excellent position, which he observed in the enemy corps was probably a contributing factor.[5] Lord Cornwallis then dispatched an order to have the regiments that he had left behind, join his force, so that he could attack the enemy the next day.

January 3. During the night General Washington marched with the greatest silence to our left without Cornwallis becoming aware of it. He detached, at the same time, a corps of 3,000 men who rounded our corps by forced marches over roads they knew well, and before dawn they attacked the English regiments in the rear of Cornwallis, at Princeton.[6] By good luck, the regiments, that had been ordered to join Cornwallis at Trenton, had set out to march already and were therefore under arms.[7]

The English brigade of four regiments at Princeton occupied a hill and defended itself very well.[8] Meanwhile, Cornwallis was informed that Washington had left, and soon after that, he heard heavy fire in his rear. Cornwallis rushed back as quickly as possible, and arrived with part of his corps not quite in time to support the English brigade, which, while defending itself bravely, lost about 300 men dead and wounded.[9] Lord Cornwallis then retreated to Brunswick, Amboy and Elizabethtown.[10]

(I forgot to report that on the 3rd [2nd] of January, the day that Cornwallis caught up with Washington at Trenton in the afternoon, he had, a few hours prior to that, attacked the rear guard of the rebels, killing and wounding about 400).[11]

The greatest loss the rebels suffered [at Princeton] was General Mercer, who commanded the rear guard.[12] This brave general, who was esteemed by the rebels and by us, was mortally wounded.[13]

If Cornwallis would have attacked Washington the 3rd [2nd], there would have been a decisive battle. If we had won the battle, Washington would have lost his entire army, for Cornwallis had a regiment of light dragoons with him. If we had lost, we would have sacrificed all the troops in Jersey, about 7,000 men, who indeed are the elite of our army, together with the Provincials of Jersey, and possibly everything, because we would have been too weak to offer considerable resistance. It should be remembered that we had sent seventeen regiments to Rhode Island.[14]

[*January 4, 1777*] *until January 31, 1777.* Up to the 21st of January, nothing noteworthy happened except that our troops stationed in Jersey have been continuously harassed by Washington. Having a sizable army, he has forced us to abandon Elizabethtown, inflicting the loss of 80 Waldeckers, and now we are occupying only Brunswick and Amboy.[15]

General Washington gave us a good scare also from the other

side of Kingsbridge, near Fort Knyphausen.[16] On January 18th the rebels summoned Fort Independence, on the other side of Kingsbridge, to surrender. They were in strength and they occupied the hills between Kingsbridge and Fort Independence.[17] General Howe intended to go there himself but there was to be a big festival because of the Queen's birthday, during which ceremony my General was to receive the Order of the Bath from Admiral Howe, in the name of the King. So I had to take orders to General von Knyphausen in Howe's place. I was ordered to accompany General Knyphausen on the mission and to bring a report back to General Howe.

I had additional orders to be delivered to General Agnew who was stationed at Harlem between here [New York] and Kingsbridge. He was in command of three English regiments, which were to march to Kingsbridge and reinforce General Knyphausen, if so requested by the General. Knyphausen had in his command only three Hessian regiments and two weak Free Corps, which small force might be called upon to face a superior enemy force.[18]

When General Knyphausen arrived on the spot and found the enemy strong, I rushed back, at his request, to get the three English regiments. By the time they arrived, Knyphausen had, with tremendous effort, placed a few 12-pounders and one 18-pounder (taken from Fort Knyphausen) on a hilltop opposite the enemy hilltop position (Kingsbridge being between us). We exchanged some cannon shots, and the rebels retreated.[19] Thereupon I hurried back to York [New York City] to report to my General. I arrived in time to see a superb fireworks and to have the pleasure of attending the ball. A crazy life it is, just having been under serious fire, and then seeing fireworks of joy and to dance.

Since General Washington continues to harass us in Jersey, as well as at Kingsbridge, orders have been sent to Rhode Island for six English battalions to return here.

February 1, 1777 until February 14, 1777. Washington's Headquarters is at Morristown. He persists with his tactics of continuous alarms, which make our men very uncomfortable. We shall be considerably weaker in the next campaign. I think he will achieve his objective if General Howe does not attack him.

The six battalions from Rhode Island arrived here two days ago and I have received orders today, on February 14th, to go to Amboy. I think, or rather, I suspect that my General will follow and that we will soon have some engagements.[20] The rebels devastate everything. Because of lack of provisions, the rebels will probably suffer from famine and we from sickness. Salt and ship provisions will keep us from dying from starvation. We are again expecting 10,000 men from Europe. I close here, to send this letter on the ships that will take our invalids back home.

Fr. v. Muenchhausen

THIRD TRANSMITTAL
February 15, 1777-April 17, 1777

[The portion of this transmittal from February 15, 1777 through a part of March 3, 1777 is missing.] of Brunswick seized a picket of 100 men of the Free Corps without firing a shot. The following night they intended to attack a picket of 60 Hessian jaegers and 40 Hessian grenadiers in the same manner. They went into action against the command with their bayonets, without firing a single shot. The command, which had just been assembled, fired one round against them and retreated hastily, because the rebels were a superior force. Two jaegers, who were late, fell into their hands. Once the campaign has started, we will again be respected by them, because they will have to learn running again, which they seem to have forgotten some time ago.

The diseases raging among them, the enormous lack of food, especially salt and of clothing, will, we hope, wear them out without our help. Here, at Kings Bridge, Fort Knyphausen and Fort Independence, and at Rhode Island, everything is quiet. It is also quiet on Long Island, where Governor Brown is posted with a Free Corps of normally 1,000 men.[1]

On March 4, 1777, Governor Brown was ordered to take his corps on a secret mission, which, however, failed. According to orders, he was to embark on boats with his corps under cover of two frigates and a few armed schooners. He was to land on the opposite shore in the province of Connecticut, roughly in the region of Branford. There he was to free the Scots and many Loyalists imprisoned there, who were suffering in chains, after which he was to withdraw at once.[2]

The rebels, who have spies everywhere, must have been informed of this, because Brown, when he was not far from land, saw the coast occupied by a strong post, which received him with cannon fire. These shots, as they claim in their excuse, plus the contrary tide, caused them to retreat hastily to Long Island. Could anything more be expected from a Free Corps recently raised?[3] Up till now, everything has been quiet at Rhode Island.

March 9. Today the January packet finally arrived.

March 10. The packet, which sailed from England the beginning of November, 1776, arrived.

March 11. The frigate *Thames* arrived together with a fleet of ships that brought provisions and ammunition. The frigate brought 300,000 Pound Stirling. By these ships I also received all letters that have been written to me from August 1776 until January 1777. Among them I received from Cassel a letter from Colonel Jungkenn with the information that the Landgrave had given orders to pay me the salary of a staff-captain for the last campaign.

March, 12, 13, and 14, 15. Nothing.

March 16. Mr. Morris, adjutant to General Lee who is in captivity here, arrived.[4] He is permitted to stay for some days and to visit General Lee. We aides have orders that one of us have to be with Mr. Morris at all times. This Mr. Morris, a very fine and cultured young man, is captain with their artillery.

March 17. Since General Howe has once again published a General Pardon extending to May 1st of this year, the rebels have had some deserters.[5] Congress has named General Washington, who is still ill, as dictator for half a year with full powers for everything.[6] News has come in that a Committee-man has been captured together with some officers. This was on the 14th, accomplished by an officer and 20 men who had crossed over from Long Island to Connecticut. Yesterday, while posted at Amboy we tried to attack a rebel post near Elizabethtown, but the enemy was on its guard and retreated with the loss of 14 captured and 12 killed.

Since several enemy parties had been seen in the region of Kings Bridge day before yesterday, we sent, yesterday, a mixed command of 150 men with orders to advance as far as possible to get information as to where and how strong the enemy was. We never know these two things because of our lack of good spies. The farmers are generally in favor of the rebels and are careful not to give us any information, especially since the English do not know how to pay spies.

This command was lucky enough to surprise a picket of 200 men in East Chester after having advanced about nine miles. Twenty-two men have been killed and 31 captured, among them a captain and the major who was in command of the post. We lost, in addition to three privates, Captain Campbell, whose loss is much lamented because of his excellent record.[7]

March 18. Nothing.

March 19. A detachment of 500 men and 50 artillerists with four 3-pounders under the command of Colonel Bird embarked on the North or Hudson River today and is escorted by a frigate of 32 guns and two sloops of 10 guns each.[8]

Nothing till March 25. The detachment went up the Hudson River. It is assumed that it is to take or destroy a very large, but not well protected, enemy magazine at Peekskill, about nine miles beyond White Plains in the Province of New York on the Connecticut side of the Hudson River.

March 26. Last night at two o'clock my colleague, aide Captain Knight, who had been sent with the [Col. Bird] detachment by General Howe, returned and brought the following good news. (N. B. On those minor expeditions, in which the General does not take part, he usually sends one of his aides and we take turns in these assignments. My turn occurred several times some while ago when the detachment was in the region of Kings Bridge, and thereabouts. It can be recollected that, at that time, I accompanied General Knyphausen).

On March 20, a Thursday, the detachment went up the Hudson River with a rather favorable wind. They halted on March 21 due to lack of wind, then proceeded on March 22. The incompetent pilot of the frigate, which was in the lead, caused the frigate and two of the transports to go aground at three o'clock in the afternoon. They remained there until the following morning, the 23rd, when the incoming tide fortunately freed the ships. (N. B. On rivers that are very deep, it is only favorable wind and incoming tide that free big ships, and it is therefore important to know the exact times of low and high tide, which causes the ebb of the tide. By low tide, the big ships must be in deep water known to the pilot, and they have to remain there until the tide comes in again, this being the way they pass through shallow water).

Toward morning, they proceeded in spite of being afraid that, because of their delays, their presence had been detected and they could expect strong resistance. They landed at Peekskill at noon, without encountering any resistance. General McDougall, who was in command there with only 400 militia men, escaped, but only after having set afire all buildings that housed stores. We set afire a powder mill, the barracks, and all boats, as well as four sloops. Nine 12-pounders were spiked. The magazine contained rum, flour, cartridges, candles, ham, butter, etc. In the evening our detachment embarked again and went back down river. They brought nothing with them except a few grape shot and the barge of General Washington, which he used to cross the Hudson River.[9]

March 27-28. Nothing.

March 29. Because diseases had broken out among our men, owing to their being so closely quartered together, a brigade of Englishmen was today transferred from Amboy to Staten Island.

March 30-31. Nothing.

April 1 through 4, [1777]. Nothing, with the exception that the frigate *Daphne,* which is on guard in the mouth of the Delaware River, sent in three prizes, among them a French ship that was to supply to the rebels 12 cannon, 6,000 pounds of powder, grape shot, and small arms. Since the last General Pardon of my General, all in all, about eight deserters arrive daily. They all agree that the lack of food and especially clothing is very great among the rebels.

April 5. The dependable news has arrived that Congress has hanged, without mercy, in Philadelphia, a young man of quality. He had corresponded with us and had special orders to send us some pilots from Philadelphia who knew the Delaware River well.

April 6. I had to deliver something to General Lee, who is in captivity here. I remained with him for lunch to get better acquainted with him. I was with him for more than three hours, which passed very quickly. Lee is a very intelligent man and a pleasant conversationalist. He speaks French very well, Italian, and some German, and reads Latin and Greek books. In the year 1764 and also in 1770 he was in Hannover and Brunswick. He remembered and described for me the honorable Prime Minister Muenchhausen, and also my brother the War-Counsellor. He spoke of the parade in Brunswick. In short, he described everything so precisely that I could not doubt that he had been there. But he did not miss an opportunity to make some casual critical remarks.[10]

April 7. Seventeen provision ships, escorted by a warship, arrived here. They had left England in November last year, but had been driven to the West Indies by unfavorable winds. They had come very close to the shores of Virginia where they were spotted by the rebels, who made 60 sails out of 17. The rebels thought for certain that these ships had troops aboard and would land there. Therefore, they hastily assembled all of their troops and sent an urgent request to General Washington urging him to send 2,000 men there. Deserters and other news sources confirm the rumor that 6,000 men from New England crossed the Hudson River a few days ago to strengthen General Washington.

For some time the enemy has been very quiet in Jersey. They no longer harass us so often as they did during the whole winter. They still do not want to exchange our captured Hessians but they did exchange a large number of captured Canadians of Carleton's army. Among them is the French partisan, St-Luc-Lucan, who made his name in the last war.[11] They have been embarked on four transports and will set sail for Quebec with the first favorable wind.

April 8. Although everything was carried out with the utmost secrecy, I discovered that much heavy artillery of the English park here was taken aboard ship in the evening. After making some inquiries I learned that twelve 24-pounders, eighteen 12-pounders, four mortars, and an especially large number of shells have been taken aboard. I always send such information to Capt. Baurmeister and also to others who keep diaries, in spite of the fact that I am sometimes reluctant to do so, so that I will have something in my diary which they do not mention.[12] Also 50 pontoons, which have been recently made here, left for Amboy today.[13]

April 9. I noticed that many transports have been made ready, have left the wharfs, and are lying at anchor here in the North River.

April 10. Nothing. Order has been issued that the packet is to sail today. Therefore, I close now. The last fortnight has been warmer here than it is during the dog days at home.

Farewell

Fr. von Muenchhausen

I hope that you can tend to my many letters as quickly as possible. But I like to write to my friends, hoping that I will receive as many letters.

April 11. The packet left this afternoon and this letter remained behind here, because of an oversight.

April 12. My General Howe rode to Kings Bridge in the company of Lord Howe, General Erskine, and several engineer officers. I noticed and also heard that their conversations concerned some fortifications, forts, etc., to be constructed there.

Late in the evening news came in that General Lord Cornwallis had set off this morning at two o'clock with the English grenadiers and light infantry, the Hessian grenadiers and the jaegers, marching in two columns, to surprise the rebel General Lincoln who, with 800 men, has been stationed at an outpost at Bound Brook.[14] Eighty men were taken prisoners, among them five officers, including the aide of General Lincoln, plus 14 were killed.[15] One 6-pounder and two 3-pounder brass cannon and the baggage were taken.[16] It must have been intended to take away the whole post. But since the two columns, which had different distances to march, left at the same time, it was not possible to arrive at their destination simultaneously.[17]

April 13. Nothing.

April 14. The frigate *Roebuck* has taken a privateer of sixteen 9-pounders in the mouth of the Delaware.

April 15. Last night the rebels captured a non-commissioned officer post of 12 men at Bonhamtown.

April 16. Another packet has been ordered to sail to England. Since one has just left, this, together with other rumors, strengthens the opinion that the enemy is near. I do not think that this is completely baseless.

April 17. From all indications I conclude that General Howe is planning a secret expedition. And I think that we will try to support the army of Carleton, since there has been no way of doing that. Everybody believes that General Howe will send a corps down into the Delaware River to land not far from Philadelphia. But, personally, I believe it would be better if we would send a corps up the Hudson River to Albany. But the rebels have strong batteries and forts on the Hudson River.

Adieu

Many rebels are still deserting. Numerous Hessians, and not the English, are now starting to get ill. From reports that I received from the General today, I see that the three Hessian regiments in the region of Kings Bridge have 1,363 ill.

FOURTH TRANSMITTAL
April 18, 1777-May 22, 1777

Dear brother, I hope that you and all of my relatives, friends, and protectors are well and happy. Thank God, I am rather well myself and will be completely happy as soon as we go on a campaign again. I cannot stand the cursed winter quarters, the continuous dining, festivities, etc.

April 18, 1777. The English frigate *Roebuck,* which is cruising in the mouth of the Delaware River, has again sent in two prizes. A rebel frigate that had too much powder on board and had tried to support the two prizes by attacking the *Roebuck,* blew up through her own carelessness.

April 19 and 20. Nothing.

April 21. At noon six English regiments amounting to 1,500 men, about 400 Provincials, and with six 3-pounders were embarked on the North River. The former governor, now Major General Tryon, is in command. General Sir William Erskine, a brave officer, who commanded the English dragoons in Germany during the last war, is also going with them.[1] The Provincials, who are deployed on Long Island had to make a move today, resulting in 500 men being stationed in the most distant part of Long Island.

April 22. At noon the ships set sail, the larger part up the East River, the remaining up the North River. Frigates convoyed both parties. Nobody knows their destination, which makes me very happy, because we have so many false friends around us, who report everything at once. At break of day our pickets at Bonhamtown, not far from Brunswick, were fiercely attacked by the rebels. But when they found all of us under arms, they at once retreated.[2]

April 23 and 24. Our ships that sailed on the 22nd encountered very unfavorable winds. The ships that had gone up the North River had many leaks, and the few troops that they had on board have been put into boats and the following night taken to the ships that had sailed up the East River.

April 25 through 27. Nothing. The empty ships on the North River are at anchor under the cover of two frigates. Deserters are arriving daily. Our Hessians are very ill and die in large numbers.

April 28. Nothing.

April 29. We received the following reliable news from our expedition: Since the wind was contrary, they did not land till Friday, the 25th, in the evening, at Compo Point, three English miles from Norwalk. From there they marched in one column the shortest way to Danbury, along the Saugatuck River, which they had to their left, a distance of 22 miles. The region that they passed through was so full of gulleys that Generals Tryon and Erskine confess that 300 good men could have stopped them. On Sunday, the 26th, in the evening, they arrived at Danbury without having encountered any resistance. The small garrison there had run away. There was no time to seize the considerable stores there, because they assumed from incoming information that the enemy was assembling to attack them. Thus, they were compelled to set fire to the town of Danbury, which was full of provisions of all sorts, and where there were 1,200 tents and much medical supplies, and to retreat as quickly as possible on a different route, which was five miles longer, but leading mostly across plains, the road passing through Ridgefield, which was also set afire because of magazines there.

On their whole retreat to the sea, where they did not arrive till the evening of Monday, the 28th, they were continuously attacked by General Arnold in the rear and by General Wooster in the front.[3] Close to the shore the enemy attacked especially fiercely because they had observed that we had run out of ammunition for the six cannon and of bullets for the privates. Therefore, General Erskine took three regiments and attacked with bayonets, which finally brought relief.

We had 144 killed, wounded, and captured, including 11 officers. We do not know the losses of the rebels, but I guess that they are considerable because they attacked very bravely and did not hastily retreat when we attacked them with our bayonets.

Generals Arnold and Wooster were seen to fall from their horses. Fifty-three prisoners have been brought in. From deserters, our spies, etc., we have the certain news that the rebels had more than 1,200 men and three cannon on Sunday morning when they first attacked us, but that they had increased so much, hour after hour, that they were 4,000 strong at the end.

They lost 500 men killed, wounded, and captured, among them General Wooster, who was wounded in the abdomen and died the following day.[4] General Arnold, whom our men had seen falling from his mount, is not wounded, but his horse was killed, for the second time. I personally surmise that it was the intention of our expedition to come back here by way of Kings Bridge, to find wagons and to take along as much as possible from magazines. The three Hessian regiments garrisoned here, therefore, had to march beyond Kings Bridge to meet the returning troops. But the enemy's unsuspected strength in Connecticut, did not permit us to carry out this plan.

April 30. Nothing.

May 1, [1777.] Last night 32 men with their rifles deserted from the rebels at Hackensack in Jersey, and came to us.

May 2. I have been on board a big ship of the East India Company, called *Empress of Russia.* This ship is being converted into a battery ship and the work is almost finished. An equally large ship called the *Britannia* has been prepared for General Howe and his suite.[5]

May 3. Again several prizes have been sent in by our cruising warships.

May 4. Orders were given to have tents and all field requisites ready for an expedition. Rumors differ. Most of them have it that we will leave Jersey, which is completely laid waste, board ships, and go as far up the Delaware River as possible toward Philadelphia.

May 5, 6, 7. Nothing.

May 8. In the evening the two aides, Balfour and Gardiner, who have been in England and who were promoted to majors by the King, arrived on board the ship of the line, *Augusta* of 64 guns. They had started their voyage from Portsmouth aboard the *Albion* of 74 guns. After sailing a few days the mainmast broke and they were forced to return to Portsmouth. This was the reason for their long absence.

May 9. My best horse, and as I believe, the best horse in our army, has stepped on a big nail. If I do not lose it entirely I am assured that I will not be able to use it again for three months. Bad luck for an aide. Several days ago an English colonel of the dragoons offered me another good horse and 100 guineas for this horse.[6]

May 10 and 11. Nothing.

May 12. The news came in that the rebels, on the morning of May 10, attacked the Hessian jaegers near Brunswick, but were repulsed. Toward evening they also fiercely attacked the 42nd regiment of Highland Scots, who occupy an outpost at Piscataway, but they also were beaten back. These two attacks resulted in nine killed and 22 wounded, and the rebels 35 captured and 26 killed.[7]

May 13-16. Nothing.

May 17. The packet for which we have been waiting for three weeks is still missing. While jumping today, I had a very bad fall.

May 18 and 19. It is reported that General Carleton has safely passed the lakes with 6,000 men, that he has taken Crown Point and is now laying siege to Ticonderoga. I do not believe a word of it.[8]

May 20. A ship's aide today gave a party on the ship *Fanny* for Admiral and General Howe as well as some other men and several ladies. They danced on the upper deck until three o'clock in the morning. Big and small boats had races and the best ones were given handsome presents by the Admiral.

May 21. Several farmers from this side of Albany have come in. They say that people in that region are quarrelling among themselves, sometimes had fistfights, and that consequently all those who were suspected to be Loyalists had to surrender their arms. Some of them have been hanged and many are imprisoned.

May 22. According to a rather reliable report, General Carleton's vanguard reached Crown Point on May 8. The reason why we have not yet opened the campaign is, as I believe, that General Howe is waiting for reliable news of General Carleton's arrival. Besides, we have to defend Rhode Island, Long Island, Staten Island, and a considerable part of Jersey. Our army, which has not yet received recruits, etc., either English or Hessian, has many losses by deaths, disease, and the Hessians captured at Trenton. Adieu. Tomorrow the ship sails, which will take these letters. My regards to each and every one.

FIFTH TRANSMITTAL
May 23, 1777-June 8, 1777

May 23. Our Leib and Prince Carl regiments together with the 63rd regiment arrived here today from Rhode Island.[1] It is said that they are to remain aboard and wait for our embarkation. Three battalions of General De Lancey's, who have been stationed on Long Island, have been taken across [the East River] and will set up camp on the hills near Fort Independence.

May 24. The three Hessian regiments who were stationed here, three of the four English regiments here, the 17th regiment of light dragoons from here, and the three English regiments who have been scattered in various places on this island between here and Kingsbridge, have all received orders to be prepared for embarkation. Today, on their ships, I visited the Leib regiment, to which, after all, I belong. I found all friends hale and hearty.

May 25. It was killing hot today, and I had to go to Fort Knyphausen, Kingsbridge, Fort Independence, and some five miles beyond that on the road to East Chester to deliver various orders from my General. He gave me 50 light dragoons for my safety, because one is no longer safe very far beyond Fort Independence. On this tour I visited Lieutenant Colonel Muenchhausen, who is stationed in the barracks near Fort Knyphausen.[2] I found him fresh and healthy in an arbored shelter, which the Truembach regiment had made on a hilltop for their beloved lieutenant colonel. From there he has the most beautiful, most distant, and most changing view.

May 26. Fourteen transports arrived from England under cover of two ships of the line. They had aboard 1,200 English recruits and 150 English chasseurs. Furthermore, they brought tents and kettles for the English. (I would like to mention, if not already known, that every year the well-paid English provide their troops with new tents and other field requisites).

In the evening a package with many letters arrived from England. As usual, we aides had to sort them out, which kept us busy during the whole night. I was abundantly rewarded for this effort when I found some mail for me. I would like to thank a thousand times all those who have sent me letters, for nothing is more enjoyable, and they make me very happy.

Please convey my humble respect to General Count Kielmansegg for the favors he has done for me.[3] I have received many letters but none from Brunswick, which I still love, and of which I never think without reverence toward my former sovereign and without fond remembrances of my former friends there. But everyone there seems to have forgotten me. I must have behaved badly to have no friends from there remember me with letters.

News arrived in the night that the rebels had crossed from Connecticut to Long Island the night before, and seized a captain and 60 men of our Provincials. They set fire to several barns containing forage, then left immediately. They were favored by a very dark night.[4]

At noon an officer came in with great speed from Brunswick with a message from Cornwallis that the rebels, who had a strong post of 1,000 men at Bound Brook and whose sentries were stationed close to ours, marched away in the greatest silence during the night at eleven o'clock. Our men did not notice this until two hours later. All reports seem to confirm that General Washington has retreated across the Delaware River.[5] Some light infantry, grenadiers, and light dragoons, under the command of General Grant, were sent after them to find out for sure which way they went.[6]

A second express rider arrived from Brunswick late in the evening with the news that our pursuing force had come upon the rebels (supposedly 10,000 strong) in camp near Princeton. When our force came close to them, we were driven back by some 12-pounders. But no human blood was shed, only the blood of a horse, for they killed General Grant's horse while he was riding it.[7]

Orders were issued this morning that three English regiments encamped the past winter here and there between Fort Knyphausen and New York, were to embark tomorrow morning. But when news came in that the rebels had retreated across the Delaware, leaving Jersey, the embarkation orders issued to the three regi-

ments mentioned above were countermanded. Then, when the second express rider arrived with the news that the enemy had not left Jersey, I had to ride at night to bring these three regiments renewed orders for embarkation. The fact that a sizable enemy corps can march away and be gone for two hours before we learn of it, shows that we are in a bad way in not having good spies among them.

May 27. The five English regiments embarked this morning. Captain Lorey of the Hessian jaegers has distinguished himself on various occasions. I asked my General if he would allow me to thank Lorey in his name; this would encourage him very much. The suggestion met with my General's approval, and I was so ordered.[8]

May 28. The regiments that arrived from Rhode Island a few days ago debarked today [at New York]. A transport that had some troops of the Prince Carl regiment aboard, sank when it was severely damaged upon hitting a rock. We saved all aboard. Wemys' Corps (formerly Rogers' Corps) of about 400 men left Kingsbridge for Jersey today.

May 29. The three English regiments that embarked on May 27th, arrived at Amboy in Jersey.

May 30. Today I brought orders to General von Heister that, of the three regiments that had been in garrison here and of the two regiments that arrived from Rhode Island, namely the Leib and Prince Carl regiments, the von Mirbach and von Donop regiments were scheduled to go with us [to Jersey], and must be prepared to embark. The Prince Carl regiment was to go to Kingsbridge at once, and the Erbprinz regiment was to stay in New York.

May 31. We were ordered to be ready for embarkation.

June 1, [1777]. Bought two horses today.

June 2. Nothing new happened.

June 3. The Anspach troops arrived here. They consist of two regiments, each having four musketeer and one grenadier companies, plus 44 artillerists and 109 jaegers.[9] Arriving with the Anspachers were 425 Hessian recruits and a troop of 50 jaegers, the Hessians having embarked at Rheinfels.[10] In the evening I went aboard the Anspachers' transport to find out their exact strength.[11] They seemed to be decent fellows. I hope they behave better against the rebels than the imperial army during the last war against the Prussian King.[12]

June 4. Three of the four English regiments that were here during the winter and the three Hessian regiments mentioned above, have received orders to embark tomorrow morning. General Howe gave a big reception today since it was the King's birthday. At one o'clock the fort fired 21 cannon shots, then the Admiral's ship fired two signal shots, which were answered by the Commodore's ship, and thereupon all the ships of the line, transports, merchant ships, etc., fired 21 shots each. You can imagine what thunderous noise it was, there being over 400 ships at anchor here. In the evening most of the houses were illuminated.

The newly arrived Anspachers give me much trouble; these dear people understand only their mother tongue. Today General Lee, for security reasons, has been taken aboard the *Centurion*.

June 5. At five o'clock this morning the 4th, 15th, and 27th English regiments were embarked, and at noon the Leib, Mirbach, and von Donop Hessian regiments went aboard ship. The Anspachers, for the time being, have been transferred to Staten Island. I had to go with them to familiarize them with their place of encampment, the position of their picket and sentries, as well as other necessary details. The Anspachers make my life miserable. Their paymaster and their quartermaster can speak only German, and I have had to trade their money, check their bills, etc. However, now I have gotten rid of this money business. I found an adventurer who speaks German, French, and English, and have had him transferred to the Anspachers. The *Somerset,* a ship of the line carrying 64 guns, arrived from England today with the English Major General Grey aboard.

June 6. The 17th regiment of light dragoons embarked, and sailed to Amboy this evening.

June 7. The English and Hessian regiments that embarked the day before yesterday, sailed to Amboy today. Nothing very definite is known regarding Carleton. I wish he were here. How happy it would make me to be with my beloved old Brunswickers.[13] Should they be incorporated into our corps, I would seize every opportunity to show them that, although I am wearing a red British uniform, and am still a Hessian captain, I am really a Brunswicker in heart and mind. In my present position I shall have many an opportunity to convince them of this.

June 8. Now, it seems, a serious attempt is being made to break camp, for the horses of General Howe and his suite left for Amboy this morning. Late last night the frigate *Ariadne* arrived from England. She did not come in all the way because of unfavorable wind, but she sent some letters by boat to General Howe. I hope that she will come in before we leave, so that I may also receive some letters.

Just this moment we are told that a packet to England is being readied and that she will sail within hours. So I will end this letter. I thank everyone who does me the honor of reading my poor diary. I am adding a distribution list of our army at the beginning of this campaign.

At Rhode Island, under the command of the English General Prescott, are four Hessian regiments, namely Landgraf, Dittfurth, Huyne, Buenau, and three English regiments, an effective strength of 2,750 men.

At New York, under the command of Lieutenant General von Knyphausen, are two English regiments and the Erbprinz regiment, a total of 900 men.

In Fort Knyphausen, Kingsbridge, Fort Independence, and on the nearby hills, also under von Knyphausen's command, are four Hessian regiments, namely Prinz Carl, Truembach, Wissenbach, Stein, and three battalions of Provincials, a total of 3,200 men.

At Powles Hook in Jersey, in intrenchments opposite New York, is one English regiment under Colonel Campbell, with 250 men.[14]

On Long Island in various corps are Provincials, about 1,000.

In Jersey are 70 cannon and troops distributed as follows:

At Amboy, under the command of English General Vaughan, are thirteen English regiments, four Hessian regiments, namely Leib, Mirbach, Donop, and the Combined regiment, the latter being the remainder of the Trenton-Rall brigade, and the English 17th regiment of light dragoons, plus 400 Provincials, total 6,150 men.

At Bonhamtown, five miles from Brunswick, under the command of Brigadier Colonel Webster, an Englishman, are three English regiments and the 71st regiment Scots, total 1,700 men.[15]

At Piscataway and vicinity, two and three miles from Brunswick, under the English General Leslie, are the Hessian jaegers, the 42nd Scots, a free-corps of Provincials (all close to the rebels), plus four English regiments and 1,000 English guards, total 3,300 men.

At Brunswick, under the command of Lord Cornwallis, who had everything in Jersey under his command during the winter, are two strong battalions of English grenadiers, two strong battalions of English light infantry, the 16th English light dragoons, and four Hessian grenadier battalions, who are under Colonel von Donop, total 3,500 men.[16] Generals Grant and Erskine stayed in Brunswick the past winter.

On Staten Island, three English regiments and the Anspachers, total about 1,950 men.

In grand total . . . . 24,700 men.[17]

This force is strong enough to chase the rebels, but is far from strong enough to penetrate deep into the country, leaving behind garrisons and ways of communication.

General Howe will go to Amboy with us tomorrow. We have exchanged all the English who were captured at the beginning of the war against the rebels captured on Long Island, White Plains, Fort Knyphausen, etc. We still held 2,000 of their men, whom we paroled so we would not have to feed them any longer.

When General Lee fell into our hands, General Howe did not want to exchange him, since he is looked upon as a deserter and not as a prisoner. Hence, the rebels did not agree to any further exchange (although they owed us 2,100 men) unless it involved General Lee.

The rebels hold of our army: 1,100 Hessians, 600 Highland Scots who came from England and landed in Boston not knowing that we had already left that place, and 400 English, total 2,100 men.

We heard that the French have recently sent cannon, rifles, ammunition, etc., to the rebels. This can no longer be doubted, since almost all of the last prisoners and the deserters that have come over to us, have had French rifles.

New York, June 8, 1777
Fr. v. Muenchhausen

SIXTH TRANSMITTAL
June 8, 1777-August 31, 1777

June 8, 1777. [continued] News has arrived that the rebels [in Jersey], who had retreated some days ago, supposedly to allure us into dangerous defiles, have again taken possession of their old reinforced camp, namely the very high and steep wooded hills.[1] At Bound Brook, where our jaegers are the closest to them, they have their first strong advanced post of 1,000 men. The few deserters who arrive now, all have French rifles. This confirms earlier speculations that the French have again sent large quantities of cannon, rifles, and clothing to the rebels.

June 9. The three English regiments and the Anspachers, who were on Staten Island, were given orders today to go to Amboy in Jersey. At two o'clock in the afternoon General Howe and one of his aides left for Amboy in a small barge, and Generals Heister, Grey, Cleaveland of the Artillery, and Erskine, and their suites, left in several sloops. General Howe arrived at Amboy at seven in the evening, and the rest of us did not arrive until 12 o'clock at night. General von Heister left Major Baurmeister behind in New York.[2]

June 10. Pursuant to their orders, the three English regiments arrived at Amboy last night. The Anspachers also had to break camp immediately and march to Amboy. Hardly had I arrived back at Amboy in the evening, when General Howe with his large suite rode through the whole encampment, stopping at each regiment and talking to the commanders and to other officers.

June 11. After General Howe had personally inspected all heights and pathways, and had given orders to put up entrenchments on various dominating hills, we started out for Brunswick with an escort of two English regiments, the Combined Hessian regiment, and some dragoons. The latter I deployed all around the General while enroute. We arrived at Brunswick after four o'clock in the afternoon without having been delayed by the rebels. At Bonhamtown Lord Cornwallis, General Grant, and others came to meet us. We dined with Lord Cornwallis, but not until almost 10 o'clock in the evening, because General Howe first had to inspect all heights, etc., and show them to the corps who were in command here at Brunswick.

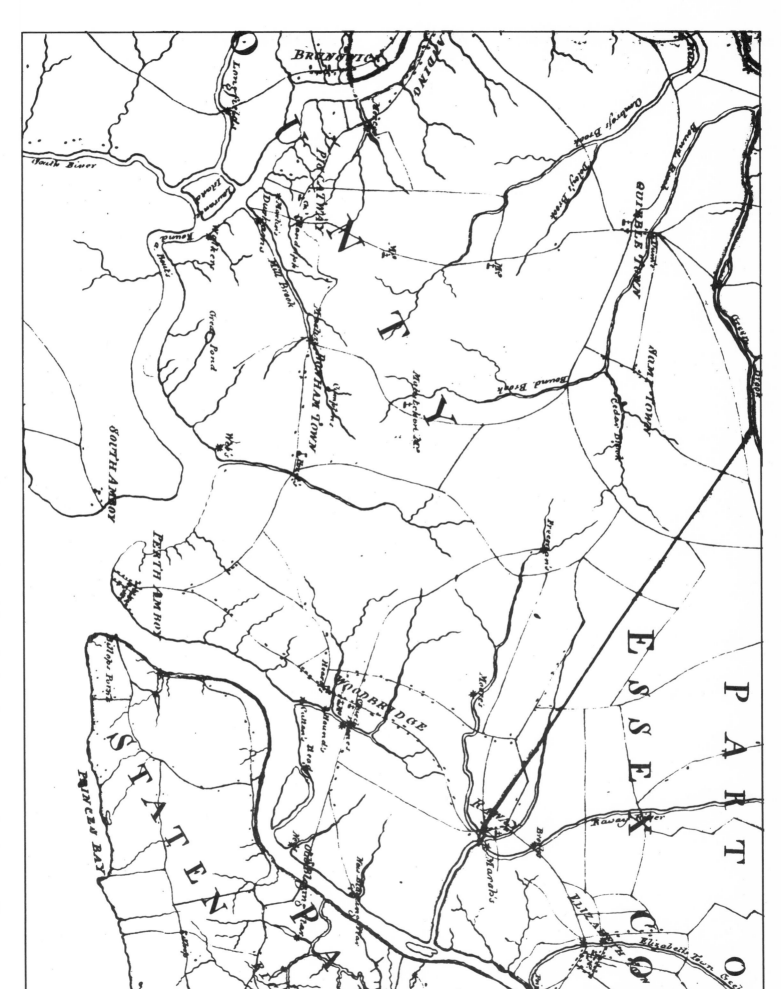

This is a section of a map made in 1781 by British Lieutenant John Hills, titled A Map of Part of the Province of New Jersey. . . . It is #11 in a twenty map atlas titled A Collection of Plans &c. &c. in the Province of New Jersey by John Hills Asst. Engr. This map

section and the section from the same map reproduced on page 17 are full scale, 3/4 inch to one mile and oriented north. The map is published through the courtesy of the Geography and Map Division, Library Congress. (See Br.M 57/34).

15

June 12. General von Heister arrived [at Brunswick] with most of the corps that had been at Amboy, and moved into camp at once. Left at Amboy as a garrison were two regiments of Anspachers, one Waldeck, and one English regiment, under command of Colonel von Eyb of the Anspachers. I have already warned the colonel to do nothing without the advice of an English captain I had left with him. The Anspach jaegers have come to Brunswick and have been incorporated into the Hessian jaeger corps under Colonel von Donop.

In the afternoon I rode to Piscataway, where the Hessian jaegers were on picket duty. At my request, Captain Lorey with six mounted jaegers did me the favor of riding forward with me toward enemy positions, particularly toward the road to Bound Brook.[3] I wanted to see the countryside, the roads, and the woods where, almost every night, the rebels had attacked our pickets during the past winter. Their outposts fired some shots at us, then ran away. Some imposing fortifications are being erected in the greatest hurry at Brunswick, an indication that our main corps will go far away, leaving this area exposed.

June 13. During these past three days, four light dragoons of the rebels have deserted. They are supposed to have four regiments of dragoons, one of them being Washington's bodyguard.[4] One of the deserters was of this unit. He wore a very nice uniform of white with blue and silver, also silver epaulettes and a nice headpiece. The uniforms of the others were red with blue, and red with black and gold. All are said to have good horses. The four I saw were well armed and well mounted.

Everyone in our army wishes that the rebels would do us the favor to take their chance in a regular battle. We would surely defeat them. I do not think that there exists a more select corps than that which General Howe has assembled here. I am too young, and have seen too few different corps, to ask others to take my word; but old Hessian and old English officers who have served a long time, say that they have never seen such a corps in respect to quality. The elite of the corps are the English grenadiers, light infantry, light dragoons, the Hessian grenadiers and jaegers. Every soldier serves with joy, and he would prefer to attack today rather than tomorrow.

At seven o'clock this evening it was ordered that all troops will set out in the morning in two corps, one under Lord Cornwallis and one under General von Heister, except that one battalion of the Guards, four English regiments, and the Combined English regiment will stay behind as garrison to defend Brunswick.[5] Tents and all dispensable baggage are to remain behind, and provisions for three days are to be carried by the troops. I believe that General Howe has planned a forced march at dawn in order to cut off and to throw back General Sullivan, who is at Princeton with 2,000 men.[6]

June 14. The following will show the course of events. Several misunderstandings, narrow passes, broken wagons, etc., resulted in our whole corps not getting started until half an hour before dawn.[7] When we did get in motion, we marched in a column formation for about three miles on the main road to Princeton, then the first corps under Lord Cornwallis marched a bit to the right, and the second corps under General Heister (General Howe went with this corps) marched on a different road still farther to the right, so that it looked as though we would be leaving Princeton to our left and were aiming to take a position between Princeton and Washington's strong encampment in the mountains. By this ruse, Sullivan's corps would have been cut off from Washington. But our late departure and the many good spies of the rebels, had allowed Sullivan to retreat to his left into the mountains toward the right flank of Washington.[8]

After we, the von Heister corps, had marched two miles farther and were not far from Hillsborough [now Millstone], it being across from us on the Millstone River, we heard some small-arms fire and later also a few cannon shots.[9] This was caused by Cornwallis' corps, which had come toward Hillsborough from the other side [of the Millstone River].[10]

A rebel major with 200 men was in the small village. Upon receiving news of the advance of our two corps, he destroyed the bridge that we had to cross to get into Hillsborough. The major with his 200 men engaged a corps of more than 6,000 men [Cornwallis'] in a woods and skirmished for about half an hour. We lost two officers and 17 men killed and wounded. After this he retreated in good order out of the woods.[11] And it was high time for the rebels to retreat, for we had just rebuilt the bridge and would have cut them off. Lord Cornwallis stayed with his corps in the region of Hillsborough, and General Heister's corps remained somewhat back on the road to Brunswick.

The headquarters was at Middlebush between the two corps, and was covered by the English Guards, Highland Scots, and one regiment of light dragoons. General Howe reconnoitered with Lord Cornwallis, General Erskine, and their suites till late in the evening. In doing so, General Howe was exposed to several rifle shots from the rebels who were hidden in the bushes.

June 15. The rebels killed two of our sentries last night. We have received certain news that last night Washington marched with his corps of 16,000 men back to Coryells Ferry, which is on the Delaware. He is said to have left behind General Sullivan (whom we had captured on Long Island) and 4,000 men, with orders not to get involved with us in a big engagement, but to skirmish around us all of the time, to cut our food supplies, and to capture small pickets, thus harassing us continuously. Toward evening, one of our jaeger patrols lost two wounded and one taken prisoner.

June 16. Four small redoubts are being erected on our hills [at Middlebush], I suppose for the purpose of securing our communications with Brunswick in case we march farther into the mountains. Many blame General Howe for not having followed Washington immediately. But I think he does not really believe yet that he indeed has left, and nobody in the world could be more careful than he is. This is absolutely necessary in this cursed hilly country. During the morning dragoon patrol, we lost two sergeants and three rank and file. General Sullivan harasses us very much.[12] A detachment of 700 men was sent to Brunswick to get provisions. Washington is a devil of a fellow, he is back again, right in his old position, in the high fortified hills. By retreating he supposedly intended to lure us into the hills and beat us there.

Two ships with Hessian jaegers, 305 men in all, have arrived in New York; a third ship with jaegers aboard is still missing. The saddles, etc., for the mounted jaegers are said to have been left behind in Portsmouth [England], because of the lack of a ship...a stupid reason.

June 17. Three English deserted last night, and three of our sentries were wounded. A packet is said to have arrived in New York. I am happily looking forward to the receipt of letters, since I do not doubt that at least one of my relatives has written me. No one writes to me from Brunswick from which place I would very much like to receive letters. I am completely forgotten there.

We hear nothing certain regarding Carleton and his crossing of the lakes; at least I know nothing. But it is possible that my General has some reliable information about him. The most widely spread rumor is that Carleton's vanguard arrived at Crown Point on May 28. We all wish they would finally arrive here, and I do especially, so I could visit with my beloved Brunswickers.

I have been on a very futile chase. It was a reconnoitering mission

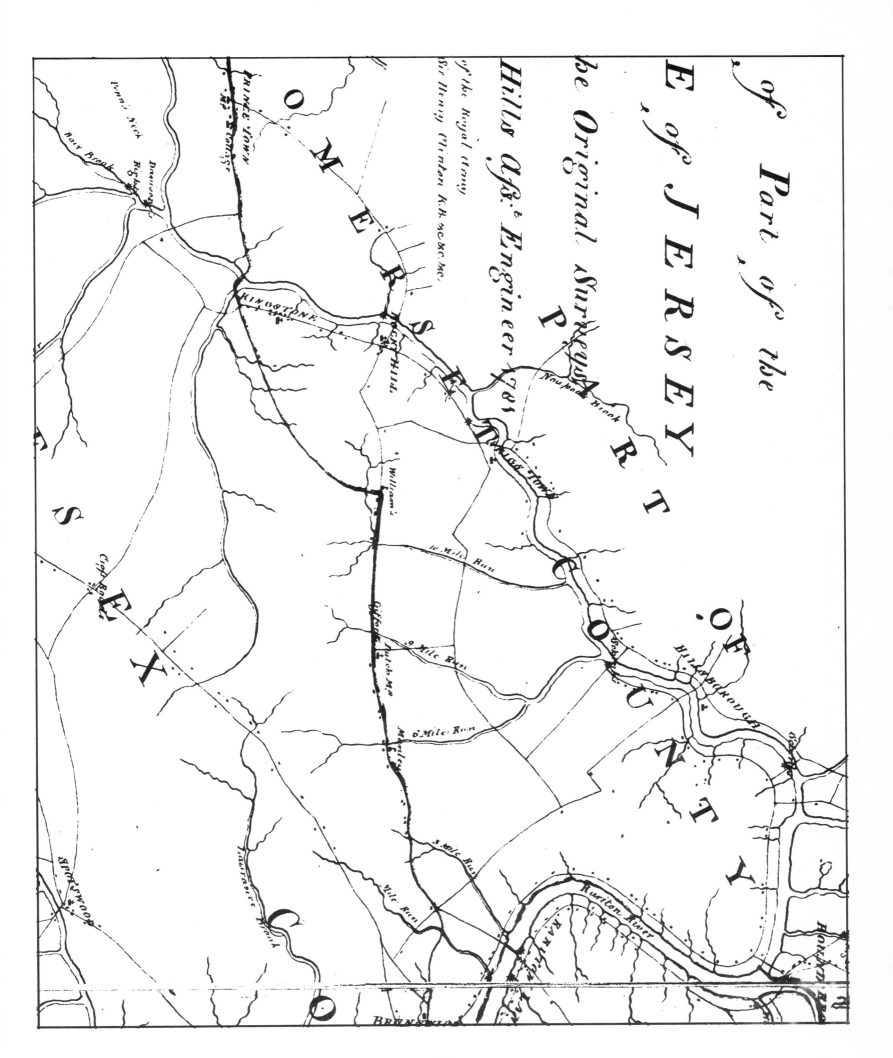

Part of the

of JERSEY

E,

SOMERSET

ESSEX

COUNTY

OF

the Original Survey in

Hills Ass.t Engineer 1781

of the Royal Army

Sir Henry Clinton K.B. &c. &c. &c.

Penns Neck

Rail Brook

Drawrings

Reg.t

Princetown

Cross Roads

Kings Town

KINGSTONE

Rock Hill

Williams

Newbork Brook

10 Mile Run

9 Mile Run

Clifsons Dutch M.g

6 Mile Run

Hills Borough

Rariton River

3 Mile Run

Spotswood

Lawrence Brook

Mile Run

BRUNSWICK

17

to gain intelligence on Washington's advantageous mountain position. I left at noon with my favorite comrade, aide Captain Knight, and proceeded rather far beyond our advance pickets. But we did not have time to observe much since a whole pack of light dragoons chased us. Some of them crept between us and our outposts along a densely wooded corner. Suddenly a whole lot of dragoons came toward us from the front, and as we were just about to turn back, the others who had gotten between us and our pickets, fell upon us and almost wore us out.

One of the many pistol shots they sent our way wounded my comrade on the arm, but only superficially. We were very scared, and narrowly escaped them with the help of some Highland Scots who had been out pillaging and came to our rescue just in time. I believe we wounded three of our attackers. At least one who was hardly three paces away and was trying to get ahead of me and was striking at me with his sword, fell from his horse when I took a shot at him. We did not tell our General of our experience for fear he would reprimand us for our ill-timed curiosity.

June 18. The road behind us in the direction of Brunswick is completely unsafe. Toward evening, a patrol of Hessian grenadiers and jaegers was fired upon from a barn. The officer was lightly wounded, and two sergeants killed, plus seven privates wounded, whereupon the rebels ran away into a woods where we could not catch up with a single one of them. In the evening, orders were issued that we were to march at dawn. No one knows where to, but since it is to be to our right, we are quite sure it is back to Brunswick.

June 19. At about four o'clock in the morning we marched in one column back to Brunswick. Since we marched off to the right by half companies, the corps of von Heister was in the lead because it was closest to Brunswick, as I have indicated before. The corps of Lord Cornwallis followed about 300 paces behind. Upon arrival at Brunswick, we went into our old encampments. We were not harassed in our march except for some shots, which the enemy fired from a distance at our rear guard and on our side patrols, causing two to be wounded.

Something very unpleasant happened, which made General Howe very angry. Last night two well-behaved young English grenadier lieutenants went about 50 paces beyond our pickets to see two sisters whom they knew during the last campaign, when we held most of Jersey. A third sister, supposedly because she was jealous, sneaked away and brought back a detachment of rebels, who made these two sons of Mars their prisoners.

Because our recent expedition seems to have failed, several rumors are spreading. Almost everyone blames General Howe, but I am convinced that many would have done worse, but none better. His idea was to take a position between Washington and Sullivan and attack the latter after a forced march, and completely annihilate him. The loss of Sullivan's corps would probably have caused Washington to leave Jersey and withdraw across the Delaware. We would then have followed him without interference and perhaps completely dispersed his troops, since we had large pontoons and large boats with us, which were carried on wagons built for this purpose. But since nothing came of our forced march because of misunderstanding and other mistakes, and because Sullivan was informed of all this, why blame my General.[13]

General Howe remained in Middlebush and Hillsborough for several days to see whether General Washington would withdraw. But since Washington did not fall back, I think that it was very wise of General Howe to return to Brunswick rather than attack General Washington, whom we could not have chased out of his advantageous position in the clouds without grave losses. Orders were issued tonight that the 17th regiment of dragoons and two regiments of English infantry are to proceed to Amboy tomorrow.

June 20. The regiments that received orders yesterday, left for Amboy early this morning. Some drunken English soldiers burned several houses. All our supplies are being taken from here to New York. Washington made a big bonfire in his mountain encampment last night.[14]

June 21. The grenadier battalion Koehler marched early this morning to Amboy and will, apparently, go to New York from there to strengthen General von Knyphausen's corps. At nine o'clock in the evening all units received orders to march to Amboy and to stay there prepared for embarkation.

When some days ago the entire corps marched forward with pontoons and boats, I surmised that the arrangements for a large embarkation, as though we were going to Philadelphia or Boston, were intended to confuse the enemy. But now I realize that without doubt, General Howe had two plans when he opened this campaign, so, that if one failed, he could start the second one immediately.

Rumor has it that Carleton has been defeated completely in the region of Crown Point and that this was the reason for Washington's recent bonfire.

June 22. A little before four o'clock in the morning the corps of General Heister, stationed on the other side of the Raritan River on the Road to Amboy, began to march toward Amboy. The rear guard was formed by the Anspach and Hessian jaegers who were attacked by about 300 rebels. We had one officer and four rank and file wounded. The corps of Cornwallis could not keep up, since being on the opposite side of the Raritan River, they first had to cross the river on a narrow bridge.[15] At the end of the bridge was a small height, where General Howe stopped with us and observed the passing troops, who looked quite sullen because of the march back. The Hessian grenadiers and the Combined Hessian regiment formed the vanguard of the column. They had just passed us when the rebels, whose dragoon parties we had seen for the past two hours on a bare hill opposite us, were observed mounting three heavy cannon on the hill. Soon they started to fire bow-shots at us from very far away. The distance was too great for their cannonade to be effective. The few balls that fell among us did no harm. General von Heister stopped when he heard the cannonade behind him, without having orders to do so. Therefore, I was sent to tell him to continue his march to Amboy.

Lord Cornwallis' force followed. The middle of this corps was between Piscataway and Bonhamtown when suddenly our side-patrols, marching at the left of our column in the woods, were so fiercely attacked by about 800 riflemen that they started to retreat toward our main column. General Howe hurriedly took the next two following regiments out of the column and personally led them toward the advancing riflemen. They skirmished with us for about half an hour and would probably have continued if General Howe had not brought up two cannon and fired several grape shot at the riflemen, whereupon they retreated. We lost about 30 men killed and wounded, the rebels, without doubt, lost many more. We captured one of their captains.[16]

The English light infantry and one dragoon regiment formed the rear guard of Cornwallis' corps. Right after the attack they reported that the rebels were still to be seen in strong force some way off.[17] General Howe probably concluded that the rebels might really have decided to give us a pitched battle on terrain of their own choosing. To keep the enemy from being able to boast that they had quickly driven us off, Howe posted the rear guard and the last part of Cornwallis' corps in two rounded lines on a small oval patch of level ground, which was surrounded by woods, there being only 20 paces between the first line and the woods. He put detachments of dragoons between the brigades and mounted cannon between the regiments of each brigade.

Shortly after this I was sent to Heister again with orders not to permit anything to detain him, but to march on, taking with him the three Hessian regiments and a few English regiments, and to put them on boats waiting at Amboy and to land on Staten Island in the region of Princes Bay, where the three Hessian regiments were also to be embarked. Then I had to order the three Hessian grenadier battalions, the Hessian Combined regiment, and several English regiments, which made up almost half of Cornwallis' corps, to proceed again toward Amboy and join Heister's corps.

When I came back, I found General Howe still in battle formation, just as I had left him. He remained in this position for two more hours, showing the rebel gentlemen that he was waiting for them with this small corps. But since they showed no inclination to come and do battle, he proceeded with great caution and reached Amboy unmolested.

If today the rebels had attacked us simultaneously at different places on our retreat from Brunswick, when we were in separate corps, I am sure that they would have beaten us up severely. Our corps was too large, and the terrain [the oval plain that Howe was in] was too small. This could easily have brought disorder.

In the evening at Amboy, I received some letters, one from the Privy Councellor von Muenchhausen, one from my mother, and three from my brother, the War Councellor, also a draft for 1,000 Imperial thalers, which I am sending back because I no longer need it.[18] I am dutifully thankful for the letters; they make me very happy.

June 23. This morning General Howe mustered the newly arrived Hessian jaegers and Anspachers. It is said to be a fact, at least the rebel newspapers report it as such, that they have taken the missing jaeger ship.[19] The Anspachers are exceedingly tall and handsome fellows. Without doubt these Anspach regiments are the tallest and best looking regiments of all those here. Time will tell how they behave against the enemy. Unexpectedly I found among the Anspach officers a Lieutenant von Donnerfeld, who served with me in the duchy of Brunswick.

Various regiments have received orders to go over to Staten Island today, but they could not do so because of the rough water. Two thousand men were sent out to cover our foraging parties; they came back without having seen any enemy troops. In the evening we received letters from New York that had arrived from England on a frigate; I did not get a single one. The recall of General von Heister, which had been expected for a long time, finally arrived. General von Knyphausen will take over the command.[20]

June 24. Early in the morning a deserter of the rebel light dragoons came in. It is said that Washington is planning to come down from the mountains with his strong corps to attack our rear guard when we leave Amboy. To this end he has already pushed forward the troops of Lord Stirling and the newly arrived French General Conway into the Short-hills, which are about six miles from here [Amboy] and are connected with the Watchung Mountains.[21]

June 25. The news that Washington is approaching has been verified.[22] In the afternoon at four o'clock, General Howe sent me to the Hessian regiments embarked at Princes Bay. I carried sealed instructions, which I was not to open until I arrived at General Stirn's side. Because of the rough water, I did not arrive until six o'clock in the evening, and then found in my instructions the order to proceed to all Hessian transports and order their respective captains, in the name of General Howe, to sail at once back to Amboy and to give their soldiers aboard three day's provisions. I was to tell the commanders of each ship to have their troops ready to disembark and march against the enemy, leaving behind their tents, kit-bags, in brief, all baggage.

Shortly before 12 at night, I had all the Hessians disembarked at Amboy without mishap. I found all troops there under arms. During my absence General Howe had given orders to take down all tents at six o'clock in the evening, and to leave these behind, together with all baggage. My General was somewhat displeased with me because I had not arrived earlier with the Hessians. Lord Cornwallis and General Erskine, however, told him that they were surprised that I had done it so quickly, without accident, and in spite of unfavorable winds and a dark night, whereupon the General seemed pleased and he praised me after first having been displeased with my conduct.

June 26. At one o'clock in the morning the first column, under General Cornwallis, set out to march for Scotch Plains region via Woodbridge. The second column, under General Vaughan, started out at three o'clock in the morning, General Howe being with this column. This column marched first along the road to Brunswick, then turned to the right, and joined Cornwallis' column in the neighborhood of Scotch Plains.

Cornwallis' column, marching to the right of Vaughan's, put a part of the Short-hills between the two columns. On his march, before the two columns could join, Cornwallis' column came upon a picket of Lord Stirling's force at six o'clock in the morning. Stirling was in that part of the Short-hills, which we had managed to place between the two columns. Stirling's picket ran off after a few shots.

Both columns continued on their march till about eight o'clock in the morning, during which time there was a steady fire on us from out of the bushes, and from behind trees. Their fire was answered by the Hessian jaegers, the English light infantry and our side patrols.[23] Then we [Cornwallis' column] met a corps of about 600 men with three cannon on a hill before a woods. They held their position until we approached them with some deployed battalions and cannon, whereupon they hurriedly withdrew into the woods behind them.

Half an hour later, on a bare hill before some woods, we came upon approximately 2,500 men with six cannon.[24] They started cannon fire early, at a distance of 1,000 paces, and then began with small arms fire. We took two 12-pounders and several 6-pounders to our left flank, where we had some rising ground. From our right flank the Hessian grenadier battalion von Minnigerode ascending the slope in deployed formation, attacked their left flank.[25] Our battalion had to move considerably to the right in order to outflank their left flank. The rebels continued a strong but not very effective fire upon us. They finally fired grape-shot at von Minnigerode's battalion, but after that, they ran away into the woods.

On this occasion the von Minnigerode battalion took two, and the English Guards one of their new French brass 3-pounders, which are very good cannon. General Lord Stirling, who was in command, had his horse shot, and General Maxwell was almost captured by the Hessian grenadiers, missing him only by a hair's breadth. The lately arrived French General Conway, with some volunteers, took part in this affair.[26]

A little while after the encounter, after nine in the morning, not far from Scotch Plains, our column [Vaughan's] joined forces with the rear of Cornwallis' and so we continued to march in one column until we arrived in the region of Westfield, where three battalions of Highland Scots were assigned advance posts. During the whole march, both our vanguard and our side-patrols were continuously harassed by shots from single detachments, which were hidden in the bushes. Westfield is about 13 miles from Amboy, 10 miles from Elizabethtown, 12 miles from Bound Brook, and 4 miles from the highest peak of the Watchung Mountain Range.

June 27. In yesterday's skirmish, or affair as it may be called, we had a total loss of 70 men, killed, wounded or suffocated in the dreadful heat. We do not know the losses of the rebels. We have taken three cannon and 82 prisoners. We also have the reliable information that they took away 37 wagons full of wounded. Therefore, I would think it not an exaggeration to estimate their losses at 400 men, at least.

About nine o'clock in the morning we started out to march back to Rahway, which is situated in the region of Woodbridge, still six miles from Amboy. We were not molested and did not hear or see any enemy. All news seems to point to the fact that General Washington with a corps of 10,000 men was advancing against us on the 26th, early in the morning, and that he had already passed Westfield to join Stirling in the Short-hills, out of which we chased Lord Stirling that same day. It is apparent that Washington's plan was to stay in the Short-hills, only six miles from our embarkation place at Amboy, until his spies should report that we were weak enough to be successfully attacked.

June 28. Today we marched in two columns by way of Woodbridge to Amboy, as unmolested as yesterday. Several English regiments and all Hessians except the jaegers went over to Staten Island today. Stirn's brigade also was embarked there. General Howe received some letters from New York, as did General von Heister, among them his recall, which we had expected for some time. General Heister's letters were sent to him on Staten Island, where he has disembarked.

June 29. Last night some English heavy artillery, and the baggage of the troops still here at Amboy, were sent to Staten Island. Several English regiments, the Anspachers, and the Waldeckers were brought to Staten Island today.

The battery ship, rebuilt in New York, formerly called the *Empress of Russia,* but now the *Vigilant,* which carries fourteen 24-pounders in addition to other guns, has been stationed at Amboy in the mouth of the Raritan River. On Staten Island, opposite us, in the same region where I had the command for such a long time last year at the beginning of the campaign, a strong battery is being erected to cover our retreat from Amboy in case Washington still has plans to carry out his first objective. But our last expedition seems to have taken away his desire to engage us here.

June 30. The 6,000 men still here [at Amboy] were put into battle formation in three lines. The last, or third line, which extends only a short distance, consists of six companies of English light infantry, both their flanks resting on redoubts they have hurriedly put up during the night. Regiments were taken out of the first and second lines, pulled back with their cannon, and embarked on 50 boats awaiting them. They were ferried to Staten Island in perfect order. Each time, twice as many troops were taken out of the first, the largest, line, than were taken out of the second line. Each time a line was so weakened, it retreated closer toward the water where they occupied less terrain, and therefore did not miss the departed troops.

The battery ship *Vigilant,* lying in the Raritan River somewhat foreward of the 1st line, pulled back at the same time that this line pulled back, maintaining the same distance. The battery ship would have given a respectable fire into the right flank of the rebels, had they tried to attack us. The first two lines were carried across to Staten Island in four embarkments. Then the last line, which had no cannon, was quickly taken across all at once. Generals Howe, Cornwallis, and their suites stayed behind on a hill close to the beach for a quarter of an hour, but we saw none of the enemy. Thereupon we also crossed over, mounted our horses, and rode to Richmond where we stayed over night. The troops had to encamp on the island.

July 1, [1777.] General Howe rode to Cole's Ferry [near what is now Tompkinsville], where we found some barges of the Admiral, which took us to New York and aboard the Admiral's ship *Eagle,* where Lord Howe treated us excellently. In the evening we rode into New York and went into our old quarters. Late in the evening General Howe paid an unpleasant visit to General von Heister, to whom he had not talked since the latter's recall.

July 2. The General rode to Kings Bridge, and after calling on General Knyphausen who is ill, he rode to Fort Independence and inspected the eight redoubts, which had been erected there.[27]

July 5. The frigate *Liverpool* of 30 guns, arrived from England with General Clinton aboard.[28]

July 6. Eleven ships with provisions and 100 recruits for the Highland Scots arrived from Cork, Ireland. Rumor is spreading widely here that Burgoyne is approaching, and it is very likely that Washington has detached three brigades, which are already on the road toward Albany. He himself is staying with his army in the region of Morristown, Woodbridge and Rahway.

July 7. Our troops on Staten Island have orders to embark tomorrow and the following days. I read a number of German newspapers today. I was surprised to find in them a lot of cruel lies about us. I have also had the opportunity to read pages of two different diaries that are being sent to Germany. I find that our accounts do not always agree. Should anyone who honors me by reading my diaries, find a difference between what I say and what is printed in the newspapers or written in other diaries, I must not be censured. Be assured that, to the best of my knowledge, I do not write anything that is not the truth, and, since I am at English headquarters, I think one can certainly put as much faith in my diary as in anyone else's.

If I were allowed to write down everything that happened here at headquarters, my readers would be extremely well informed, for much information not available to me before, is available to me now that I am with General Howe. But I fear that I would make some enemies if my letters are read in England, because I, for the sake of truthfulness, mention losses which in other diaries are not mentioned at all or else are diminished.

July 8. A big part of our army embarked today. When our troops first took possession of New York, there were all in all, fewer than 400 inhabitants here, including children, etc. Now, we have nearly 14,000 people here, including the military. Upon General Howe's proclamation, many older inhabitants and other loyal people came back and settled down here.[29] Also many English and Dutch merchants have come here.

July 9 & 10. Embarkation from Staten Island continued, and all troops are now aboard. General Clinton will remain here [in New York] and take command over the troops that have been under General von Knyphausen. The latter will go with us. It is rumored that 2,000 Indians have completely annihilated three regiments of rebels on the Indianfield and are now waiting for Burgoyne to join up with them.

The frigate *Daphne* arrived from St. Augustine in the evening, together with two other ships that had aboard the English 14th regiment. This regiment, which has been very much weakened by the war and by sickness, will go to England to have its ranks filled again. The news from St. Augustine is that the English Major General Prevost has, with 150 men, completely dispersed the vanguard of the approaching rebels. The American Indians there are said to be our good friends. They sent two scalps to General Prevost.[30] It is said that General Howe will go aboard on Sunday and that all will leave on Monday [the 14th]. Then we shall see where we will go, which is not known to anyone. Everyone surmises that we are going to Philadelphia.

July 11. Three light dragoons of the rebels came across from Jersey, swimming. The General gave them a good present for their extraordinary boldness.

July 12. We eight aides have been at General Howe's. A few days ago he dismissed one of them in a very polite manner, and today another, so that now there are only six of us.[31]

July 13. Rather reliable news makes us believe that Ticonderoga, 268 miles from New York, is in Burgoyne's possession. No one seems to be able to figure out why we are waiting here so long, considering the fact that everyone, except Howe and a few officers, are aboard ship. Some malcontents have given some rather unfounded and unworthy reason for this delay.[32] I, for my part, am sure that we will depart when we get reliable information from Burgoyne. I would give anything if he were here. Then I would have the pleasure of seeing my dear Brunswickers again.

July 14. Some deserters have arrived and brought confirmation of the news of the capture of Ticonderoga and of the consequent restlessness of the rebels. We also received from these deserters a Philadelphia newspaper of July 2, in which they report that the northern army had passed the Lakes and was on the march to Ticonderoga. The General sent me to Kings Bridge to tell General Knyphausen that he would today be replaced by General Clinton, and that he should return to New York and prepare for momentary embarkment.

In the afternoon we received the unpleasant but reliable news that during the night of last Thursday to Friday [the 10th/11th], 24 rebels came from Connecticut to Rhode Island in two small boats, eluding all sentries, and at one o'clock in the morning, seized the English Major General Prescott, together with an aide and one picket, and took them away. Revenge for Lee.

General Prescott had taken quarters in a house a quarter of an hour behind the camp, about half an hour from the coast. His guard consisted of one noncommissioned officer and eight men who were staying in an outbuilding 30 paces from the house. The sentry at his door must either have been asleep or was bribed, since not a single shot was fired.[33] General Leslie who commands the Highland Scots, has broken his leg. It is a pity that we have to leave behind this very able and upright general, the like of which the English have only a few.

July 15. The English General Pigot is to go to Rhode Island to take command there. General Howe is in a difficult situation because he has but few capable generals under his command here. It is said reliably that we are going to board our ships tomorrow. We have no longer any reason to doubt the news of the capture of Ticonderoga, for my General personally received letters today from Burgoyne.[34]

General Washington has marched up the North River and camped last night opposite Fort Knyphausen. Upon receipt of this news, the battery ship *Vigilant* and two galleys were sent up the North River to anchor close to Fort Knyphausen, thus increasing its safety. Eleven ships with provisions and 200 recruits, mostly for the Highland Scots, arrived from Ireland. There were twelve ships making the voyage, but one of them, whose captain was well disposed toward the rebels, stole away during the crossing.

July 16. Washington has marched still farther up the North River to Clarkstown [Rockland County, New York], 30 miles from Powles Hook. It is said by some that he intends to go farther up to meet Burgoyne, and to beat him while we are amusing ourselves with navigation.[35] I believe that General Howe would like to see General Washington cross the North River, and proceed on our side.

General Knyphausen is aboard the *Nonsuch,* a ship of 64 guns. Lord Cornwallis and General Grant are aboard the *Isis* of 50 guns.

A younger brother of Lord Cornwallis is captain of the *Isis.*[36] General Grey is aboard the *Somerset* of 64 guns. The artillery ship, *Brilliant,* arrived in the evening from Portsmouth [England] with 164 artillerists, of whom we have great need, because till now we have had not more than two or three artillerists with most of the cannon.

July 17. Since all our belongings were aboard ship, General Howe had to eat in a tavern today. All the invited English generals and their adjutants, but not a single Hessian officer, dined with us, there being 56 seated at a long table. In the evening at seven o'clock, General Howe, two of his senior aides, and his first secretary, went on board his brother's flagship, the *Eagle.* The other three aides (attrition has brought our number down to five), went on board General Howe's ship the *Britannia.* She was a big ship of the East India Company before purchase by the Crown. Rebuilt and luxuriously furnished, she was sent over here two years ago for the use of General Howe and his suite.

The ship has two decks, each of which has a hall and four state rooms, in addition to various small rooms. The two halls and eight rooms are lacquered white, with gold skirtboards. Built into the walls are several mirrors and beautiful copper engravings. It is difficult to imagine how beautiful it is to see the undulating light green sea with many ships reflected into the mirrors through big port holes.

All wood is mahogany, and all furniture is luxurious. From the hall of the upper deck one can go to a gallery, which is very pleasant. The gallery leads outside around the quarterdeck of the ship. If anyone who has not seen a ship of 700 to 800 tons, doubts my description concerning the spaciousness of the *Britannia,* let him bear in mind that she is as large as a ship of the line carrying 50 guns and 400 men, plus much ammunition, provisions, etc. Yet, she has nothing like this aboard, other than 30 sailors. Thus, the ship serves only the ease and comfort of the General.

July 18. We are lying at anchor while attempting to divide the large number of ships into divisions and agent's flotillas. I have not yet received the final count, nor have I been able to count them myself, but we are estimating that their number slightly exceeds three hundred.[37]

The 17th, 26th, 35th, and 38th English regiments and a regiment of Anspachers that was embarked with the English regiments, were disembarked yesterday and will stay behind on the island of New York to reinforce General Clinton. General Howe, who is very cautious, does this, I believe, because we have received reliable information that Washington is very strong (many claim more than 25,000 men), and is quietly positioned somewhere opposite Peekskill. In this position he is threatening Kings Bridge and the approaching General Burgoyne.

I wonder what kind of maneuver Washington will carry out once he is convinced that we are going to his capital, Philadelphia, which, I have no doubt, is now our objective. I fear that he will make some forced marches and attack Burgoyne who is believed not to be very strong, and, from what I hear, is eager to do battle, and that after this, Washington will return to us. It would have been better if we had not stayed here so long, but had gone to Philadelphia four weeks ago—these are my ideas. We could then be returning by land to support Burgoyne. Nevertheless, I hope that everything will turn out well.

I noticed some days ago that several men were sent to Burgoyne with tactical orders. Heaven may render that one of them will get through, and that Burgoyne will be careful. I believe that General Clinton could make a diversionary march along the North River to assist Burgoyne, because Clinton now has more than 7,000 men, including the Provincials. He may already have instructions to do just that.

A few days ago I had an opportunity to copy the following list of our embarked regiments and their strengths, including servants, laborers, and some washer-women with each company.

ENGLISH

16th mounted regiment of light dragoons	300
English Guards	945
Light infantry	1424
Grenadiers	1271
4th regiment (1st brigade)	352
23rd regiment (1st brigade)	416
28th regiment (1st brigade)	379
49th regiment (1st brigade)	400
5th regiment (2nd brigade)	400
10th regiment (2nd brigade)	300
27th regiment (2nd brigade)	333
40th regiment (2nd brigade)	320
55th regiment (2nd brigade)	274
15th regiment (3rd brigade)	378
17th regiment (3rd brigade)	233
42nd regiment (3rd brigade)	624
44th regiment (3rd brigade)	366
33rd regiment (4th brigade)	363
37th regiment (4th brigade)	362
46th regiment (4th brigade)	335
64th regiment (4th brigade)	446
71st regiment Scots (5th brigade)	1218
Chasseurs [Ferguson's rifles] (5th brigade)	130
Provincials [Queen's Rangers, unbrigaded]	278
Sappers	210

HESSIANS

Grenadier battalion von Linsing [Von Donop's brigade]	425
Grenadier battalion von Minnigerode [Von Donop's brigade]	446
Grenadier battalion von Lengerke [Von Donop's brigade]	420
Leib regiment [Stirn's brigade]	710
Regiment von Donop [Stirn's brigade]	624
Regiment von Mirbach [Stirn's brigade]	705
[Combined regiment] Von Loos' brigade, consisting of the pitiful remains of the regiments von Knyphausen, von Lossberg, and von Rall	517
Hessian and Anspach jaegers [von Loos' brigade]	594
Total (not including artillery and sappers)[38]	16,498

July 19. In the morning the Admiral's ship gave the signal to set sail.[39] The skipper of the ship of the line *Nonsuch,* being the ranking captain, serves as commodore; he therefore repeats all the signals of the Admiral's ship, which is especially necessary with such a large fleet.[40] Anchors were weighed, but the wind was too weak and too unfavorable, so that we were forced to drop anchors again without having advanced much.

During the afternoon four frigates came in, two from Quebec, one of them was the *Apollo,* which had brought General Burgoyne from England in the Spring. Another had cruised in the West Indies, and still another off Boston. In the evening I went aboard the Admiral's ship. Our ship had orders to keep, at all times, close to it. There I heard that the four frigates that arrived today will go with us.

It has been rumored for a long time that the 32 gun frigate *Repulse* was wrecked in a storm last winter while cruising off New York. She was the ship that had escorted to New York the rest of the 1st Hessian division under Major General von Mirbach, that had

been left behind at Bremerlehe.[41] I did not want to mention this before, but I do so now, because even Lord Howe does no longer have any doubt about it.

The Hessians, especially, deplore the loss of Captain Davis of this frigate.[42] He was an outstanding, upright man, who every day invited several Hessian officers to his quarters while on the voyage from England to New York. He was in every respect an exception to the run of English ship captains. The *Repulse* had been taken from the French during the last war when she was called the *Bellona.*

July 20. The wind was more favorable, and all transports were signaled to set sail under guidance of their agents. They took the same route by which we arrived last year, moving slowly toward Sandy Hook. The wind was too weak to permit the ships of the line to come along. In the evening the men on our ship [the *Britannia*] were joined by a Mister Robinson who had escaped from Philadelphia to New York for fear of being hanged by the rebels, since they had intercepted one of his letters to my General.

July 21. The Admiral's ship, the other large ships, and some transports that had been left behind yesterday, plus more than 50 small craft with horses of our army, got under sail with a good wind at five o'clock in the morning. But the wind became weaker and weaker, and we hardly made it to Sandy Hook, where the ships that had set sail yesterday were lying at anchor. The English frigate *Sphinx* met us on its way to New York, whereupon it received orders to go with us.

July 22. The wind was contrary; we therefore stayed at anchor. It is said with assurance that the English frigate *Fox* of 28 guns, which has been on station near Newfoundland, has been taken by two rebel frigates. She is said to have been lying at anchor and was careless enough to allow the two rebel frigates, which were flying English flags, to come close, without making a thorough inspection. Thus, the rebels were able to fire several broadsides at the unsuspecting *Fox,* whereupon she surrendered. If this story is true, it does the English as much honor as the Hessians gained at Trenton.[43]

July 23. A very good wind; we weighed anchor and sailed along the coast, which we could see very clearly on our right.

July 24-July 27. We have had either no wind or a contrary wind. It is 20 English miles from New York to Sandy Hook, 120 miles from there to the mouth of the Delaware, and from there to Philadelphia 110 miles.

I forgot to mention that on July 16th, General Washington asked to exchange General Lee for the English General Prescott. He offered to include the Hessians in the exchange for Lee. Needless to say, his offer was turned down.

July 28. Such a thick fog this morning that it was almost impossible to see a ship at a distance of 20 paces, and a ship is not a small object. At ten o'clock in the morning we had a thunderstorm accompanied by a heavy rain, which chased away some of the fog. At noontime we finally had some good wind. In the evening we had another thunderstorm. Lightning struck the top (about a yard long) of our mainmast without setting it afire or causing any serious damage.

July 29. Unfavorable wind, but a little better in the evening.

July 30. We had continuous good wind all last night so that by six o'clock this morning we could distinctly see Cape Henlopen, as well as the light-tower. At nine o'clock we sighted two rebel privateers in the mouth of the Indian River, which empties into the sea between the Delaware River and Chesapeake Bay, yet somewhat closer to the Delaware. In the Delaware, not far from Cape Henlopen, we saw the *Roebuck* of 40 guns, and two English frigates, all lying at anchor. The first one, the *Roebuck,* came toward us, and we saw her captain going aboard the Admiral's ship, supposedly with news. The wind was favorable, yet we did not run up the Delaware River, but in the evening, laid toward Cape Henlopen, which is opposite Cape May.[44]

July 31. In the morning we saw Cape May; after a short while we changed our course toward the mouth of the Delaware, then toward the sea, and then toward Chesapeake Bay. The width of the Delaware, that is, the distance between Cape Henlopen and Cape May, is judged to be 20 miles, from Cape Henlopen to Cape Charles, 100 miles, and from there to Cape Henry on the opposite side of the Chesapeake, 16 miles. From the mouth of the Chesapeake to Philadelphia is estimated to be 240 English miles. The last 50 miles will have to be on foot in case we want to go up the Chesapeake to get to Philadelphia, because our big ships can go no farther than the Elk River.

August 1, [1777.] I did not let the day pass without celebrating with my comrades the birthday of the Duke of Brunswick. I will never forget the grace that he has shown toward me.

August 2. Today, no less than yesterday, the Admiral changed our course several times, and it was difficult to tell where we were heading.

August 3. Today we are apparently heading for the Chesapeake. We had a big thunderstorm and considerable wind in the evening. The storm drove the frigate *Tuscan* very close to our ship, nearly endangering us; she was no farther than a foot from us when good luck and good maneuvering turned her away.

August 4. Almost no wind. We paid a visit to the two brothers Howe.[45] Wherever we land, a general pardon and proclamation will be issued.[46] If this does not work, we will presumably be more ruthless and will burn and ravage a bit to see if that will help.

August 6. Last evening a strong thunderstorm came up, which exposed our ship to great danger, and at one o'clock our foremast was shattered down to the keel, damaging the decks and knocking down the sails and yards. The whole forepart of the ship, which was set afire, was sunk into the sea by the force of the blow. Thus, the fire was extinguished and we were saved. Whether this episode, short as it was, was a pleasant one, I leave it to the judgment of others, for until the fire was out, we considered ourselves lost, because no ship will come to the assistance of a burning vessel for fear of catching on fire.

As soon as the fire was extinguished, we worked pumps hard and constantly to keep our ship from sinking until other ships could come to our aid, for we had supposed that she had suffered sufficient damage to take on much water. There was no ship in the vicinity, because during the storm, ships always spread out to avoid collision. We, therefore, put up beacons to signal that we were in distress. Soon after we had been hit, the storm ended. A complete calm followed, which lasted several hours. About three o'clock many boats arrived to help us.

The Admiral ordered the nearest ships of the line to send their carpenters to us, who at once began to repair our damage by putting up a new mast etc. General Howe immediately sent his senior aide to inquire whether anyone was injured. With the exception of a sailor, who is not expected to recover, no one was injured. Before seven o'clock in the morning some wind came up, but because we were not able to get under sail, the ship of the line *Reasonable* of 64 guns took us in tow. By four o'clock in the afternoon our ship was completely repaired.

During the afternoon we had a visit from the two aides of General Howe who were with the General on board the *Eagle,* namely his first secretary McKenzie and Admiral Howe's chaplain. They brought the following news: General Washington has gone to Philadelphia with his whole army, and General Burgoyne, who got

wind of this, has advanced to Fort Anne, 22 miles this side of Ticonderoga, after two prior skirmishes with the rebels.

The rebels are said to have fortified, with 52 heavy cannon, an island in the Delaware, which is seven miles from Philadelphia.[47] Furthermore, they have made the Delaware, which is dangerous enough because of its bars and flats, completely unpassable by sunken ships, chains, and cheveaux de frise.[48] In addition they are said to have many fireships, branders, galleys etc. ready to receive us should we enter the Delaware.[49] The *Roebuck,* which has been stationed in the Delaware, brought this news. This was undoubtedly the reason for cancelling the plan to go to Philadelphia by way of the Delaware, and deciding to go up the Chesapeake, which has so far not been possible because of continuing contrary winds.

August 7. Unfavorable wind. Since it was not foreseen that we would be aboard ship so long, the horses were given very little space; this is the reason they are beginning to die. This evening a rebel frigate could be seen in the distance. She was apparently trying to learn where we had stayed so long. Two of our frigates chased her, but could not catch up with her as she sailed extremely well.

August 8. Very slight wind.

August 9. A good wind. The *Roebuck,* which had been in the Delaware, sailed with us, because the crew knows Chesapeake Bay. In her place, the *Liverpool* was left in the Delaware.

August 10. Very unfavorable wind.

August 11. A rather brisk wind, so we hope to reach Chesapeake Bay by noon tomorrow, provided the wind continues.

August 12. Unfortunately the wind changed early this morning and came straight down the Chesapeake, the way we were heading. We, therefore, had to turn about, although our lead ship had already clearly seen land.

August 13. Unfavorable wind, somewhat better in the evening.

August 14. At noon we were at a position where we were about to turn into the bay, directly across from it, about 30 miles away. The slightest constant wind would bring us into the bay. An English sloop of 12 guns, which together with several other ships had been in the bay, joined us. Finally, a medium wind brought us to within 12 miles of Cape Henry, where we dropped anchor at eleven o'clock at night.

August 15. The wind was not good enough to run in, although we did weigh anchor at six o'clock in the morning. The Admiral led us past Cape Henry in a southerly direction until eight o'clock in the morning, when he turned about on another tack, which took advantage of the contrary wind, bringing us closer to the Chesapeake. We saw Cape Henry to the south very clearly. We could also see Cape Charles, which was 16 miles from Cape Henry, but not so clearly by any means. Our foremost ships came into the bay at four o'clock in the afternoon and dropped anchor, having gone about eight miles into the bay with the support of an incoming tide. Here we had to wait for other ships, most of which could not make it because of the contrary wind.

August 16. Before noon the wind allowed the lagging ships to run in, and about three o'clock in the afternoon they joined us, whereupon all ships proceeded under the lead of the Admiral until seven o'clock in the evening, when we again dropped anchor, because thunderstorms were threatening. The storm soon caught us, and by midnight we experienced the heaviest rain and thunderstorm I have ever seen.

August 17. At seven o'clock in the morning we weighed anchor and advanced before a favorable wind. During the day we received reliable news that the English ship *Rainbow* of 40 guns has captured, on July 8, near Halifax, the rebel ship *Hancock* of 34 guns, after a chase of 39 hours. The rebel commodore, Captain Manley and 230 men were aboard. He is the same Manley who a short time ago, with the support of the rebel frigate *Boston* of 30 guns, had taken the English frigate *Fox*.[50]

Manley had kept the captain of the *Fox*, together with 40 men, as prisoners aboard, so that these men have now been freed. We have great hopes to regain the *Fox* frigate as well, for she was with the *Boston* in company of the *Hancock* when she was chased by the *Rainbow* and the two other ships, one of them the English frigate *Flora* of 32 guns. Commodore Manley has been brought to New York. This is undoubtedly a big loss to the rebels, since he was the first and best skipper in their navy.[51]

The heavy thunderstorm has killed seven horses in a horse ship. We dropped anchor at two o'clock in the afternoon since neither tide nor wind was helping us. Soon thereafter I and one of my comrades (the other has been ill for some time), went to the Admiral's ship where we lunched. We learned that a packet from England had arrived, but there were no letters for me, which is hard to take. The Admiral has the reliable news that the English frigate *Fox*, which the rebels had manned with a crew of their own, has been recaptured by the frigate *Flora*. The *Boston* escaped.

General Washington is said to be heavily entrenched in the hills not far from Brandywine Creek, between New Castle and Philadelphia, but closer to New Castle. He has sent General Putnam with 6,000 men to Albany to stop Burgoyne.

While we were still aboard the Admiral's ship, two white and three black men came from shore in a boat; they brought melons, apples, and other fruit to the Admiral, assuring us that they were Tories (Royal minded citizens) and did not wish to go back. Thus, they stayed with us. These people told us that everyone is anxious (since hearing of our arrival) to join the force of General Washington in order to be in the great fight against the Tories, as they say. Almost all people, women and children, have left their homes and moved farther into the country. They had also heard that heavy cannon have been brought to the shores to fire on us as we pass, but they do not know where these cannon are mounted.

A small ship and three rebel sloops with salt, tobacco, etc., sneaked into our fleet at sunset a few days ago. Their intention was to leave the fleet the following night, and proceed into a small river, that was well known to them. They sailed with our fleet the whole day without being discovered, but when they stole away the next night and took a different direction, they were discovered by one of our side frigates, and were chased. The three sloops escaped but the ship was caught. In the evening we had a thunderstorm.

August 18. Good wind, and we sailed on. During these days we have often seen fire and heavy smoke coming from high elevations on shore. They are probably signals of the rebels. At 10 o'clock we saw several small and one larger rebel ship near shore, flying their flags. They were too far away to chase. Even though we might have wanted to capture these ships, it would have been almost impossible along their shores, with which they were very familiar, and we not at all. The ships were soon out of sight. In the afternoon a rebel galley was daring enough to fire some shots from a great distance at our lead frigate. When we later dropped anchor because of lack of wind, two frigates and one galley received orders to stay as close as possible to the mouth of the river so that the rebel galley could not come out during the night and disturb us.[52]

So far we have been sailing along the shore north of Cape Henry. I think that much of this land is under cultivation because many houses can be seen, in spite of the fact that there are woods along the shore. I am forced to complain about the intolerable heat we have been having to bear so far. If I could own the whole of America, I would refuse if I had to live in these hot regions. We console ourselves in the hope that it will be cooler on shore.

August 19. We sailed, with medium wind, at seven o'clock in the morning. At 11 o'clock we arrived off the Potomac River, which is said to be at least 12 miles wide [at its mouth]. The river forms the border between Virginia and Maryland. We passed the river on the left side and went up to the Patuxent River, where we dropped anchor in the evening.

August 20. Very good wind today. The Chesapeake averages about 22 miles in width at this point. At nine o'clock this morning we were, for at least an hour, in a narrow part about eight miles wide, which, in the distance, widened out again. While in this narrow part, we could very clearly see both shores and large wooded areas.[53]

At noontime the advance ships tied their anchors at the point of their cutwaters. This is done as a precaution against attack by branders, etc., which are impossible to sink or turn off their course. The heavy anchor is then dropped on an advancing brander, which would normally sink it, or at least cause it to be delayed for a while. At noon we had a calm, which lasted two hours, then the incoming tide carried us farther. We passed Sharps Island on our right and anchored at six o'clock in the evening in the region of Kent Island, also on our right.[54]

August 21. At five o'clock in the morning we sailed up the bay with a good wind. By shortly after seven we passed Annapolis, the capital of Maryland, which we could see to our left. We saw several large and handsome buildings in the town. The city is said to have 800 houses. In the city and on the fort are flown big rebel flags (Union flags, as they call them). They are white with purple stripes.[55] There has not been a fort here before, so the rebels must have built it. This is borne out by the fact that we saw them very busily at work on the earthwork in front of the city and on a battery atop a hill to the right of the city, both not yet finished. We were too far away for them to salute us with their cannon.

Shortly before noon we heard two strong cannon shots coming from the shore off to our left. They were repeated farther and farther away, in the direction of Baltimore. In spite of a favorable wind and a favorable tide, we dropped anchor at one o'clock in the afternoon to have soundings made for sandbars, which we would now encounter. This was done by sending ahead smaller boats, which we observed dropping lead lines to find a safe channel for our large fleet.

August 22. At half past five in the morning we started out and passed North Point, where the Patapsco, on which 12 miles farther up Baltimore is situated, empties into the Chesapeake. Two rebel galleys appeared here, but turned around as soon as they saw some of our vessels coming toward them.

At eight o'clock we sailed by Pooles Island, after having passed on our left the mouths of Black, Middle, and Gunpowder Rivers. Here the channel that we had to navigate was extremely narrow. The Admiral, therefore, placed small ships on both sides, with orders to fire at any of our ships that would venture farther out.

This morning, as we weighed anchor, we heard two cannon shots from the left shore, just as we had heard yesterday noon. These were repeated from one position to another, each one farther away, until the sound was lost. These are definitely signals by which the enemy are informed, in a very quick manner, how far we have progressed to that moment.

In the evening the entire fleet passed the Admiral's ship, and the first transports advanced within two miles of Turkey Point and the mouth of the Elk River. The Admiral's ship and the other large ships could not venture that far because of the shallow water. The battery ship [*Vigilant*], several frigates, and the *Roebuck*, the latter of which is of especially shallow draft, proceeded farther up

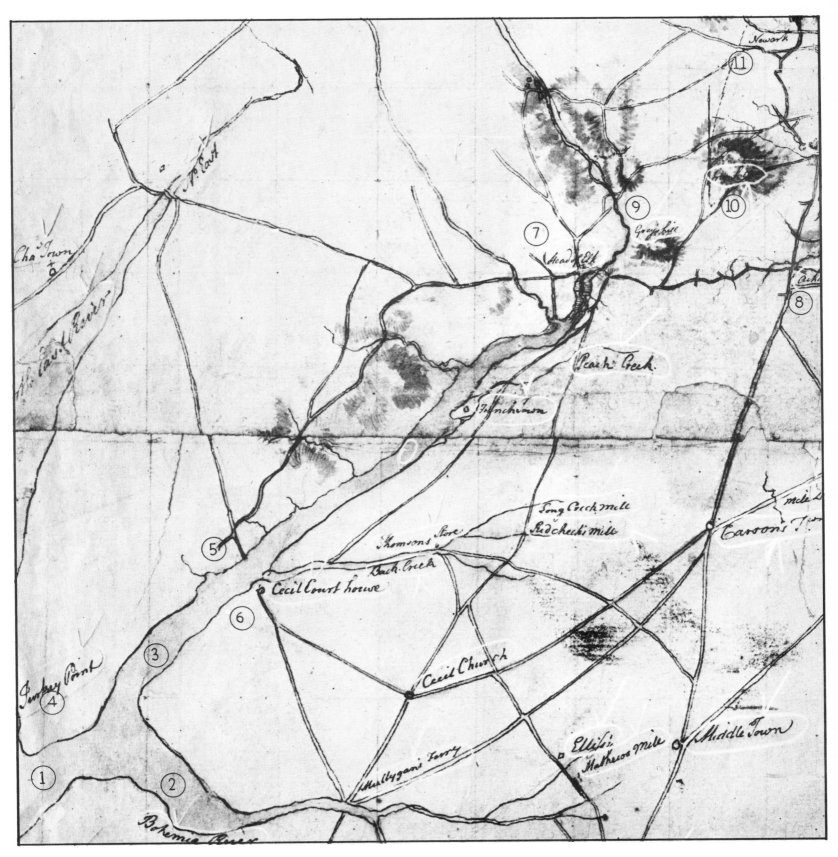

This section of an undated and untitled map is described in the Guide to the Manuscript Maps in the William L. Clements Library, *by Christian Brun, Ann Arbor, 1959, map #556, as Part of the modern counties of Philadelphia, Bucks, Montgomery, Delaware, Chester, Lancaster, in Pennsylvania; New Castle in Delaware; and Cecil in Maryland. (Br.M 132/8) This, and the sections reproduced on pages 29, 33, and 37 are published through the courtesy of the William L. Clements Library, The University of Michigan. The sections are full scale, one inch to two miles,*

oriented north. It is believed that this map is the product of a British cartographer, and was made during the fall or winter of 1777/1778, at Philadelphia, as a record of the route of British-Hessian march from Elk Ferry, Maryland to Philadelphia, beginning August 25, and ending September 26, 1777. Circled numerals are additions to the map indicating place names as follows: 1. Chesapeake Bay, 2. Bohemia River, 3. Elk River, 4. Turkey Point, 5. Elk Ferry, 6. Cecil Court House, 7. Head of Elk, 8. Aiken's Tavern, 9. Grey's Hill, 10. Iron Hill, 11. Newark.

and spread out in the mouth of the Elk.[56] We had expected an enemy battery on Turkey Point, but found everything quiet.

August 23. From five o'clock in the morning until noon the Admiral and General Howe explored the mouths of the Susquehanna and Elk Rivers, advancing especially far up in the latter.[57] In the afternoon the English light infantry, the grenadiers, and the Hessian jaegers received orders to prepare for disembarkment. One of our sloops that had gone up the Susquehanna as far as Spesutie Island, had, unexpectedly, several cannon shots fired at her.

August 24. [Burgoyne] is said to have advanced to within 30 miles of Albany. There was no disembarkment today.[58]

August 25. At three o'clock in the morning the light infantry, the English grenadiers, and the Hessian jaegers were put into boats. At five in the morning the Admiral and General Howe, together with his aides, went aboard the *Roebuck,* which was stationed close to the mouth of the Elk River. The Admiral's flag was then hoisted on the *Roebuck,* accompanied by the customary signals, and the *Eagle,* which the Admiral left because she drew too much water to proceed farther up, struck the Admiral's flag at the very same moment.

The battery ship and five other light frigates, galleys etc., were ordered to proceed up the Elk River. The flatboats with the troops, and then the transports followed slowly. Admiral Howe, his brother, and all of us [staff] went aboard the battery ship, which was in the lead. In this manner we proceeded very slowly until we reached Elk Town [Elk Ferry], eight good miles from the mouth of the river, where we landed at 10 o'clock in the morning without the slightest interference.[59]

My General advanced with the jaegers and light infantry for three miles and then made a halt. We found almost all houses deserted, except that some women and children were left behind. Disembarking of troops and of the light artillery continued the whole day.

August 26. General Washington is said to have come down with some men, most of them dragoons, to the head of Elk, eight miles from here, in order to observe our advance.[60] Disembarkment of troops continued throughout the day, ending in the evening. The heavy artillery, wagons, horses, etc., will be disembarked next. Major Balfour, one of my comrades, was almost captured this afternoon when he was carrying orders to one of our foreposts. In the late afternoon we had a heavy rain. During the evening orders were issued that we will set out marching at three o'clock in the morning to our right, with the exception of General Knyphausen who will stay here with 13 battalions.

August 27. Since the heavy rain continues, and the roads are bottomless, and since the horses are still sick and stiff, we had to ride out at two o'clock in the morning to countermand the order of march. At nine o'clock in the morning one of our boats, which had come quite close to the opposite bank, was fired upon with small arms. Our battery ship sent two 32-pound balls over, and the affair was ended.

August 28. By three o'clock in the morning everyone was under arms, and at four we marched off, with the exception of Knyphausen's corps, which was ordered to change camp after our departure. Since the region here is heavily wooded and cut up with ravines, we marched very slowly and carefully. It was 10 o'clock when the head of our column got beyond the pretty little town of Head of Elk [Elkton], where we halted for an hour to repair the bridge so that our artillery could cross. While the bridge was being repaired, the troops marched through the water up to their knees.

We observed some officers on a wooded hill opposite us, all of them either in blue and white or blue and red, though one was dressed unobtrusively in a plain gray coat. These gentlemen observed us with their glasses as carefully as we observed them. Those of our officers who know Washington well, maintained that the man in the plain coat was Washington. The hills from which they were viewing us seemed to be alive with troops.[61]

My General deployed 3,000 men and marched forward. As soon as they observed our advance, they retreated; we caught only two dragoons. These dragoons and some Negro slaves confirmed that it was Washington with his suite and a strong escort that was looking us over. Most of our troops halted on and around this height.

General Washington spent several days in the same house where we are now lodging, and did not leave it until yesterday morning. So he must have known, or at least suspected, that we intended to come here yesterday. From talk said to have been from the lips of Washington and some of his officers, we learn that Washington believes our objective to be Lancaster rather than Philadelphia.

While here, Washington received the pleasant news, though unpleasant to our side and particularly to us Brunswickers, that a corps of 1,500 men, mostly Brunswickers that had been detached by General Burgoyne, has suffered very much in an engagement on the 16th of the month. One lieutenant colonel, one major, five captains, 14 subaltern officers, and more than 500 men are said to have fallen into the hands of the rebels. A General Stark was in command of the rebels, and a Brunswicker, Colonel Baum, was in command of our troops.

Here, we have found all houses deserted, as at Elk Ferry. This morning we captured 15 small vessels in the Elk River, most of which were loaded with grain.[62] Our wagons, provisions, etc., have been put on small craft in the Elk River.

August 29. Because of increasing acts of pillage in our corps, last night we lost several men who had advanced too far and were captured. Early this morning our jaeger picket was alarmed. In the afternoon Brigadier General Grey, sent by General Knyphausen, arrived from Elk Ferry and reported that everything was quiet there. Since tents were unloaded there, they are now in Knyphausen's camp. The tents, provisions, etc. for the corps here arrived in small boats this evening. Lord Howe also arrived here under cover of an escort, then went back to Elk Ferry in the evening to board the *Roebuck.*[63]

August 30. Again last night some of our men, while pillaging, fell into the hands of the enemy.[64] Tents are being put up here. At noon about 200 dragoons appeared in front of our jaeger picket; many of their officers are said to have observed our positions very closely, but without approaching us. It was possibly Washington or one of his first generals, reconnoitering.[65] The officer of the jaeger picket lobbed a few shots from an amusette at them.[66] They were too far away, but it caused them to withdraw.

August 31. Nothing new. We will probably stay here today and tomorrow to give our horses, which suffered exceedingly because of the unexpectedly long voyage, a chance to recover, and also to shoe them. I presume we will then proceed in two corps, one under the command of General Knyphausen, to Philadelphia by way of New Castle, Wilmington, etc.

Some country-people have just arrived. According to them, and other information received, General Washington with his whole army is again in the hills behind Wilmington, where he wants to do battle, since, if he should allow us to proceed to Philadelphia unharmed, the greater part of his army would leave him.

He is said to have several small corps in front of him and close to us, who are operating without fixed positions but under orders to skirmish continuously around us. General Howe wishes very much that a battle will ensue. Otherwise, this war will not end for a long time.

I must finish here, since the letters will be taken to the *Roebuck* today, and from there will be sent by packet to England. I obediently commend myself to everyone.

Head of Elk, August 31, 1777
Friedrich v. Muenchhausen

SEVENTH TRANSMITTAL
September 1, 1777-October 26, 1777

September 1, 1777. Still at the Head of Elk. Late last evening three deserters came in. They tell us the following: 700 men, commanded by a French count, are close in front of us; an additional 1,800 to 2,000 men are but five miles away; Washington is with this force; the main rebel army of 38,000 men is at Wilmington.[1]

Last night seven of our pillagers were captured. A picket was also attacked, and we had one killed and five wounded. At noon another of our pickets was attacked, but a strong patrol, which happened to pass by, supported our picket.[2] The rebels left behind a few dead, and one captain, one lieutenant, and four rank and file taken prisoners. These prisoners were from the Free Corps of Colonel Marquis d' Armand, whose corps consists of 700 men, all Germans. They have been the ones skirmishing with us around here.[3]

My General wanted to gain information from the two captured officers by resorting to both threats and promises, for these were the first officers captured during this campaign. I was given the task because they were Germans. The lieutenant, who seemed to be a true rebel, was either too smart or too dumb, for I could get no information from him.

The captain, von Uechtritz by name, was an aide to the Marquis d' Armand.[4] At first he was uncooperative, but when I promised him in the name of my General that he would be treated well and be sent to Germany a free man, he spoke freely.

Following is the information received through the interrogation, which I transmitted to my General. His name is von Uechtritz; he was born in Saxony, where an older brother is said to be the owner of the estates of Wilsdruf and Cune. He hoped to make a fortune in America, which caused him to leave his Saxonian lieutenant post to go to France, whence he came to America five months ago, together with several French officers.

He says, "Washington's army, which came to the hills back of Wilmington, when they learned we were in the Chesapeake, consists of 15,000 regulars, well armed and most of these well dressed. They are mostly Germans from the provinces of Maryland, Virginia, and Pennsylvania. A fourth of them are Irishmen, Scots, and Englishmen. In addition to these, they have four light regiments of dragoons each consisting of 250 men. They have about 12,000 militia who are arriving and departing whenever they please.[5] They are badly dressed, poorly armed, and undisciplined.

"The Americans lack salt and rum, but they compensate for the lack of rum by another strong drink that they produce in quantities. They do not lack food, nor good horses, nor cannon. In addition to the 50 pieces of cannon they received from France this winter, they have cast numerous brass 6-pounders this winter in Philadelphia.

"After Washington received the news that we had landed at Elk Ferry on August 25, he called his generals to a council of war. The French generals and also two German colonels, both colonels being very highly regarded by Washington, especially Armand, urged an immediate attack on us before we could recover from the long voyage. They figured that we would have many sick, and that we would not be able to use our cavalry nor our artillery because of sick horses.[6]

"They pointed out that in any event Washington would soon be compelled to engage us. The Germans would quit the army, as they had already threatened to do, should Washington withdraw and yield to us Philadelphia and the regions where most of them have their homes. Now, that they have all sorts of advantages, is the time to attack us, and, it is hoped, defeat us.

"It was also brought out in the council of war that, if General Howe was an expert at his trade, they would soon have to deal with three corps, those of Burgoyne and Clinton, in addition to Howe's.

"Contrary to this view, the American General whose opinion Washington finally backed, maintained that it would be much better to remain in the hills [back of Wilmington] until they had reliable information as to whether Howe was headed for Lancaster or Philadelphia. Others argued against a battle but recommended a plan designed to slow us down and diminish our strength continuously by small skirmishes and harassments. In short, the objective should be to prolong the war because of the belief that England could not, and would not, continue such a costly war much longer.

"Furthermore, there was some reason to believe that various situations in Europe would very soon lead to war between England and France. It was alleged that, as far as this campaign is concerned, there was nothing to fear from Burgoyne after his last defeat, and that General Clinton is not as strong as he is reputed to be, and cannot put a sizable force into the field without endangering the security of New York.

"After the council of war, Washington left with his escort and supposedly rode toward our position. During the evening of the 27th, information had been given to Washington that Howe was marching to the Head of Elk with 8,000 men, and that he had left behind 4,000 at Elk Ferry. (Of course this march was delayed a day by the rain). It was also reported to Washington that many of our troops were sick, and that the horses that had survived the trip were in very bad condition.

"With this new intelligence, Washington returned to Wilmington the same day and held another council of war. During this council, the views of the French, which had been to attack us, now were so much more forcefully asserted, since the Germans in the army were very dissatisfied because we were not prevented from pillaging their land.

"As a result of this second council of war, at 10 o'clock in the evening, three brigades under the command of Lord Stirling and General Conway, as well as the Free Corps of Marquis d' Armand, were ordered to march from Wilmington toward the Head of Elk. The three brigades not exceeding 2,000 men, after marching all night, came to a halt in the hills, six miles from us. The corps of Armand was ordered to advance farther.[7]

"While Armand's corps was moving forward, General Washington passed them with his escort and ordered Armand to follow as quickly as possible. After Washington had finally arrived at a position about two miles from us, he returned. On his way back he met Armand and told him to look for a secure outpost in front of our lines and to harass us as much as possible. Armand carried out this order, and continuously sent out patrols around us. These patrols captured many of our pillagers. Captain Uechtritz was sent out yesterday morning with 60 men to make a violent attack on one of our pickets, and so molest our army, but on this occasion he fell into our hands.

"Many of the French officers are dissatisfied and want to go home to France. Especially disgusted is a French brigadier of artillery, Monsieur Coudray, who this winter had brought from France 50 cannons, rifles, etc.[8]

"One of the German officers is Colonel Baron v. Arendt, who had formerly been a major in Prussian service, and had also been aide to the Crown Prince. He commands a strong regiment of only Germans, who are so well drilled that Washington often shows them off as an example for others."

September 2. Some deserters came in. We had orders in the evening that the entire force was to march at four o'clock tomorrow morning, with the exception of six battalions under General Grant, who were to stay here [at the Head of Elk]. We will take no tents with us, except those for the officers.

September 3. We marched off at five o'clock in the morning on the main road to Philadelphia. Our advance was without enemy contact until we arrived in the hilly region, that they call Iron Hill. Here skirmishing began with the jaegers, who were our vanguard, under the command of Lieutenant Colonel von Wurmb. The fire was weak at first, but it steadily increased.

General Howe concluded from this increased fire that the rebels were strong at this position, and he ordered that a battalion of English light infantry support our jaegers on each flank. They were to attack simultaneously the flanks of the enemy who were hidden in the woods.

At the same time my General sent me to the jaegers to see how they were doing, and to learn where the enemy was stationed and how strong they were. I was to tell Colonel Wurmb not to advance too fast so as to give the light infantry time to support him. A handsome 18-year old English engineer officer, Haldane by name, who was normally in our suite of aides, and who was a good friend of mine, rode with me. We saw several rebels behind trees, firing at our advancing jaegers, then retreating about 20 yards behind the next tree, then firing again.

It would be unfair not to mention that Colonel von Wurmb was continuously in front of the jaegers, encouraging them in every way, both by actions and by words. I talked to him for a moment; then rode back. The fire was very strong at this time, and to my great sorrow, my accompanying engineer officer received a shot that splintered his right arm, which was amputated in the evening.[9]

While I was returning to the rear, I met my General, who in the meantime, because he had heard nothing of the light infantry that he had sent out and because the fire was increasing, had formed two English grenadier battalions, and advanced with them. He had also sent ahead two 2-pounders to support our jaegers.

About this time we heard firing from somewhere on our left, but directed forward. This was from one of the dispatched light infantry battalions, which had gone too far to the left and encountered a small party of rebels instead of coming to the aid of our Hessian jaegers. The other dispatched light infantry battalion also was prevented from supporting the jaegers because they ran into a deep morass, which forced them to retrace their steps.

Before General Howe arrived at the front with the two grenadier battalions, the jaegers had already finished the whole affair themselves, chasing the rebels through the thick woods, then across the barren hill and the Christiana Creek bridge, which led them across a second creek and a deep ravine.[10] The rebels stopped at this second creek and made music with half-moons and other (wind) instruments.[11]

My General had, in the meantime, sent me back to the front to tell Lieutenant Colonel von Wurmb the reason why he was not supported in the action, and to extend to him his compliments and thanks on the excellent behavior of his men. A short time later, my General followed me to the front, and when he arrived, he dismounted and thanked and praised Lieutenant Colonel von Wurmb and all the other jaeger officers.

Then my General crossed the ravine to the other hilltop from which position he saw in the distance the rebels slowly retreating on the way to Christiana. According to reports, the corps of Ar-

mand numbering 700 men, had confronted our jaegers; also a force of about 300 militia had opposed the battalion of light infantry.[12] The latter [militia] fired only one round; then they left the field.

The English losses are three officers and nine rank and file wounded, one noncommissioned officer killed. We had 14 Hessians wounded and two killed. We buried 41 of the rebels, among them several officers, including a captain who was still alive when I rode by. He asked me to get him something to drink. Since I could not do it at the time, I hurried back to him, but I found him already dead. We do not know the number of rebel wounded because they carried them away. We have taken only four prisoners. They can run so fast that one can not catch them without taking a chance on being cut off.

General Knyphausen, who had ordered a brigade of Englishmen under General Grey to cross to the other side of Elk Ferry on August 30th, personally, crossed over with the whole corps on the 31st, and marched several miles deeper into the country the same day. He stopped for a rest on September 1. He marched again yesterday, the second, and joined the rear of our column today on the road in front of the woods where we had skirmished.

The jaegers and grenadiers who had been pushed forward, had to withdraw. General Howe encamped on this side of the small Christiana Creek, which is not to be confused with the Christiana River that is five or six miles in front of us.

Only the jaegers and English light infantry are on the other side of the creek, yet very close to it. We have Iron Hill on our left flank and the nearest slope of this hill is occupied by the English grenadiers.

September 4. Our wounded and our invalids were sent to the Head of Elk this morning under the protection of a strong escort. From there they will be taken to the hospital ship. At noon my General rode out to reconnoiter; one of the places we went to is a slope of Iron Hill, which is more than three miles from the left extremity of our camp.[13] From this elevation we could clearly see the Delaware River.

In the afternoon we received the very unpleasant news that the rebels, under the command of General Sullivan, had embarked from Elizabeth Point in the Jerseys on the 22nd of August at 10 o'clock in the evening, and landed on Staten Island, where they captured more than 350 men, among them four colonels, six majors, and many other officers; all of them were Provincial forces. They set on fire several forage magazines, and retreated at three o'clock in the morning of August 23. Our regular troops of English and Waldeckers, encamped on the other side of Staten Island toward New York, came to the rescue, and arrived in time to capture one colonel, two majors, several other officers, and 123 men of the enemy rear guard.[14]

In the evening we sent a party under strong escort to procure food, oats, etc., at the Head of Elk. These stores had been sent from our ships on small craft up to that point. Because of lack of horses, we will be forced to stay here for a few days. The 120 horses that the Knyphausen corps had gathered on its march (in addition to 200 head of cattle and 600 sheep), cannot compensate for the 400 horses that perished on our unfortunately long voyage, or after landing here. I was more lucky than most officers since I did not lose a single horse at sea, but two of mine have died since we landed.

September 5. Last night two of our patrols fired on each other by mistake; one dragoon was wounded, and two horses were lost. The rebel patrols, which usually consist of 10 to 15 dragoons and 20 to 30 infantrymen, now appear more often, and they fire at our posts occasionally. Two battalions of English light infantry under General Erskine advanced three miles in the direction of Christiana Bridge. They were on patrol in search of information on enemy positions, as well as to round up horses. They returned without horses and without seeing the enemy. In the afternoon a letter ar-

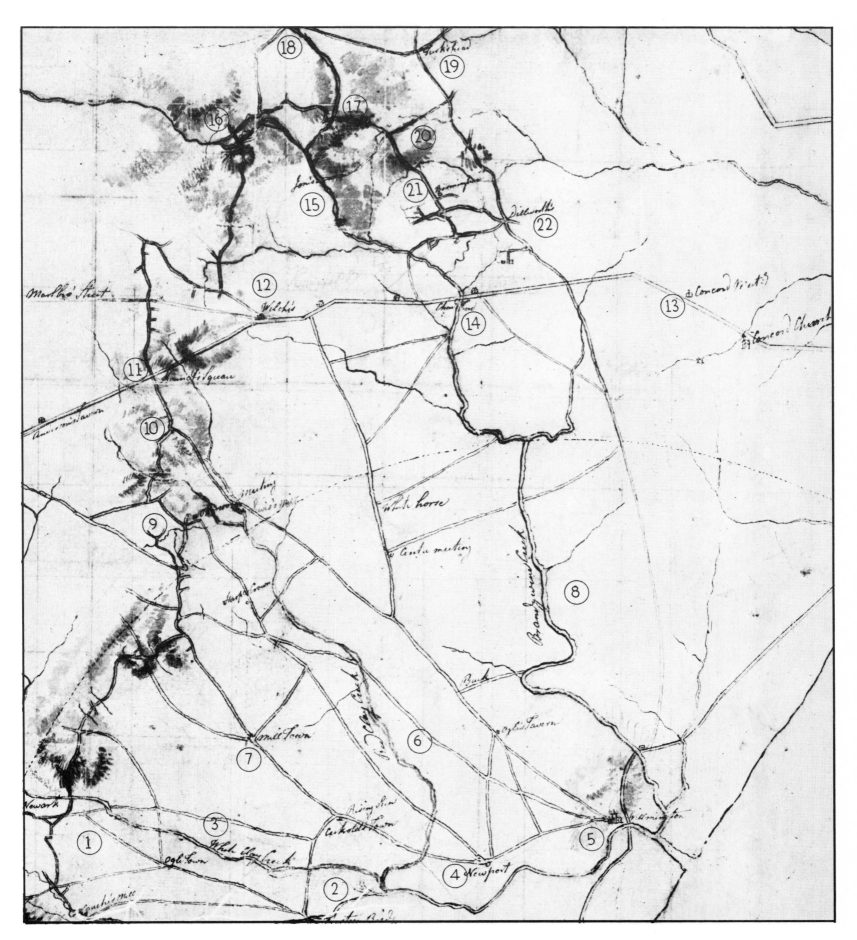

1. Newark, 2. Christiana Creek Bridge, 3. White Clay Creek, 4. Newport, 5. Wilmington, 6. Red Clay Creek, 7. Mill Town, 8. Brandywine Creek, 9. Hokkeson Meeting, 10. New Garden Meeting, 11. Kennett Square, 12. Welch's Tavern, 13. Concord Meeting, 14. Chad's Ford, 15. Jones Ford, 16. Trimble's Ford, 17. Jeffries Ford, 18. Taylors Ford, 19. Turks Head, 20. Osborne's Hill, 21. Birmingham, 22. Dilworth.

rived from General Washington. I understand it was an impudent letter, stating that he would not exchange General Lee for General Prescott.[15] Today I bought three horses, and rather cheaply for local conditions, since I paid no more than 113 Guineas for them.

September 6. Everything was quiet last night. General Grant arrived in the afternoon from the Head of Elk with his six battalions.[16] Intelligence reports indicate that Lord Stirling has arrived with 1,200 men at Newark, two and a half miles from our left flank, where he intends to harass us. In the evening the English light infantry and the light dragoons received orders to march at once and, as I believe, to surprise the rebels who have arrived at Newark. Rainy weather that started soon after they had set out, plus the lack of certainty as to their strength, caused the light infantry who had already started out, to be called back. A patrol of only 50 men was sent to Newark, where on their arrival during the night, they learned that Stirling had already left. Many dragoons of the rebels have deserted. Undoubtedly the amount of money they get from us for their mounts is the reason.

September 7. Today an ensign and five dragoon deserters arrived in camp, from whom we learned for sure that Washington is marching to Newport, three miles from Wilmington. So he is now closer to us, and is also in better control of the main road from Wilmington to Lancaster.

Everyone believes—and it is very plausible—that we shall take the main road by way of Christiana Bridge to Wilmington where we will meet our fleet in the Delaware, which will furnish us with provisions, etc. Washington who certainly suspects such a move, has put up some fortifications and abatis at Christiana Bridge, and has posted militia in the woods around there. At midnight, orders were issued that everyone must be under arms at two o'clock ready to march.

September 8. At 4 o'clock in the morning the van of the 1st division under Lord Cornwallis, accompanied by General Howe, started to march. Then the 2nd division under General Grant followed; after this came the 3rd division under General von Knyphausen, which had with it all our baggage, a lot of cattle, provisions, and other wagons. All marched in one column, and to our great surprise, instead of taking the road by way of Christiana Bridge to Wilmington as expected, we went to our left by way of White Clay Creek and Newark. We halted near Nicolson's, the only house on the main road from Newport and Wilmington to Lancaster.[17] Knyphausen's rear guard did not arrive until two o'clock in the morning. Everyone is pleased with the good march and the fact that it was kept a secret, thus cutting off Washington from Lancaster.

When our vanguard arrived here, it seemed that the rebels were also on the move. We were only five miles away from them and only five miles from Newport. There was much activity in front of us. We saw two regiments coming from Newport on two different roads, with their flags flying, and in very good order, as if they were heading for the road to Lancaster.

I was ordered by the General to ride quickly so as to lead the Hessian jaegers diagonally through the woods to cut off these troops, if possible. At the same time General Howe, with the light infantry, marched directly toward them for the same purpose. But the rebels, who had become aware of all this, retreated quickly. Notwithstanding this, the jaegers got close enough to send a few amusette balls at them.

We impatiently look forward to the end of these maneuvers. It is hoped that, unless Washington withdraws by forced marches the coming night, we can either force him to do battle on an advantageous terrain or to make a precipitous retreat. Either would mean the ruin of his army.

September 9. Unfortunately Washington marched away last night; it is uncertain what his destination is. The General has two conflicting reports. According to the first one, which is generally believed, Washington marched from Newport back to Wilmington, crossed the Brandywine, then recrossed at Chads Ford, and proceeded on the road to Lancaster. According to the second report he went up to Chads Ford along this side of the Brandywine, his main force being stationed in the hills on the other side of the Brandywine.[18]

At one o'clock in the afternoon, soon after this intelligence was received, Knyphausen was ordered to march with his division, including baggage, cattle, provisions etc., on the road to Kennett Square. It was almost six o'clock before his rear guard left the camp grounds.

At six o'clock General Howe marched with the division of Lord Cornwallis and General Grant on another road to Kennett Square, to the right of the one Knyphausen took. The road that we [Howe] took was so bad, and it was getting so dark, that the General halted five miles from Kennett Square.[19]

General Howe sent me and one of my comrades, Captain Knight, together with 12 dragoons, back with orders for Knyphausen's division to stop at New Garden Meeting, which we would have to pass. The General assumed that he would be able to catch up with General Knyphausen before he reached New Garden Meeting because his march would be slowed down by the large amount of baggage, cattle etc. We also were instructed to inform General Knyphausen that he should march early the next morning toward Kennett Square with the greatest precaution, because Washington's foreposts were already at Welch's Tavern, two miles from Kennett Square.[20]

The good, honorable General Howe, who is never concerned about himself but always about others, warned us to be careful not to be taken by one of the rebel dragoon parties, and to make sure that at least one of us got through to Knyphausen with the orders. Although we rode for 10 miles in territory we did not control, and twice came upon rebel dragoons who fired at us, we luckily got through. General Knyphausen's vanguard was already at Kennett Square, and it was absolutely impossible for him to return to New Garden Meeting because of the loaded wagons and the ravined roads.

We two aides rode back as quickly as possible to report this to our General. General Knyphausen permitted no fires, and was as quiet as possible, so that Washington who was nearby, would not discover his presence. On our way back we met two English brigades with heavy artillery and the baggage, that General Howe's corps had taken along. They were on their way to General Knyphausen at New Garden.

While we were away, the General had sent forward with a few dragoons, a Scottish Captain Campbell, who was a deputy aide, more properly a courier, to get reliable information about Washington's position. Campbell, who had been told that Knyphausen was at New Garden Meeting, unfortunately ran into a patrol of the Knyphausen corps on the other side of Kennett Square. Since neither party supposed the other to be there, they fired at each other, and our poor Campbell was shot through the belly and will probably die.

September 10. We got back to General Howe [at Hokkeson Meeting] at about two o'clock in the morning and at five o'clock we started out for Kennett Square where we joined General Knyphausen at eight o'clock.[21] Knyphausen's rear guard had not arrived until just then because of the many wagons and cattle. It was ordered that all should march at once in two columns, one under Howe and the other under Knyphausen, but this was impossible, since the men, and even more the horses, were completely exhausted. Counter orders were therefore given, calling for a march tomorrow morning.

September 11. Nous avons des chapeaux à vendre. [We have hats to sell.] Last night General Howe received the reliable information that General Washington has retreated somewhat, that he now has 3,000 men on this side of the Brandywine, in the hills before Chads Ford, and that the main army is positioned also in the region of Chads Ford and higher up in the hills that come close to the Brandywine. Since Washington learned that we are at Kennett Square, he is said to have sent back his whole baggage to Chester, but is keeping ready to march.[22]

At six o'clock in the morning General Knyphausen set out to march with his column, which consisted of four regiments of Hessians, two brigades of Englishmen under General Grant, the 71st regiment of Highland Scots, one squadron of dragoons, the Hessian mounted jaegers, and 350 Provincials, as well as the English riflemen, plus all the baggage, including cattle.[23] His route was toward Chads Ford by way of Welch's Tavern.

At five o'clock in the morning General Howe marched off to his left, up the Brandywine. Our column consisted of two battalions of English light infantry, two battalions of English grenadiers, two battalions of English Guards, two brigades of English infantry, two squadrons of dragoons, the Hessian jaegers and the Hessian grenadiers.[24]

Since our column had no baggage, but did have a number of sappers in the van, we moved forward quickly in spite of the great heat. During the march, we heard some small arms fire about 10 o'clock in the morning, and later, cannon shot, which continued almost during the whole march. At noon our vanguard came upon 200 rebel dragoons, who wounded some of our men by their fire, but they soon retreated.[25]

We crossed the Brandywine seven miles up from Chads Ford, where the river is divided into two branches; the bridges were destroyed. The men had to cross these two branches in up to three feet of water.[26] We then continued our march a short distance straight ahead, and then suddenly to the right down along the Brandywine toward the region of Chads Ford.

After a march of 17 miles we finally arrived on a steep, barren height, where we formed into lines by brigades.[27] We were now on the other side of Chads Ford, although it was still three miles to the left. Here we paused for a long hour to give the men some rest and to enable the last of the battalions to come up.[28]

We noticed strong movements from the rebels' right wings to their left ones. They formed two lines in good order along their heights; we could see this because there were some barren places here and there on the hills, which they occupied.[29]

At four in the afternoon our two battalions of light infantry and the Hessian jaegers marched down the hill. They marched first in a column, but later, when they approached the enemy, in line formation, deploying to the left. Soon after this the English grenadiers did the same in the center, almost at the same time; just a little later, the English Guards formed the right wing. Behind the English grenadiers were the Hessian grenadiers; behind the light infantry and the jaegers was the 4th English brigade. The 3rd English brigade was in reserve on top of the hill. The two squadrons of dragoons, who were close to us [Howe and his staff], halted behind the left wing of the Hessian grenadiers.

If I get a chance, I shall secure a good plan of the whole region and the battle, and will enclose it. But to give you some idea of our positions, I made the following sketch. I have not yet seen a good drawing of it; it only shows that which I can remember. (Page 53)

As soon as the third column had formed, the signal to march was drummed everywhere. When we got close to the rebels, they fired their cannon; they did not fire their small arms till we were within 40 paces of them, at which time they fired whole volleys and sustained a very heavy fire. The English, and especially the English grenadiers, advanced fearlessly and very quickly; fired a volley, and then ran furiously at the rebels with fixed bayonets. They drove them back three miles with their bayonets without firing a shot, in spite of the fact that the rebel fire was heavy.[30]

By six o'clock our left wing still had not been able to advance. Here the rebels fought very bravely and did not retreat until they heard in their rear General Knyphausen's fire coming nearer. Knyphausen had chased the rebels from the heights on the other side of the Brandywine at about 10 o'clock in the morning. After taking the heights, Knyphausen halted, and engaged in an almost continuous cannonade with the rebels, until he heard our fire. Then, at about six o'clock in the evening, he crossed the Brandywine at Chads Ford and attacked the rebels from this side.[31]

Now the rebels found themselves between two fires. This probably caused them finally to leave their strong post and retreat from their right wing to the right on the road to Chester. A pity we could not pursue them, for it was already completely dark and Howe's corps had marched 17 miles before the engagement, and consequently was very tired.

Washington was here with his entire army, and even yesterday showed the first gentlemen of Congress around. It is said that he was very pleased, au moins il a fait semblant [at least he made it appear so] that we should dare attack him in his strong and defensible positions.

He rode through the lines and encouraged his men, telling them that this could be their last campaign. He said that they have 40,000 men (he cannot add very well), and we have only 8,000; that we are fresh and in the most advantageous position that could be found, and that they have very tired troops.[32] Washington concluded by saying, "For God's sake and our freedom's sake, do not stop firing too soon, and try to be brave; than I'll vouch that you will achieve complete victory over the enemy."

After these admonitions, Washington must have moved to a position on his right wing, in the hills, where the roads lead to Chester, for neither we nor the men whom we captured saw him during the battle. Undoubtedly he was in the action with Knyphausen in the morning.

As far as I can tell, Washington executed a masterpiece of strategy today by sending columns from his right to his left wing in the beginning, without attempting to veil these movements. This was to give us the impression that his strength was there, which would probably cause General Howe to support the Guards and English grenadiers on our right wing with the Hessian grenadiers as well as the light infantry, the jaegers and the 4th brigade.

Soon after this Washington withdrew from his left wing, where we now supposed his main force to be, by filing off a large number of troops to the rear and toward the right wing where he had his cannon. All this was done with great speed and especially good order.

But the sharp eye of General Howe noticed this as the firing started, and at once ordered the 4th brigade to advance from the second to the first line, on the left wing. At the same time, the 3rd brigade, which at first was in reserve, was ordered to take the place of the now advanced 4th brigade. The new front was somewhat more sloping.

These movements, however, could not be carried out quickly enough to prevent our left wing from suffering somewhat initially, and for this reason the battle lasted longer than it should have.

This delay benefited Washington, who, in case he should be defeated, could not be pursued by us because of darkness, and, should we lose, his still fresh men, who knew the terrain very well, could have the same advantage they would have in daylight.

In all, we had 62 cannon, Knyphausen's included, of which we used not even 20, nor were more than half of our troops under fire. The Hessians, who except for the jaegers were in the second line, had no losses, but had a few grenadiers wounded. The jaegers lost 30 men. The enemy is said to have been 25,000 strong and to have had 58 cannon. Our losses were 579 men dead and wounded, among them 58 officers.[33]

The losses of the enemy, as much as we know, are close to 400 dead, whom we have buried. We also captured 497 during the day and the following days, most of whom were hidden in the bushes. Among them are almost 100 seriously wounded. We also took 11 good cannon, two of which were Hessian cannon taken at Trenton, and a lot of rifles that had been thrown away, and many very good ammunition wagons.[34]

If daylight had lasted a few hours longer, I dare say that this day would have brought an end to the war. Without doubt we would have taken half of Washington's army and all of his cannon. It was very advantageous for us that we did not take many prisoners during this, our first battle. We were cut off from the fleet, had provisions only for a few days, and were in a country in which we could not obtain the smallest amount of victuals. Further, we had good and strong forces around us who had no lack of anything, and whose sole objective was to keep us away from our fleet for as long as possible. Thus, we would perish because of want.

We all admire the strong and unexpected march of General Howe, and the special bravery, which the English showed in the battle, and I am convinced that everyone in Europe would admire General Howe if they were as familiar with all the obstacles he faces, as we are.

As usual, the General exposed himself fearlessly on this occasion. He quickly rushed to each spot where he heard the strongest fire. Cannon balls and bullets passed close to him in numbers today. We all fear that, since he is so daring on any and all occasions, we are going to lose our best friend, and that England will lose America.

September 12. General Grant was ordered today to march on the road to Chester as far as Concord [Concordville], with two brigades of English and the 71st regiment of Highland Scots.

September 13. Deserters came in yesterday and today. They all say that Washington marched throughout the night after the battle and continued his march until he crossed the Schuylkill near Philadelphia, where he finally halted. This morning Lord Cornwallis followed Grant with the English light infantry and the English grenadiers, but after reaching Grant, he marched a good distance farther, close to Chester.

September 14. Aside from dragoon parties, who frequently skirmish around us, there are none of the enemy nearby. It is certain now that Washington is on the other side of the Schuylkill, with his left wing between Philadelphia and the Schuylkill. His baggage is in Germantown.

Hessian Colonel Loos had to leave for Wilmington nine miles from here, at six o'clock in the morning, with the rest of the Rall brigade.[35] He took along all our wounded and prisoners, and at Wilmington he will find the 71st regiment of Scots, which General Grant pushed forward to that place yesterday.

September 15. Some stupid people are dwelling on the fact that our General does not quickly follow Washington with his whole force. Of course this would be a good thing to do if it were possible, but it is definitely not, because the General first has to send away the sick and wounded on the wagons, which carry our provisions and baggage. It is not possible to procure enough wagons here to do both at the same time, and neither of the two could be left behind.[36]

At noon, in his report from Wilmington, Colonel von Loos informed us that he found the 71st regiment of Scots there, and that they had found the entire town deserted by the enemy. In a fort near Wilmington they found two 12-pounders, four 9-pounders, and one 4-pounder in addition to many other items of war materiel. Governor McKinley of Delaware, who was late in leaving the city, was captured by the Scots.[37]

Colonel von Loos further reports that our fleet has not yet arrived at Wilmington, but that several frigates had come up as far as New Castle, without incident. Two rebel frigates came down from Philadelphia yesterday on their way to New Castle, but retreated very quickly. Von Loos' pickets were alarmed last night. Spies and other rumors suggested that efforts would be made to surprise him at Wilmington and force him out of that place. Lord Cornwallis, whose position is two miles from Chester, and General Grant, who is a few miles back on his right, have picked up some flour and fresh provisions, but nothing to drink.

At about 11 o'clock this morning, with an escort of 50 dragoons, General Howe rode to Lord Cornwallis, about eight miles from here. We cannot give a name to our present headquarters.[38] Less than a quarter of an hour from us is a small village of 11 houses, called Dilworth. The battle, which was fought around here, is called the Battle of Brandywine. Two Englishmen were hanged in the camp of Cornwallis for marauding.

It has been reliably learned that the strength of Washington's army has been reduced by 4,000 men since the battle, owing mainly to the fact that a lot of men left the army and went home during the battle, and that even more left during the long forced retreat. Late in the evening my General received news from Philadelphia, of which I have learned only that Washington has moved his right up along the Schuylkill River, at the same time advancing to meet a corps of 8,000 men being sent to him as reinforcements from Maryland, Virginia, etc., but perhaps mainly to keep clear the middle road to Lancaster.

September 16. We marched at five o'clock in the morning, not toward Chester, but in the direction of Goshen, that is, closer to the Middle Road to Lancaster.[39] Lord Cornwallis headed for the same place, and since he was stationed not far from Chester, he had to march much farther.[40]

About two o'clock in the afternoon, in the region called The-Boot-Sign, our vanguard, consisting of the Hessian jaegers, and the vanguard of Lord Cornwallis, encountered about 1,500 rebels, being the vanguard of Washington's army, which was in full march on the road to Lancaster.

The Hessian grenadiers and Hessian Leib regiment were put in line on a height. But the rebels retreated, and there was only some skirmishing with the jaegers, who were in the van of our column.[41] Colonel von Donop, who had advanced a little too impetuously with a company of jaegers and 40 mounted jaegers, was almost surrounded and only narrowly escaped capture.[42]

Since 10 o'clock this morning we have had the heaviest rain imaginable. It has made the roads so bad that our cannon, baggage, etc., remained over three miles behind us. This made it impossible for General Howe to follow General Washington, who has many good horses, and to force another battle, much as he wanted to do it. We had a few wounded and no dead. We found nine rebels dead, and captured a lieutenant colonel, a major, four officers, and 19 rank and file. Because of the bad weather, we simply had to stop. Our headquarters was established in a miserable small house, called The-Boot-Sign, which has given this region its name.[43]

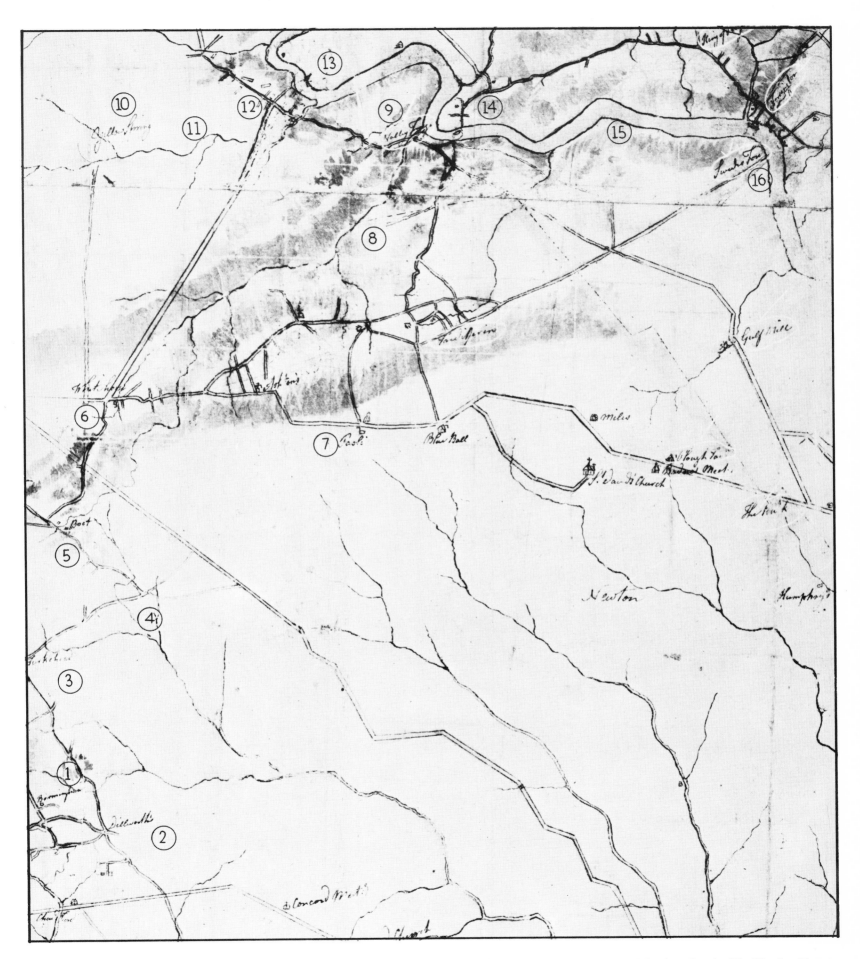

1. Birmingham, 2. Dilworth, 3. Turks Head, 4. Goshen Meeting, 5. Sign of Boot, 6. White Horse, 7. Paoli, 8. Valley Creek, 9. Valley Forge, 10. Yellow Spring, 11. Pickering Creek, 12. Charles Town, 13. Gordon's Ford, 14. Fatland Ford, 15. Schuylkill River, 16. Swedes Ford.

There are three wide roads that lead from Philadelphia to the regions of Lancaster, Reading and Carlisle, etc. These roads are called the Lancaster Roads, and to differentiate one from the others, they are referred to as the Lower, the Middle and Upper Lancaster Road. Washington, whom we saw today marching on the Middle Lancaster Road, is said to have halted not far beyond White Horse [Planebrook], which is three miles from us.

It can be deduced from this, that Washington did not want to get trapped between our army and Philadelphia, the Delaware, the barren Jersey, and perhaps Burgoyne's or Clinton's corps. Since he has lost control of the Lower Lancaster Road by Howe's movement to his [Washington's] right, and by losing the Battle of Brandywine, he has tried by forced marches, most of them during the night, to gain the Middle Lancaster Road, pass our left flank, and so get behind us. He would thus have plenty of maneuvering space to his rear and would be able to make unhindered use of support and provisions from Maryland, Virginia, etc.

Early this morning, as we were starting out, the Mirbach regiment was sent to Wilmington to reinforce Colonel von Loos. It is certain that six of our frigates have luckily reached Wilmington. Steady strong rain continues, which caused General Howe to cancel his plans to march at three o'clock in the morning.

September 17. In the afternoon, the rain, which has come down steadily since yesterday morning, let up somewhat, and at three o'clock marching orders were given. Everybody was already on the move when the heavy artillery, which was somewhat ahead, took the wrong road, a mistake of one of our guides. It took until nine o'clock in the evening before the artillery, over ravined and bad roads, was brought back to the main force. This unhappy mistake made us halt, and kept us from attacking Washington's army, which is in full march on the big road, in order to get on our left flank, as well as to get behind us.[44] In spite of all this, Lord Cornwallis had to march late in the evening to White Horse with the English grenadiers, two brigades of English, and one battalion of light infantry. He arrived there after midnight.

September 18. At half past two in the morning the General left with all the troops for White Horse, where we arrived a little after dawn and met Lord Cornwallis. Here we halted until 10 o'clock, when all forces continued the march, first in one, then in two columns. The roads were extremely bad, partly because of the heavy rains and partly because Washington, with the large part of his army, artillery, and all his baggage, had passed this way last night, thus reaching his destination before Lord Cornwallis arrived at White Horse, all owing to the fatal mistake of our artillery.

We are told that several thousand men are still stationed in front of us behind the Schuylkill in the region of Swedes Ford, which is supposedly eight miles from here. Washington is said to be awaiting support from Maryland, Virginia, etc., after which, as the rebels say, he will hem us in completely at the Schuylkill.

We marched through the Great Valley to Tredyffrin. They call this region Great Valley because there are chains of high hills covered with woods on both sides of the valley. The Valley Creek, part of which flows through our camp, has the best water I have tasted here in America.[45]

In the evening Colonel Harcourt left with two squadrons of dragoons, three companies of light infantry, and 200 dismounted dragoons. His destination is Valley Forge, four miles from here, at the end of Valley Creek, where it empties into the Schuylkill. He plans to seize a deserted magazine there. Except for a few shots, the detachment luckily arrived without incident. They found 4,000 barrels of flour in addition to quantities of axes, horseshoes, and other small items. We also got 123 horses, but unfortunately no rum or other beverages, which we need most of all.

September 19. At noon news arrived that our detachment at Valley Forge was being attacked. Two English regiments were sent off at once; they arrived there in an incredibly short time, whereupon the enemy retreated. In the afternoon the English grenadiers and the 1st battalion of light infantry left for Valley Forge, and the detachment under Colonel Harcourt, as well as the two English regiments sent there today, came back here.

In the evening it was reported that General Wayne had been detached by General Washington with 800 men to make the region behind us insecure. Consequently, the 2nd battalion of light infantry and the English riflemen were dispatched to break camp quietly and attempt to surprise these gentlemen. They found General Wayne two and a half miles behind us, and they had almost surrounded him when fate intervened. Two drunken Englishmen fired at a picket, which touched off an alarm, and permitted their escape, though in great confusion. At two o'clock in the morning the light infantry returned, without having attained its objective.

September 20. Early in the morning the Guards marched to Valley Forge. Washington, having achieved his aim by his forced marches and by the unfortunate mistake of our artillery, has now gained our left flank. He has uncontested access to supplies as well as a route of retreat to the lower provinces. He himself is positioned behind the Schuylkill with a strong force in the region where, opposite him, Valley Creek empties into the Schuylkill, his line extending a little beyond Swedes Ford. He has sent all his baggage etc. to Reading.

It is said that he intends to prevent our crossing the Schuylkill, which is wider and deeper than the Brandywine. In order to achieve this more effectively, he has detached 4,000 men to this side of the Schuylkill, 2,000 of whom are on our left flank and 2,000 are close behind us, under the command of General Wayne. Both corps have orders to attack us if we march again, and, particularly, if we try to cross the Schuylkill River.

In the evening the General received reliable information that General Wayne, who is said to be highly regarded by Washington because of his personal bravery, is only three miles behind us. We are informed that his 2,000 men are not militia but the best troops Washington has in his entire force.[46] We are further informed that Wayne intends to attack our rear guard and our baggage, as soon as we are in march again.

It was ordered that all troops would march early in the morning. At 10 o'clock in the evening five battalions of English under the command of General Grey were sent off in two detachments, with the strictest orders for quietness, to surprise Wayne.[47] Under the threat of the death penalty, quiet was ordered and all were warned not to load their muskets so that no soldier could create an alarm by firing.

Success was ours; our men surprised Wayne at one o'clock in the morning. More than 400 were found dead on the terrain, 123 were wounded severely, and 76 were taken prisoners, among them one major, and several other officers.[48] We also took 10 good wagons and horses.

General Wayne had taken quarters in a house some 100 paces to one side. He had with him some 100 men and his cannon, which we did not know. This was the reason that he was able to escape with his men and cannon. The rest of his corps, which I personally verified as numbering 599, was completely dispersed.[49] We would surely have taken his entire corps had Wayne not already ordered his men to march at two o'clock in the morning, as we learned later. Thus, most of his men were awake and dressed, and could therefore get away more easily. We lost one captain and two rank and file killed and two officers and seven rank and file wounded.

September 21. Very early in the morning a trumpeter was sent off with a letter to General Washington, who was on the other side of the Schuylkill River. The letter informed him that there were more than 100 severely wounded from Wayne's corps and that it was necessary for him to send surgeons to take care of them, since we had no surgeons to spare.

The main reason for sending this trumpeter off, probably was not only to acquaint Washington with the bad news, but also to have the trumpeter secure information on the depths of the water at Valley Forge. Giving Washington the news of Wayne's defeat before he might learn it himself, might induce him to leave his position and allow us to cross the Schuylkill unopposed.

At about six o'clock in the morning we marched off to Valley Forge in one column, where we found the English grenadiers, the 1st battalion of light infantry, and the Guards, who were already encamped and who remained there. We passed Valley Creek without being opposed by the rebels, whom we could see very clearly. They were wise not to attack us because the heights on which the English grenadiers and four 12-pounders were posted, completely commanded the low terrain on the other side of the Schuylkill.

Upon arriving between Valley Creek and Pickering Creek, the four English brigades and the light mounted and dismounted dragoons, as well as the artillery park, took position next to the English grenadiers, Guards, and the 1st battalion of light infantry. Our headquarters was also in this region.

The Hessian grenadiers, the Leib and the Donop regiments, with the Hessian jaegers and the 2nd battalion of light infantry were stationed together with the Provincials, commonly called Wemys' corps, on the other side of Pickering Creek. The region hereabouts [at headquarters] is called Charles Town.

I forgot to mention that the English riflemen, who were 140 strong in the beginning, have melted down to 42, and ceased to exist some days ago; they are not incorporated into the light infantry.[50]

September 22. It is reported that Washington, upon receiving word of the defeat of General Wayne, retreated from his position to the right along the Schuylkill, to the region of Reading, and that he left only 500 men to observe our movements.[51] At noon a noncommissioned officer and 12 men crossed the ford that is called Fatland Ford, or more commonly called Gordon's Ford, where the English grenadiers were encamped and where the Valley Creek empties into the Schuylkill.[52] The area is called Fatland. The men crossed to see how deep the water was and to determine whether we would face many of the enemy in case we should attempt to cross the Schuylkill there. They came back with the news that they had seen nothing of the enemy except a patrol and that the water was three feet deep.

At five o'clock in the evening 30 Hessian grenadiers and some jaegers crossed a ford [Gordon's] where the Hessians were encamped, that is on the other side of Pickering Creek, for the same purpose. They sent some cannon shot across the creek. Soon strong parties of rebels advanced toward the 30 grenadiers, and more assembled farther back.

Two English cannon were immediately emplaced and several shots were sent at the rebels. At the same time, the 30 Hessian grenadiers were reinforced by as many as 100 grenadiers and 60 jaegers, whereupon the rebels retreated into the woods about 500 paces from the bank. The Hessian detachment then took a position 200 paces farther forward. One grenadier and two jaegers of this detachment were wounded.

I was then ordered to go and tell Colonel Donop to send a patrol of mounted jaegers closer to the woods. On this occasion we lost several horses without being able to judge the strength or weakness of the enemy because it was completely dark by this time.

At the same time the Hessian grenadiers went across, three companies of English went across at Fatland Ford, which they accomplished without the least opposition. These two fords are about six miles apart.

At eight o'clock in the evening everything was packed, and the order was given to march immediately. My companion was sent to the ford where the three companies of English had crossed, and I was sent to the ford where the 160 Hessians had crossed. We had orders to get precise information on the depths and width of the water and on the nature of the bottom. My comrade came back with the news that the stream there was very wide and three feet deep, with an island in the middle, which separates the Schuylkill into two streams.

The ford that I went to was not very wide and only 1½ feet deep, with a hard bottom and an island in the middle. But the rebels had put up a small abatis, which would have to be cleared away before cannon and wagons could cross. The rebels appeared to be still in the woods into which they had retreated, but they did not harass our command.

At 11 o'clock at night the English Guards started to cross the Schuylkill at Fatland Ford. The English grenadiers, the English light infantry, artillery, dragoons, etc., followed.

September 23. The crossing of the Schuylkill delayed us considerably because the water was three feet deep and the men had to walk about 300 paces in the water owing to a bend in the ford. Sometime after three o'clock in the morning, three brigades of English crossed, then General Stirn's brigade of Hessians, then the Hessian grenadiers and jaegers, then the complete baggage, cattle, etc. After this came two brigades of English, and at the end came Wemys' corps of Provincials, which did not cross till four in the afternoon.

As soon as the individual regiments had crossed, they formed into line some 100 paces from the water, and lighted big fires to dry their clothes. The 100 grenadiers and 60 jaegers who last night had crossed the Schuylkill six miles farther up, were ordered to come back before dawn; they crossed the Schuylkill at Fatland Ford where the entire army crossed.

We halted until an hour before noon, which was about the time the baggage was crossing. Then we proceeded about seven miles from the ford to the Norrington house, where the main Lancaster Road goes to Philadelphia by way of Reading.[53] Our position was then about 16 or 17 miles from Philadelphia. The van of our column was stationed here, and the Hessian jaegers and Wemys' corps were about three miles from the ford. The other troops were spread between these two points, along the road.[54] Today we got hold of a hidden large flag, a couple of drums, 5 dragoons, 13 infantrymen, and four iron 18-pounders, that were mounted in the region of Swedes Ford, where we were expected to cross.[55]

September 24. Last night rebel parties harassed our outposts. A good mile from our advance posts we found, last evening, stores of gun powder, bullets, and large quantities of cartridges and grapeshot. It took nine wagons to carry away what we could use; the rest we destroyed. This morning the light dragoons found another store of various provisions, including several barrels of wine, which upon orders from the General, was divided among the officers. Although it did not make even one full bottle for each officer, they were all happy for most of them had not had any wine for three weeks. Today two more 6-pounders were found on elevated ground close to the Schuylkill. Washington is said to remain stationed in the vicinity of Reading, trying to reinforce his army. He sends only small parties to harass us.

September 25. A little after six o'clock in the morning we set out to march in two columns, the baggage in front of each column, by way of Chestnut Hill to Germantown. Lord Cornwallis' column, with which our General rode, had an exceedingly pleasant march, because the road from Chestnut Hill to Germantown is lined with many houses, most of them nice buildings. Along the way we found many inhabitants, mainly Germans, who spoke only German among themselves.

General Knyphausen's column marched two miles from us on our right and joined us at Germantown. Knyphausen's column took a position extending from the Schuylkill to Germantown. Some of Cornwallis' column was posted on the right side of Germantown, almost in line with Knyphausen's corps and to the rear on the road to Philadelphia.

A battalion of light infantry was placed two miles back, between Germantown and Chestnut Hill, where they had their first picket. We captured five men and the captain commanding a patrol of light dragoons. His name was Fons-Roi. He was a handsome man, handsomely dressed, and was so perfumed with scented water and pomade that one could easily guess his fatherland.

Cornwallis' corps came to be stationed closer to Philadelphia, in fact so close that its van, which included our headquarters, was only four miles from Philadelphia.[56]

Two squadrons of dragoons were detached this evening to Frankford, three miles from here, to seize a rebel commodore, Master Seymour and Colonel Potter, together with some commissioners who were reported to the General to be there. The dragoons came back after a little more than two hours and brought with them these gentlemen, together with 32 empty wagons on which these gentlemen had intended to carry away various provisions.[57]

It is said reliably that six rebel galleys, etc., are stationed close to Philadelphia, in such a way that they can fire upon the main street. Hence, these galleys must be chased away before we can enter Philadelphia in safety.

September 26. After eight o'clock in the morning, all English grenadiers and two battalions of Hessian grenadiers, as well as two squadrons of dragoons under the command of Lord Cornwallis, set out for Philadelphia. They took with them six 12-pounders and four mortars, in addition to the 6-pounder of their battalion. With these they will put up batteries on a height close to the city, and chase away the rebel ships.

General Howe left with these grenadiers, who were all dressed as properly as possible, having tied greenery and bands to their hats and on the horses pulling the cannon. He accompanied them half way and then rode back after the grenadiers had passed in review to the accompaniment of martial and other music.

Before Cornwallis marched off, my General sent me to an estate on Chestnut Hill to see the Messrs. Allen, three brothers, who left Philadelphia during the last winter and came to us in New York, where they have been useful to the General.[58] These Allens, who own the estate and came back as soon as we arrived, are the first and richest family in Pennsylvania except the Penn family. One of their sisters, who is said to be very beautiful, is married to Mr. Penn, Governor of Pennsylvania, whom the rebels have taken with them because they considered him our friend.[59]

I unexpectedly met this beautiful Mrs. Penn, who was with her sister and five other beautiful ladies, while they were having tea. I confess that this very unexpected sight of seven very pretty ladies disconcerted me more than the bullets of the battle at Brandywine. I had expected to see not a soul except the three brothers, whom I knew quite well, and, being an aide to the commanding general, I proceeded unabashed, without many compliments.

How completely I lost my poise is illustrated by the fact that, at first, I completely forgot the order from my General, which was to bring back with me to Lord Cornwallis, two of these brothers, who were to go to Philadelphia to gather information. After composing myself I was anxious to leave this dangerous place as soon as possible. To this end I urged the Allens to get ready to ride with me. We were able to catch up with the grenadiers this side of Philadelphia.[60]

The rebel galleys that were in the Delaware near the main road from Philadelphia, left as soon as they heard of the arrival of Lord Cornwallis and the 12-pounders and mortars he had with him. They sailed back toward their fortified island, where they also have cheveaux de frise, etc.[61]

Lord Cornwallis marched into Philadelphia to the accompaniment of fifes and drums. The inhabitants, who are said to still number 10,000, (normally 40,000) came to meet us and showed in various ways their pleasure at our arrival. Lord Cornwallis, without loss of time, began work on three batteries close to the Delaware, as he had been instructed to do.

In our camp at Germantown we were, in the meantime, harassed by a party of 300 rebels, who attacked our pickets fiercely, but were eventually driven back.

September 27. In the morning after eight o'clock we heard a strong cannonade at Philadelphia, and soon after this we received news from Lord Cornwallis that two rebel frigates and several galleys had come up the Delaware and tried to pass Philadelphia on their way to Bristol, whither their merchantmen had retreated before our arrival. Our batteries fired at them so emphatically that they turned around and sailed back. When turning around one of the frigates is said to have run onto a sand bar, and we were able to capture it. She carries 24 guns and is named the *Delaware*. The other frigate and the galleys returned to their stations under heavy fire, which, however, did little damage to them.[62]

Washington is still stationed on the main road this side of Reading. In the afternoon we were alarmed again, as yesterday. This time we had several wounded, among them three officers.

September 28. In the morning my General rode to Philadelphia for the first time. After passing through the main streets and visiting the captured frigate and our batteries on the Delaware, he stopped at Lord Cornwallis' headquarters, where he stayed until four o'clock in the afternoon, whereupon he returned to camp.

All the streets in Philadelphia are laid out rectangularly. Several buildings, among them especially the State House where Congress held its assemblies, are very large and attractive.

In the evening a detachment of 250 grenadiers was sent to Chester to escort to Philadelphia the naval officers and 50 sailors who were detached from the *Roebuck* to complete the complement of the *Delaware*. She was already manned by 59 good seamen that were found in the corps, and by 60 grenadiers.

It is still not possible for our frigates (the fleet is still far back) to come up to Philadelphia, because the rebels have in addition to the fortified island, one frigate, 13 galleys, some of which carry 24-pounders and some 18-pounders, several floating batteries, and two big row galleys mounted with 32-pounders. In addition to this they have, two miles farther down, two batteries on the Jersey shore. This shows how wisely the Howe brothers acted when they decided not to go up the Delaware on our voyage from New York.

September 29. Two Englishmen were hanged today, one for desertion and the other for pillaging. Some 30 men of the enemy sea forces have deserted since last night. They tell us that the rebels, if it comes to the bitter end, intend to set fire to their naval vessels after dismounting the guns, etc., and taking them to Jersey. This action is planned because they see themselves surrounded, in front by our frigates, in the rear by our batteries and the captured frigate

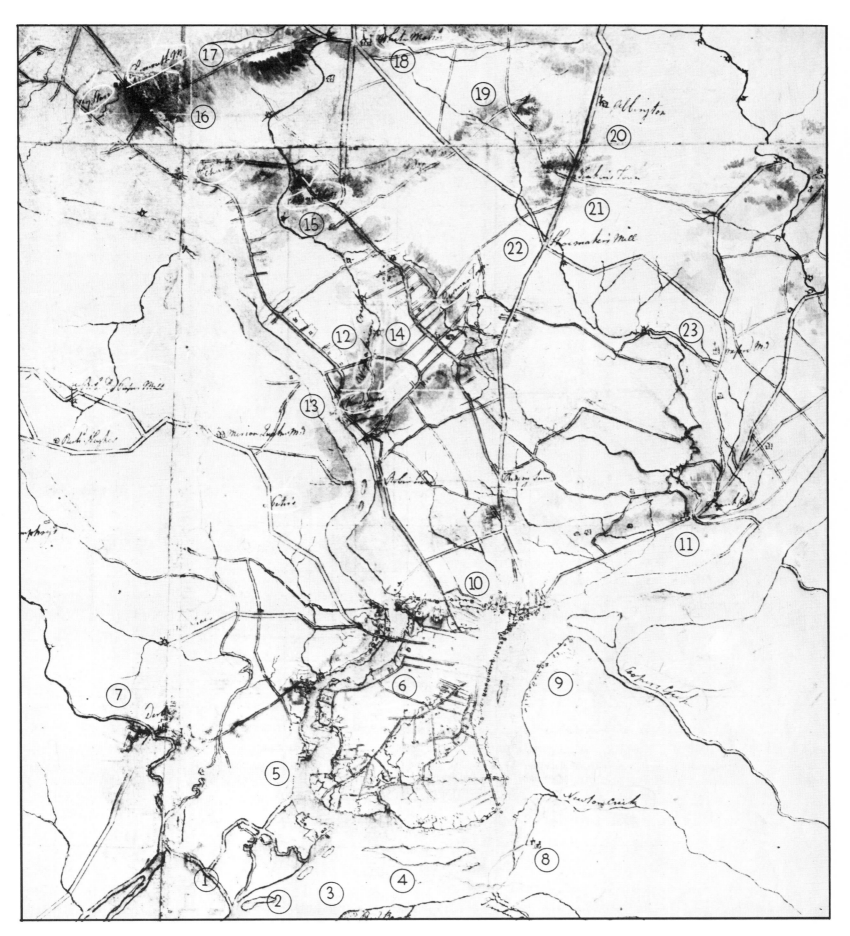

1. Province and Carpenters Islands, 2. Fort Mifflin (Mud Fort), 3. Fort Mercer (Red Bank), 4. Delaware River, 5. Schuylkill River, 6. Philadelphia, 7. Darby, 8. Gloucester, 9. Coopers Ferry, 10. Chain of British redoubts, 11. Frankford, 12. Wissahickon Creek, 13. Vandeering's Mill, 14. Germantown, 15. Chestnut Hill, 16. Barren Hill, 17. Plymouth Meeting, 18. Whitemarsh, 19. Edge Hill, 20. Abington, 21. Jenkins Town, 22. Shoemaker's Mill, 23. Oxford.

at Philadelphia.

We now know for certain that the French General de Coudray was drowned while retreating across the Schuylkill on the night after the battle of Brandywine. Also, more than 20 Frenchmen, who served mostly as volunteers with the rebels, have gone to Boston, to proceed from there safely back to France.

September 30. Some deserters say that Washington has given rum to his whole army and made bonfires because he claims to have received the reliable news that Burgoyne was decisively defeated and personally wounded.[63] The 42nd regiment of Scots and the 10th regiment of English under Colonel Stirling were detached late last night.

October 1 [1777]. News is spreading that Burgoyne has defeated the rebels in the region of Stillwater, 25 miles on the other side of Albany, and that the following day he advanced several miles farther. Washington who yesterday told his army that Burgoyne was defeated—we hope they believe it—has advanced farther down from Reading, and is now 24 miles from us.[64]

In a Philadelphia newspaper that came out while we were roaming at sea, before we landed at Elk Ferry, appeared the following article: "Whereas a certain William Howe, alias Sir William, alias anything or nothing, has gone off, greatly in debt to sundry persons in New Jersey and other parts of the Continent, and has not left wherewithal to make payment for the same; this is therefore to caution all persons not to trust him on any account, as they will certainly lose their money. Said Howe is charged with having, in company one Cornwallis, not yet taken, broken into several houses in New Jersey, and stolen and carried off many valuable effects.

"Likewise he is charged with counterfeiting currency of this continent, and of having starved to death several good subjects of these states. He has a chief jailor at New York who is a very despicable looking person, and he is the indented servant of a certain George Whelp, alias Guelph, alias King George. Whoever will secure said Howe in any jail on this continent, or will give notice where he is to the American Army, will be handsomely rewarded. N.B. He has lately been seen skulking about Amboy, Westfield, and Spank Town in the Jersies and has not been heard of. Should he attempt to practice his villany in this city, 'tis hoped all persons will be on their guard to apprehend him."[65]

October 2. At nine o'clock in the morning we heard cannonading. Later we learned that it came from Billingsport, situated on the Jersey shore about two good miles farther down than the cheveaux de frise, where the rebels have a battery, which they fired at our frigates. At one o'clock noon we heard some more firing, which however stopped soon.

October 3. Last night we heard the following news: The 42nd regiment of Highland Scots and the 10th English regiment, both under Colonel Stirling, which were detached from camp on the 30th of September, went down to Chester where they were taken aboard our five frigates that Lord Howe had sent in advance and, which are under the command of sea Captain Hamond of the *Roebuck*. Here they found the 71st regiment of Scots, which, under the command of the Hessian Colonel von Loos, had been at Wilmington and had come up from there with the frigates.

These three regiments, which constitute six battalions, landed under the cover of the frigates near Billingsport at noon yesterday, and took the battery there without suffering any losses. The rebels, 300 strong, ran away after some small arms fire on their side and some cannon shots from our side. They left behind in the fort, nine spiked heavy iron cannon. This morning two additional regiments were detached from camp to take a position near Philadelphia, on the other side close to the Schuylkill.

October 4. At my General's request, I rode to Philadelphia to arrest a man named Reichell, who was hiding there and who, in the last [Seven Years'] war, had been a lieutenant and regimental quarter-master in the Brunswick battalion Wittorf. He came here two years ago and since then has continuously been with the quartermaster general of the rebels, by name of Lutterlough, who was also in Brunswick service and was Reichell's commander.[66]

I was close to Philadelphia about half past five in the morning, when I heard cannon shots behind me. I immediately rushed to Lord Cornwallis' quarters and asked one of his aides to report the firing to his lordship, who was still asleep, and to have Reichell arrested. I then rushed back to my General. Since I knew that the General would always be where firing was heaviest, I rode, without asking where I could find him, in the direction of the heaviest fire, and there I found him.

Yesterday at noon Washington had once again assured his army, which was up to 20,000 men again, that Burgoyne had been completely defeated; that we had less than 6,000 men in our camp [at Germantown], because so many detachments had been sent to Philadelphia, Wilmington, Billingsport, etc., and that our best troops were in these detachments.[67] This would be the time to defeat us as completely as Burgoyne. And if they would behave like real soldiers, and keep quiet, he promised to lead them into Philadelphia in the morning. He then had them given rum, and at six o'clock in the evening, he marched off in three columns in our direction, leaving a few thousand men, baggage, tents, etc., at his camp about 15 miles from our advance posts.

A short time before his departure, he detached 600 men with four cannon under orders to make a lively attack on our left flank, where the jaegers are posted on the Schuylkill, one hour before dawn the next morning. Washington himself marched with his army the whole night. A few miles from our outposts he halted, had rum distributed again, and then formed one column in line, ready to attack our right wing, namely our Guards and the 1st battalion of light infantry.

The other two columns, advancing first in column formation, and then in line, attacked our 2nd battalion of light infantry. As previously noted, this unit was somewhat ahead of our line on an advance post; it did not detect the enemy approach until they were upon them because of their extreme quietness and also because of the thick fog.[68] Thus the light infantry was forced to retreat, as can be imagined, but they soon fell into line again, since the 5th regiment of the 2nd brigade arrived in good order. They held off the vehemently attacking enemy for a time, but then had to retreat, after heavy losses. I arrived just at that time, and was astounded to see something I had never seen before, namely the English in full flight.

Upon orders from my General, who was here, the 40th regiment arrived at this very critical moment. Colonel Musgrave, who commanded it, saw the light infantry and the 5th regiment falling back toward him, whereupon he detached half his regiment forward to support the retreating troops.[69]

Musgrave, with the other half of the 40th, threw himself into a massive building that was situated close between the two roads on which the two enemy columns were advancing. This maneuver by Colonel Musgrave was extremely helpful to our corps.[70] The enemy, who brought up cannon and tried to force him out, took so much time that General Howe, who had hurried to the rear, had enough time to form in line the rest of the 2nd brigade, as well as the 1st, 4th and 3rd, together with the Hessian Leib regiment. This eased the situation, and soon caused the enemy to flee.[71]

Our jaegers, in the meantime, were attacked on the left flank by 600 men whom Washington had detached across the Schuylkill. This caused the General to send to the support of the jaegers a

Hessian grenadier battalion that had remained in camp. The regiment von Donop, as well as the grenadiers, who were initially to advance with the line, had to cover the left flank of the Hessian Leib regiment, though a little farther back, forming a hook on the height.

During this period they attacked in line our Guards, the 1st battalion of light infantry, and Wemys' corps, while moving to the left as if they wanted to outflank our right wing, but they were compelled to retreat there also.[72] The retreat may have been caused largely by the arrival of the English grenadiers and one battalion of Hessian grenadiers, whose approach the rebels could see. (One battalion of Hessian grenadiers had been left behind in Philadelphia by Cornwallis, as were also the two English regiments that had been detached to the other side of the Schuylkill yesterday, but called back to Philadelphia). The Hessian grenadier battalion that had come from Philadelphia took a position between the regiment von Donop and the jaegers, the latter being with the von Minnigerode battalion.[73]

[Text accompanying Muenchhausen's plan of battle.] (Page 53)
No. 1 first column of rebels, which came by way of Chestnut Hill, No. 2, pushed back the light infantry, No. 3, which was positioned in the upper part of town, No. 4, and then formed into line, No. 5, where they were delayed a long time by Colonel Musgrave in the house, No. 6. The second rebel column, No. 7, came into the flank of the light infantry, No. 3, and drove back the light infantry and the advanced 5th regiment, No. 8, and also attacked the house, No. 6, in which Colonel Musgrave was stationed with half of the 40th regiment, No. 9, eventually this column also formed into line. Nos. 10 and 11 are the third rebel column, which formed into line at No. 12, and then attacked our Guards, No. 13, and the 1st battalion of light infantry, No. 14, and Wemys' corps, No. 15. a. are the Hessian jaegers, supported by the grenadier battalion von Minnigerode, which were attacked by 600 rebels with four cannon stationed at b.; c. Hessian Leib regiment; d. 3rd brigade; e. 4th brigade; f. 2nd brigade; g. 1st English brigade, completing the line with which General Howe dislodged the enemy and marched forward. Note: The line stood in camp as it is shown in c, d, e, f, g, 13, 14, and 15, h. is the regiment von Donop which formed a hook; i. are the English grenadiers, and k. the Hessian grenadier battalion that came from Philadelphia; m. militia with two cannon; n. militia, which alarmed Philadelphia; x. and y. are the two roads on which most of the rebels retreated and over which we pursued them.

On one road General Howe and Lord Cornwallis pursued the enemy with the English grenadiers, dragoons, two brigades of English, and the 2nd battalion of light infantry. On the other road General Grant pursued them with two brigades of English, one battalion light infantry and Wemys' corps.

The Hessian jaegers and two battalions of Hessian grenadiers remained to cover the left flank. Donop and the Leib regiments of Hessians and the 40th regiment of English under the command of General von Knyphausen, remained in the region of Chestnut Hill and spread-out to the rear in the direction of Germantown. The English Guards, under General Matthew, remained dispersed on the right flank, extending toward Philadelphia.

The pursuit of the enemy over both roads continued for about nine miles from our advance posts. But it was impossible for us to catch up with them, even less possible to take their cannon, which they had taken away before their corps retreated. Furthermore, the roads were very good and they did not suffer from lack of good horses.

We have 387 dead and wounded, among them 35 officers, and among these the British General Agnew and two colonels, who are

dead. The Hessians have only 14 dead and wounded, among them General von Stirn, who was the only officer wounded, having a contusion on his left arm. So, our losses are really very low.[74]

We have buried more than 300 of the rebels and have taken 438 prisoners, among them 47 officers. The rebels have carried with them a great number of their wounded, which was evident from the great amount of blood we could see along the entire road on which we pursued them. Their losses are very considerable when you add to the above those who normally run away into the country when their forces take a whipping. Some of their ammunition wagons fell into our hands.[75]

Everyone admits that Washington's attack was very well planned. He knew our exact positions through his very good spies. He was also aware that all regiments stood in one line in our camp, which by now was not quite as large, several detachments having been sent off. He was further aware that we could not send any regiments to places where he might attack without breaking our line.

He had based his plan on first alarming us by a false attack on our left flank, since we would then move in that direction as soon as we heard his four cannon firing rapidly. (His men had special orders to do just that). Then his two columns would attack us in the center and would either throw us back, or, in case we would take our right wing to support the center, his third column, which was poised for attack, would throw back our weakened right wing and get in our rear, through Germantown.

To alarm our garrison at Philadelphia, Washington, immediately after he started to attack us, had some 100 men of the militia show themselves on the other side of the Schuylkill and on the other side of the Delaware, on the Jersey shore. Lord Cornwallis, who soon realized that these were feints, came flying to Germantown, as I reported above.

In the evening the grenadiers went back to Philadelphia. After the evening meal, General Howe once again offered me an English commission, stating that, due to the losses this day, there would be a very good opportunity for advancement, but I want to wait to find out whether General von Jungkenn, in Cassel, who has taken good care of me up to now, will find a company for me.[76] This I would rather have than a major's patent in English service.

October 5. News arrived that our frigates had raised the first row of cheveaux de frise. Lord Howe, with his whole fleet, is reported to have come up-river. But they still cannot come as far as Philadelphia where we are, owing to the second and third rows of cheveaux de frise, which the men of the frigates cannot raise because they are within range of the enemy cannon. (Page 53)

October 6. In the evening the 42nd regiment of Scots and the 10th regiment returned from Billingsport. The 71st regiment of Scots went to Wilmington. In the evening between half past seven and nine o'clock we heard a heavy cannonade coming from the direction of the fortified island [Fort Mifflin].

October 7. The cannonade of last evening was an attack by the rebel navy upon our ships, which were trying in vain to raise the second row of cheveaux de frise. This afternoon the two regiments [the 42nd and 10th] that had been detached on October 3rd, came back to camp [at Germantown]. Redoubts are to be built on this side of Philadelphia.[77]

October 8. Among the prisoners taken on the 4th was a lieutenant who had deserted from the English at Boston, as a private.[78] He was hanged this morning, along with three marauders. This evening a battery is to be erected in the corner on this side of the Schuylkill.[79] News from Lord Howe arrived, informing us that a packet with many letters from home had arrived, and I learned with pleasure that tomorrow two squadrons of dragoons will be sent there [probably Wilmington] to pick up the mail.

At nine o'clock in the evening some rebel galleys and floating batteries approached our newly erected battery and they tried, but in vain, to destroy it by continuous fire, which lasted until the next morning at eight o'clock, at which time they were forced to retreat with the tide. During this attack they detached other armed boats up the Schuylkill and burnt some new boats we had there. We had intended to use these boats last night to go to Province Island and put up a battery.

October 9. Early in the morning, out of idle curiosity, I rode down to see the newly erected battery, and had the pleasure to see not only Mud-Fort [Fort Mifflin] and Province Island, but also the entire American Navy, which was in clear view.[80] All ships flew very large flags. Here for the first time in my life I heard chain-shot coming in.[81]

At noon a number of letters arrived. I was very happy to receive not only a gracious letter from General von Jungkenn, but also a very gracious letter from my sovereign, in which was enclosed my patent as wing adjutant with rank and pay of captain of a grenadier company. I need not tell you how happy I am over this double and unexpected advancement. Now, I do not feel sorry for having turned down the several kind offers of General Howe.[82]

October 10. Last night we almost completed our redoubt on Province Island, and we have already moved a 12-pounder into it. A mortar that we attempted to take over, sank in the process. Two hundred men were left as a command in the Province Island redoubt and in the vicinity. They were 40 Hessian grenadiers and 160 men of the 10th English regiment whose commander, Major Vatass, was in over-all command.

Toward noon the rebels landed about 200 men on Province Island under the heavy fire of their floating batteries, galleys, etc.[83] A captain, who was in the first line, and Major Vatass, with almost all of the 10th regiment, threw away their rifles and ran off; some of them let themselves be taken prisoners.[84]

The Hessian grenadiers, who were farther back, and only 40 strong, forced them to retreat to their boats from the redoubt, which they had already taken possession of, and which was very much in ruin. The grenadiers received a present of 20 guineas from General Howe. Two officers and nine men fell into the hands of the enemy during the engagement.[85]

October 11. We had a false alarm last night.[86] The entire army left camp, and two battalions of grenadiers were summoned from Philadelphia. A jaeger patrol, which had pushed too far out, lost two men. We did not return to camp until seven in the morning. But before we took positions, we made some changes in camp. The right wing was pulled back toward Germantown, and the center was moved forward, so that our camp occupied less terrain. Our headquarters was moved to Germantown.

Yesterday we completed two batteries on Carpenters Island and we have also put up a redoubt farther up toward the road to Darby, etc. It is said for certain that General Clinton moved up the North River from New York the beginning of the month, with 3,000 men.

October 12. About noon the rebels landed again at three places on Carpenters Island (locally Carpenters and Province Islands are called Province Island although they are in fact two separate islands).[87] Captain Stamford of the Hessian Leib regiment, commanding 25 Hessian and 25 English grenadiers distinguished himself on this occasion by driving back the enemy with losses.[88]

October 13. Last night our pickets were attacked. An English dragoon patrol lost one sergeant and two men.

October 14. Washington continues to stand 16 miles from us, but is said to have a few thousand men in the region of Chester with

orders to send more troops over to Red Bank.[89] We observe more activity at Red Bank, and some tents have been erected there.[90] It is said that they are working day and night to make the fort there as strong as possible. I recently gave an erroneous report on the number of rebel ships stationed at Fort Island and thereabouts, for I counted nearly 30 sails myself today.

Last night we heard heavy cannonading, owing to the fact that the rebels sent two fire rafts, fully ablaze, down upon our fleet. (These fire rafts are able to pass over the cheveaux de frise, which are nine feet under water). They were destroyed by the *Roebuck* and *Vigilant* before they could do any damage.[91] The rebels have again made fires to celebrate, as they claim, the complete defeat of General Burgoyne.[92]

October 15. In the morning we heard a heavy but not sustained cannonade. In the evening we were informed that it came from our batteries [on Province and Carpenters Islands], firing all at once at the rebel ships, which were forced to withdraw toward Red Bank out of reach of our batteries. If we had 24-pounders, we could even chase them away from Red Bank. In this engagement, an 18-pounder that we found here, exploded. Many bombs were thrown into the fort on the island but they did not set it afire.[93]

October 16. In the morning we fired hot-shot at the fort, but in vain.[94] Despite the fact that only two sides are of masonry construction and the others of wood; nothing caught fire.

October 18. Last night our pickets of the jaegers and those of the light infantry were attacked. We are told that Washington is moving with his army. At nine o'clock in the morning eight regiments of English and 50 dragoons under General Grant were pushed forward by way of Chestnut Hill for a distance of about nine miles, to get precise information on Washington.[95] In the evening they came back without having met any of the enemy, except some strong patrols. Washington's position is said to be 16 miles from here on the Reading Road.[96]

In the evening [Colonel Francis] Lord Rawdon, aide to General Clinton, arrived with the following news: General Clinton, with five English, one Hessian and two Provincial regiments, together with some dragoons and 200 Hessian jaegers (of the contingent of 400 Hessian jaegers who arrived in New York after our departure for Philadelphia), has attacked and taken Fort Montgomery and Fort Clinton in the evening of October 6. We had 187 killed and wounded.

The enemy then deserted Fort Constitution situated higher up the river, after first spiking their cannon and setting fire to their barracks and provisions. We took 400 prisoners out of 1,200 men distributed in the garrisons of the forts. Two hundred are said to have been killed in the first heated onrush, and they lost close to 70 iron cannon.

Our Wilmington garrison, which embarked several days ago, disembarked again in the region of Chester, together with many convalescents. Without delay they marched to Philadelphia and will encamp close to the Schuylkill, where we are constructing a bridge.[97]

October 19. We marched in two columns to Philadelphia, where we moved into a very strong camp on the side of Philadelphia facing Germantown.[98] The ten newly erected but not completed redoubts, which lie scattered from the Delaware to the Schuylkill, are in front of our camp.

October 20. Last night Lord Howe, upon request of his brother, sent 12 flatboats up [the Delaware] along our shore. This proved to be almost disastrous because one of our pickets, not having been informed of the expected arrival of the flatboats, fired on them. This alarmed the rebel ships and the forts so they fired a few cannon shot toward our flatboats, which, fortunately, were almost all the way up the river.

Lieutenant Colonel von Wurmb was almost captured this morning when he made a short patrol. A much stronger rebel patrol of dragoons pursued him as far as between our pickets. We caught one dragoon captain, while they caught two of the jaegers accompanying Colonel von Wurmb.

Last night most of the Guards were detached to Chester to convoy to Philadelphia provisions and ammunition that had been unloaded there from boats.[99] The convoy arrived here this afternoon, without mishap.

October 21. At five o'clock in the morning the grenadier battalions Linsing, Minnigerode and Lengerke, as well as the regiment Mirbach and the Hessian jaegers, all under the command of Colonel von Donop, crossed over to Jersey at Coopers Ferry [now Camden], with orders to take the batteries and the fort at Red Bank.

October 22. At noon 200 English grenadiers were put into boats prepared to land on and storm Fort Island at the same time when some of our ships would come up the Delaware as close as possible to the cheveaux de frise and begin to fire on the fort at Red Bank and on rebel ships, as they were ordered to do. I believe that all this was to take place simultaneously with Colonel von Donop's attack. But a completely contrary wind prevented the war ships that had received orders, from coming up the river.[100] Consequently, General Howe requested Donop not to attack this afternoon. Unfortunately, shortly after four o'clock we observed a strong fire at Red Bank, and, after it had ceased, we still saw the rebel flags flying.

October 23. Last night the following report arrived from Lieutenant Colonel von Linsing: Colonel von Donop stormed the fort at Red Bank yesterday afternoon with two grenadier battalions and the regiment von Mirbach, leaving behind in reserve the jaegers and the grenadier battalion Lengerke.

The fall of Colonel Donop, who was severely wounded, and of Lieutenant Colonel von Schieck, who was shot to death, as well as the fall of von Minnigerode, who was also wounded, together with many other brave officers, is a grave loss.[101] The dreadful cannonade of the ships, which fired on our flanks, and especially the desperately steep height of the parapet (which had been palisaded), and the parapet on one fort made it completely impossible to take the fort.[102]

Our force, with the loss of almost 400 men, among them 23 officers killed and many more severely wounded, was compelled to withdraw, and are now on their way back. After the receipt of this news, two English regiments were ordered to cross [the Delaware] at dawn to cover the retreat of Donop's detachment. They took with them 30 wagons for the wounded as well as provisions.[103]

I had to go with this detachment. It took till nine o'clock in the morning until I had all of them across [to New Jersey]. Then we marched about two miles, when we met many wounded officers and common soldiers, who were followed by the battalions. I cannot describe my feeling, especially when I saw the company to which I had just been assigned and which is very dear to me. It came back with the loss of 37 men. All were across the Delaware by 11 o'clock in the evening. The three battalions, which had lost almost all their officers and nearly 400 men, were lodged in the barracks, for they could not possibly do service very soon.

This morning, before nine o'clock, the ships, *Augusta, Roebuck, Merlin, Vigilant* and a few others took a position close below the cheveaux de frise, and began a terrible fire. The English grenadiers had already been put into boats to land on Fort Island when suddenly the ship *Augusta* of 64 guns and the *Merlin* of 20 guns caught fire.[104] At once the other ships had to withdraw in order to keep them from catching fire, although they tried to save as many of the unfortunate men as possible aboard the two burning ships.

October 24. All the Hessian rank and file and all the officers under Colonel Donop, as well as Colonel Donop himself, were publicly praised by General Howe in his orders of the day.[105]

October 25. General Howe sent his chief surgeon to Red Bank to look after Colonel von Donop, who is said to be still alive.[106]

October 26. Several Hessian surgeons were sent to Red Bank today to attend to our poor wounded who have not yet been bandaged.[107] According to reliable news that just arrived from General Clinton, he marched back to New York with 600 men, after having razed Forts Montgomery and Constitution and having left behind three battalions in Fort Clinton, which fort is said to be the strongest of the three.

Clinton has sent General Vaughan up the North or Hudson River with 1800 men on large boats and schooners. He landed 40 miles this side of Albany in the region of the town of Esopus [Kingston, N.Y.], which was burned down because the rebels dispersed themselves in houses and thus used them as forts. Many rebels were burned, and some were captured along with 15 cannon. Vaughan then boarded ship again and sailed to Albany to ease the situation for Burgoyne, whom he assumed to be at Stilwater on the other side of Albany and who was opposed by General Gates and Schuyler with 7,000 men. But unfortunately we have rather certain news that Burgoyne has already gone back [toward Canada] because of lack of provisions. If this is true, it is very unfortunate.

The English doctor has just come back from Red Bank; he says that, though Donop is still alive, he will not recover under the circumstances. Also, a flag of truce from the enemy has just come in with open letters from our captured officers, which I sent at once to General von Knyphausen. Since they were open letters, I read them and learned that Lieutenant Colonel Brethauer has died.[108]

As far as I know, there are the following rebel generals; although there is no printed list of them: [George] Washington, [Charles] Lee, captured, [John] Sullivan, [Samuel] Parsons, [Seth] Pomeroy, [   ] Steel, [John] Paterson, [Benedict] Arnold, [Horatio] Gates, [Philip] Schuyler, [William] Livingston, [   ] Hern, [   ] Stephenson, [Robert] Howe, [Alexander] Mc Dougall, [   ] Crofts, [Andrew] Lewis, [Lewis] Morris, [Charles] Scott, [William] Thompson, [William] Maxwell, [Anthony] Wayne, [William Alexander Lord] Stirling, [Thomas] Mifflin, [John] Cadwalader, [John] Dickinson, [Philemon] Dickinson, [Daniel] Roberdeau, [George] Clinton, [James] Clinton, [Joseph] Reed, [Artemus] Ward, [William] Woodford, [James] Ewing, [John] Armstrong, [Arthur] St. Clair, [George] Weedon, [Francis] Nash, killed at Germantown, and [James] Irvine.[109]

No one knows what we will do now; most are of the opinion that we simply must take Red Bank and Fort Island as well as their ships in the Delaware in order to have communication with our fleet. Then we could chase Washington across the Susquehanna. Homo proponit, Deus disposit [Man proposes but God disposes].

Philadelphia, October 26, 1777

v. Muenchhausen

EIGHTH TRANSMITTAL
October 27, 1777-January 22, 1778

October 27, 1777. It has been raining hard since last evening. This afternoon a packet sailed from here.

October 28. The heavy rain, which will not stop has completely inundated areas on the Schuylkill and especially Carpenters and Province Islands. This causes considerable difficulty for our pickets posted in these regions. A communication bridge, which we constructed across the Schuylkill was torn away by the water. With 400 men, we again occupied Billingsport in Jersey, which we had razed. They have orders to construct a redoubt there.[1]

October 29. The flooding on Province Island, owing to the continuing rain, has caused our posts on that island, and in the vicinity, to have some men drowned while many others are becoming ill.

October 30. The rain, which began on the 26th, finally stopped this morning. I was given orders by my General to go down to Red Bank by water. One of my instructions was to inquire about Colonel von Donop. A major and a captain came to meet me and took me blindfolded in their boat and through their fleet near Fort Island and past Red Bank to a house about 600 paces beyond Red Bank, where I found two of our severely wounded officers. Colonel von Donop had died the evening before at seven o'clock. Because I was aide to General Howe, I was urgently invited to dine with the rebel commander at Red Bank, Brigadier General Greene, and General Putnam's son, who is a captain, and a French major, which invitation I declined, mainly because General Greene, although he was very polite, betrayed signs of arrogance, partly because he had repulsed our attack on his fort, and partly because of the news that Burgoyne had been captured with his entire corps.[2]

The two wounded officers were eager to be taken to Philadelphia. I therefore asked Greene in the name of my General to send them there, which he did. Then I took leave, although they insisted that I stay to attend the burial of Colonel von Donop, who, the same evening, was put in the soil with military honors at the same place where our other officers and privates had been buried, in accordance with the wishes Colonel Donop expressed shortly before his death.

We are now constructing two floating batteries. They are to be equipped with 32-pounder cannon taken from the Admiral's ship *Eagle,* which guns are to be debarked at Carpenters Island then towed up the Schuylkill to the spot where the floating batteries are being built.

October 31. At Red Bank and on Fort Island (also called Great Mud Island) we see the rebels laboring unceasingly to strengthen their positions with new works. We are building a large entrenchment close to the Delaware, this side of Coopers Ferry, at the place where Donop crossed over.

In the afternoon, with Washington's permission, the General had a visit from our officer sent by Burgoyne, who reported that Burgoyne, being completely surrounded, was compelled to surrender.[3] The main points of the surrender are: All cannon, rifles, weapons, and munitions are to be turned over to the enemy; the troops must proceed to Boston, where they will stay until General Howe either sends them to England or releases them; until then they are not allowed again to serve against the United States of America.[4]

How unfortunate this event is for us, is easy to imagine. At Ticonderoga there is said to be a garrison of 3,000 men, together with provisions for six months. If this garrison could hold out, our enemy could undertake nothing in the northern part of America this year, since winter is approaching fast. New York and Rhode Island, however, will do well to be on the alert. Many of us hope that England will give in, or else send 20,000 men early next spring. The first would be the most desirable, because I fear that England cannot accomplish the latter.

November 2, [1777.] Yesterday and today the General spent several hours on the Schuylkill, to promote, by his presence, the work on the floating batteries.

November 3. Last night we luckily brought to Province Island six 24-pounders on two large gunboats. At the Day's orders, the capitulation of General Burgoyne was read without changing the story very much. Aside from very poor and little hay, our horses have had nothing for the past two weeks so that they are all perishing.

November 4. In the morning two rebel ships approached Fort Island from Red Bank, supposedly to land munitions, etc. Drawing fire from our batteries on Carpenters Island, they withdrew.

November 5. Last night six 32-pounders were taken from the *Eagle* to Province Island, in addition to much provisions, ammunition, etc. Four of the guns are being taken to the Schuylkill to be employed on our floating batteries; the two others are to be used on Province Island, where the six 24-pounders that had been brought the day before yesterday are to be mounted in a battery that is almost finished.

Shortly before noon General Howe rode down to Province Island, inspected the works we had constructed there, and ordered many changes. He also posted the English 27th and 28th regiments some distance behind the batteries. They had been taken out of the line this morning and marched there. The report that Washington was to attack Province Island from the direction of Darby probably led the General to make this decision. A daily command of 470 men will continue to be taken out of the line and posted there.[5]

The rebels on Fort Island and several of their galleys with 32-pounders, who must have seen the General on Province Island, directed some of their cannon on a spot from which we had just come and to which we would have to go on our way back. When we passed this spot (it was really a dam) as we rode back, we got a whole salvo of cannon balls, but none of them fulfilled the hopes of the enemy in spite of the fact that the General stopped at this place for several minutes.

Later we rode up the Schuylkill, where our two floating batteries were being built. One of them had just been finished. Two 32-pounders were then put on it, and the floating battery was pushed into the water with great effort, and with the aid of many devices, but it did not seem to come up to the General's expectations. The other battery will be ready within the next two days. While there we heard loud cannon fire for ten minutes, which, the General was informed, came from a newly opened battery of the rebels a good distance beyond Red Bank, close to the Cheveaux de Frise. By their fire, they forced our nearby anchored warships to retreat.[6]

From here the General rode through the pickets of the entire line and he found them all awake and alert in spite of the fact that it was raining hard and it was very dark. After 10 o'clock in the evening we finally arrived [at headquarters] soaking wet, and we had our noon meal at 11 o'clock at night.

November 6, 7 and 8. Nothing special, except that we are hard at work on our batteries on Province Island.

November 9. Last night the pickets of our right flank were very much molested. A patrol of 10 dragoons and 12 grenadiers of the Guards, who had been sent off at dawn, fell into enemy hands. Lord Howe informed us that more than 3,000 men, including some convalescents and recruits, under the command of the English

General Sir Thomas Wilson, arrived in ships from New York.[7] Further, the General received the reliable information that the rebels have assembled 7,000 men in Connecticut opposite Rhode Island, that they sent more than 70 boats full of troops to the Rhode Island coast, but that they withdrew after they had been welcomed by several heavy cannon balls, and then found our troops, rifle in hand.

November 10. In the morning shortly after eight o'clock our batteries on Province and Carpenters Islands began firing.[8] These batteries consist of two 32-pounders, six 24-pounders, one 18-pounder, one mortar of 13 inches, two of 8 inches, and two howitzers of 8 inches. There are also two 12-pounders, which were not firing, as well as one 18-pounder and two 12-pounders in the corner of this [the north] side of the Schuylkill, which are not firing either. The latter five pieces are placed in such a way as to prevent rebel ships from coming up to Philadelphia. The first-mentioned pieces played the entire day at the side of the fort nearest to us, about 900 paces from our batteries. The enemy answered from the fort quite powerfully and accurately; for example (something that happens very rarely), they fired a 12-pound ball directly into the barrel of one of our 24-pounders, without damaging our cannon because it went in so accurately.

This morning one of our patrols of 30 dragoons attacked an enemy patrol of 50 dragoons, who, led by General Pulaski (known from the Polish Confederation but now in the service of the rebels), gave our dragoons a good fight. We captured a French major and a dragoon, and they captured three of our dragoons; besides, we lost five horses.[9]

General Vaughan, after having burned the town of Esopus, was back in his boats again and moved farther in the direction of Albany to relieve the pressure on General Burgoyne, but when he heard of the capitulation of Burgoyne he hastily withdrew. Before his retreat he razed Fort Vaughan, former Fort Clinton, which he had reinforced and intended to defend. He is now back on York Island. On his retreat he did a lot of burning and pillaging.

November 11. Last night and today the fort was continuously fired upon to prevent the enemy from repairing the damage.

November 12. Last night four sloops full of provisions and much ammunition came up the river under cover of our fire. Despite the heavy fire from the enemy, three of them fortunately got through.[10] The fourth was severely damaged, but all of its cargo was saved. The sloops brought three weeks' supply of salt provisions and ship biscuits. Cannonading and bomb-throwing continues day and night. I wish we would finally capture this cursed fort; it makes us aides ride around so much. It is especially inconvenient to ride during the night because everything is swampy, and, besides, one is very exposed to enemy shells if one does not happen to be standing in a battery.

Finally, in the afternoon, our two floating batteries, each carrying two 32-pounders, were finished. They were taken down the Schuylkill and were placed in the mouth of the river. In addition to the battery that the enemy had opened beyond Red Bank on the 5th of November, they have been working the past three days on a new one, on the Jersey shore, farther down toward Billingsport. This drew a very heavy cannonade from our fleet, and it seems that they gave up this dangerous work this evening. I have had a slight fever for some days, and because I could not take care of myself, it became worse yesterday and has forced me to stay in my room.

November 13. Our batteries are playing all the time.[11]

November 14. Our floating batteries, which tried their luck today, were so warmly received by the enemy that one of them was so close to sinking that it took its cannon ashore on Carpenters Island to be used in a new land battery we shall construct tomorrow night.

The other floating battery was forced to go back up the Schuylkill River.

The battery ship *Vigilant,* which for several days has been trying to pass through, will certainly come up tomorrow morning with the high tide, and then there will soon be a decision respecting the fort.[12]

November 15. About eight o'clock in the morning the *Vigilant* luckily worked herself through and anchored about 200 paces from the fort. With her, a small sloop arrived, aboard which Admiral Howe had a battery of three 18-pounders mounted.[13] At the same time five large warships moved as close as possible to the cheveaux de frise and covered the battery ship with a continuous strong fire, for the rebel ships that were near Red Bank tried to come around [Fort Island] to ruin the *Vigilant* and the sloop with their much heavier fire.[14]

At this time the fire from our land batteries started again, with new vigor. The fire of our ships stopped the rebel ships from coming around, after which our ships turned their fire on the fort. The rebel floating batteries, galleys, sloops and one of their frigates answered our fire well, and the *Isis,* whose captain was a brother of Lord Cornwallis, was badly damaged, having taken 34 shells that went right through her. Their fort on the island fired only a few shots.

Everyone expected that they would surrender because their parapets and log houses had suffered so much from our continuous fire since the 10th of the month that one could see through them and because they now receive the strongest fire from all sides.[15] On the *Vigilant,* English riflemen were posted on the masts; they fire from up there, quite accurately, into the fort.

General Howe as well as Lord Howe, who had come up by boat early this morning, were in the mortar battery till seven o'clock in the evening. As the General rode back [to Philadelphia] he ordered the cannonading and bombing to continue throughout the night. Four hundred English Guards under the command of Colonel Sir George Osborne, and necessary boats, have been prepared since morning to storm the fort. (In spite of not being well, I was there all the same; the intense fire was too beautiful a spectacle to miss by staying home. In the army it is forbidden for anyone to leave his post or regiment to watch something). Everyone believed and wished that the General would give the command to storm any moment. But he did not do so, for he maintained that the enemy could not stand our dreadful fire much longer and would leave the fort voluntarily the following night, which they did after one o'clock at night, and then after setting the barracks, etc. afire, they went over to Red Bank in boats.[16]

The fort garrison of 200 men was commanded by a French major, in spite of the fact that one of their colonels, named Smith, had the title of commander.[17] One man of the garrison hid himself in order to desert to our lines. They intentionally did not strike the rebel colors, because they believed this to be more respectable than to let them fall into our hands.

November 16. Early in the morning a command of ours occupied Fort Island. We found some cannon balls and 28 cannon, only five of them spiked. The fort was put in a dreadful condition by our cannon balls. Almost every cannon had spots of blood on it. Many of their killed were buried, many of them not. Last night their ships moved up 500 paces in the direction of Gloucester.[18]

November 17. With the 32-pounders taken to the fort, and with the two 24-pounders and four 18-pounders that had been left in good condition by the rebels, we began to construct a battery on Fort Island. It will be finished tomorrow. The other usable cannon are being taken to Philadelphia where they will be distributed.

Our first adjutant, Major Cuyler, who was still a captain last year and who had been sent with the last packet to England with the news of the Brandywine and Germantown affairs, was today promoted to lieutenant colonel by the General, since a lieutenant colonelcy was vacant. If I were in English service, the General could promote me just as quickly.

November 18. Last night ice froze solid. At nine o'clock in the evening the 1st battalion grenadiers, the 1st battalion light infantry, the 27th and 33rd regiments English, 50 jaegers, and the Hessian grenadier battalion Lengerke, all under the command of Lord Cornwallis, marched to Chester. In the evening they started to cross over to Jersey to join the force of the English General Sir Thomas Wilson, who, as previously reported, had arrived from New York and disembarked in Jersey this morning with three English [regiments], two Anspach [battalions], and the 17th regiment light dragoons, as well as two companies of Hessian jaegers.[19] Lord Cornwallis' vanguard came upon a rebel picket in the Darby region and captured one officer and 19 men.

November 19. According to information received from several deserters and confirmed through other sources, Washington is still 15 miles away from us, standing behind earthworks thrown up on heights along the main road to Reading, having a bridge across the Schuylkill at his right flank, by which he maintains communication with detachments of about 3,000 men on the other side.

Yesterday and the day before Washington received several reinforcements, partly from Gates' northern army, including the light infantry that had been taken away from [the attack on] Burgoyne, partly from the southern provinces. A General Morgan with 600 riflemen of whom heroic deeds are expected, are among them.[20] It is rumored that General Gates himself may be with them.[21]

These reinforcements amount to about 5,000 men, but according to rebel reports 18,000, which probably accounts for the rumor that they intend to attack us. This we doubt very much because of our well fortified camp, the right flank of which is anchored on the Delaware and the left on the Schuylkill. In the front we have 10 well placed redoubts, which are connected by parapets.

Toward New Year, the Delaware and the Schuylkill normally have high water, and if Washington's now strong army should not be dispersed by then, we will, if the water stays high, have to be careful. It is certain that during this winter our headquarters will be in Philadelphia, and that the General will not go back to New York, as had been suspected. Washington is said to have sent two brigades to Jersey.

November 20. Two brigades of rebels crossed over to Jersey last night in the area of Burlington.[22] In the afternoon the rebels set fire to two of their ships.[23]

November 21. Last night the rebels set fire to four of their ships, and at the same time five of their best galleys crept up with the high tide and a good wind, and got past our frigate before they were noticed.[24] Nevertheless, they were subjected to the intense fire from the frigate and from our shore batteries near the city. One of the galleys was destroyed, but the crew made its way to the Jersey shore after it had set fire to the galley.

There was never a more beautiful fireworks than the one caused by 15 burning ships during the dark night. They moved up and down with the tide, and as soon as the fire reached the powder magazines the ships blew up with loud explosions. It was the most spectacular sight I have ever seen, and it was augmented by our batteries and our frigate firing upon the passing galleys. It is certain that last night seven of their galleys got through without being discovered. According to my calculation, they must have saved 11 galleys and burned and sunk 20, among them their frigate.[25]

A narrow passage through the cheveaux de frise, which was un-

known to us, but was closed up with a very strong chain, was opened by our ships today, so that they can come up now.[26]

November 22. At seven o'clock in the morning we felt some rather strong tremors of an earthquake. At that very time, the enemy attacked the Hessian jaeger pickets, but they soon retreated because the entire jaeger corps opposed them. Toward 12 o'clock noon they attacked Simcoe's light corps (formerly Wemys' corps) on our right flank.[27] The English Guards, who were close by and hastened to Simcoe's support, again drove back the enemy, who was probably not more than 600 strong.

A good mile from our pickets they made a stand again in some houses. After we had driven them out of these houses we set them on fire. Since enemy detachments are harassing us often and since they are posted in the buildings before our front, General Howe ordered all these houses to be burned down by our patrols whenever the opportunity offers. Lord Cornwallis, who yesterday had taken possession of Red Bank after the enemy had deserted it and left behind some cannon etc., was this morning ordered to raze the fort completely.

November 23. During the last few days we have been busy dismantling our batteries, redoubts, etc., on Carpenters and Province Islands. We finished this today and have now completely evacuated this region. Some of our dragoons deserted last night. A corps of 2,000 rebels is said to have taken a position on Chestnut Hill, beyond Germantown, last evening.

November 24. When we received the news that 600 riflemen with three German cannon from Burgoyne's troops, under the command of General Morgan, had arrived this side of Germantown last night after midnight, 600 light infantry and 200 dragoons were ordered to proceed there along two different roads. But they found the post was already deserted, General Morgan having retreated yesterday evening.

November 25. This morning the baggage, etc. of Lord Cornwallis' corps, which is encamped on the banks of the Delaware close to Gloucester, began to come across. Toward noon the General visited Lord Cornwallis on the other side of the river, at Gloucester.

November 26. Last night the rebels attacked our Hessian jaegers in Jersey.[28] Since they outnumbered our jaegers considerably, and also had a few hundred dragoons with them, the jaegers were compelled to retreat at first, but they were soon supported, and drove away the enemy. The jaegers had two officers and 28 men killed and wounded during this affair.[29]

A large number of various ships have come up the river and are now at anchor close to Philadelphia. Some of them were damaged considerably when they passed through the very narrow channel between the cheveaux de frise.

November 27. Today the rest of Cornwallis' corps crossed the river.[30] Two ships have been stationed close to the Jersey shore to cover the rear guard.[31] Their fire caused the enemy, who showed up in strength to harass our rear guard, to retreat very quickly, wounding only a few of our men. Cornwallis' corps was placed partly in barracks in town and partly on the outskirts of the city, for there was no room in our line. Lord Cornwallis was unable to collect as many cattle in Jersey as General Howe had expected and hoped for.[32] We shall have to live on salt provisions during the coming winter.

November 28. The battery ship *Vigilant* and some other sloops of war have orders to join the frigate *Delaware* above the city of Philadelphia, that is, more toward Burlington so that she can keep galleys and other ships, of which the enemy still have many in the Delaware at Bristol and Burlington, from sneaking through and alarming our fleet. To prevent the enemy from sending fire ships down the river, a strong chain is being made, which is to be placed in the water, up-river of the frigate *Delaware,* toward the enemy. Yesterday Lord Howe moved into a house in the city close to us, and, since it is not furnished yet, he and his suite have all their meals with his brother.

November 29. The troops that Washington had in Jersey have returned, crossing last night at Bristol and proceeding up the Pennypack Creek.[33]

November 30. It has been raining very hard since the evening before yesterday, and this seems to be the main reason that we have not moved again. It is speculated that Lord Cornwallis with his corps will cross the Schuylkill here. We hear that Washington is no longer on good terms with Congress. The English General Sir Thomas Wilson, who has just arrived, will return to England.

December 3, [1777.] A fleet of 27 ships with provisions, straw, oats, etc., and many convalescents arrived here from New York yesterday. In the evening we marched in two columns, one under General von Knyphausen and the other one under Lord Cornwallis. At 11 o'clock at night the orders were countermanded.[34]

December 4. The enemy is said to be still in his old position in the hills near Whitemarsh, a very advantageous position about 14 miles from here. Orders to march were given in the evening. Toward 10 o'clock we left in one column, headed for Germantown.[35] There was an extremely heavy frost. Three miles from here our vanguard met the first enemy picket. This picket and others that we met, at and beyond Germantown, fired on us and then retreated. We continued to march without a halt. Shortly before four o'clock in the morning we heard the enemy's alarm cannons being fired, first in one place and then in another.

December 5. A short time before dawn the van of the column arrived on the foothills beyond Chestnut Hill and halted there. This was 11 miles from Philadelphia. By a little after seven o'clock our whole corps of 12,000 men had arrived; we formed in one line along our height. We did not have a second line but only a few reserve regiments posted here and there behind the first line.

The enemy, who was in position on the very high and wooded hills behind Whitemarsh, had extended their front considerably.[36] In front of him, Washington had swampy water spanned by two bridges by which he maintained communication with some light troops on this side of Whitemarsh. Between him and us was a deep valley, which was also wooded, except that there was some rather level ground before our right flank, as well as some close to our left flank.

At nine o'clock in the morning a detachment of our light infantry took a mill in the valley in front of our right flank, where an enemy picket was posted.[37] Thereupon their light troops retreated to the other side of the water and destroyed the bridges behind them. Our troops stacked their rifles and made campfires, but they were not permitted to move around.

At this time General Howe went out to reconnoiter. Opposite our right wing there was a church, to the left near Whitemarsh, where we clearly saw a strong abatis with many embrasures and cannon.[38] According to deserters and other information, Washington's headquarters is at that church, and the abatis has been put up because this was the only weak spot of their camp, since the creek could easily be crossed here.

At about noon the enemy attacked our right flank with 1,200 men under the command of General Irvine, but was soon repelled, and General Irvine, who had been wounded, was taken prisoner.[39] This caused our right flank to stir, and undoubtedly a total engagement would have ensued if the General had not given repeated orders for the light infantry to retreat, since he believed that the enemy was intent on engaging us here, where they had the abatis

and many cannon. During the night we rested on our arms. It was a beautiful spectacle to see the great number of our and Washington's fires.

December 6. The enemy detached from their center a strong column and moved it toward his right flank, which they had pulled back last night and made unassailable with a very strong redoubt. Our armies were separated at the most by three miles. All information leads to the conclusion that Washington wants us to attack, because he has 30,000 men and is in a good position behind the abatis.[40] At six o'clock in the evening we were ordered to march at three in the morning. Contrary to expectations we set out to march back to Germantown at nine in the evening.

December 7. Everybody supposed that we were marching back to Philadelphia, but we turned to the left in Germantown, and after a few miles, again to the left, and thus again toward Washington whom we now approached on his left flank.[41]

General Grey with one brigade of Englishmen, all the jaegers, Simcoe's light corps, and 120 light infantry, was detached when the van came parallel to Washington's left flank, so that later, when we should attack, he could fall upon the enemy's left flank, and then align himself with the main corps.[42] (This is the way we were deployed yesterday, but now, because we had marched around Washington, his left flank had become his right one).

We [the main column] marched another short distance straight ahead and then to the left again.[43] We halted from nine until eleven o'clock in the morning, during which time rum was given to the men. General Howe rode out to reconnoiter and found that the enemy's position here was even stronger than on the other side of Chestnut Hill. A range of heights called Edge Hill, in which the enemy had some 1,000 light troops, riflemen, etc., was between us and Washington's encampment.

At noon the English and Hessian grenadiers formed into a line together with the English Guards, and set out for Edge Hill. The corps followed close behind in column formation, the English light infantry forming the van.[44]

At this time General Grey, who had been detached, attacked the enemy's right flank. The enemy, who had only a few troops in these hills of Edge Hill, skirmished with us for some time, which resulted in our having 89 killed and wounded.[45] Then the enemy retreated to the very high and wooded hills of their real camp. We then formed in line on the hills of Edge Hill, which the enemy had deserted.[46] It was now about three o'clock in the afternoon. General Grey had by this time formed in line with our left wing. General Howe reconnoitered until eight o'clock in the evening. He found everywhere strong natural and man-made obstacles, which prevented any hope of success.

December 8. The enemy has worked during the night making additional barricades, etc. At noon we set out to march on the most direct road to Philadelphia, where we arrived at 11 o'clock at night without being seriously pursued by the enemy, which, I assume, the General had hoped for.[47] We moved very slowly in two lines with one column in between, so we could be ready for a surprise attack. The troops moved into their old camp near Philadelphia.

December 9. The ships that are to take away Burgoyne's army are said to have left.[48] The Hessian von Mirbach regiment and three battalions of Scottish Highlanders, i.e., the 71st regiment, will be sent to New York.

December 10. Most of us assume that we shall now move into winter quarters. Some believe that we shall make one more expedition with perhaps 4,000 or 5,000 men toward Wilmington to bring in some cattle. Many transports are leaving for England to bring over fresh troops, as we are told. There is much talk about 20,000

Russians.[49] General Washington is said to have detached still more troops to his right across the Schuylkill, so that almost 3,000 men are now under the command of General Potter.

December 11. Last night about 4,000 men received orders to march; they crossed the Schuylkill this morning at three o'clock, under the command of Lord Cornwallis.[50]

General Potter, though in very favorable position, retreated when our corps approached. Following him on his heels, our troops came upon some 800 men who did some skirmishing with the vanguard of Lord Cornwallis, during which the enemy lost many killed and prisoners. Lord Cornwallis pursued General Potter to within three miles this side of Swedes ford, where Potter hastened to join Washington, crossing over the communication bridge, which he demolished behind him.[51]

December 12. Lord Cornwallis came back and brought 200 tons of hay and 400 head of cattle.

December 15. The Hessian regiment von Mirbach and the 71st regiment of Highland Scots were embarked into boats to gather provisions in the region of Chester under the cover of some sloops of war. The provisions will be brought here in boats, which were taken along for that purpose. Thereafter these two regiments will embark on transports and leave for New York.

December 16. This morning Lord Cornwallis went aboard the *Brilliant* to go to England. We expect him back next spring.

December 18. It is certain that Washington has marched with his main army from Whitemarsh across the Schuylkill to Valley Forge.[52]

December 20. Admiral Howe left and went aboard his ship, the *Eagle,* and will depart if the wind is favorable. Where he will go is a secret, but it is assumed that it is to Rhode Island.[53] Undoubtedly the two brothers would have liked to stay here together, but the fact that the Delaware River will freeze over, which normally happens in December and often lasts till the middle of February, does not allow this. One of the two King's commissioners must therefore leave so as to receive dispatches from England as soon as possible, which will probably be important after the Burgoyne affair. During this time we shall be cut off from all communications.

December 21. A detachment was sent across the Schuylkill by way of a bridge, which we had constructed on the left wing of our line. But this detachment had to retreat along the river to Grey's Ferry, where we were building a pontoon bridge to cover the working party. In the evening about 8,000 men received orders to march the next morning.

December 22. In the morning General Howe marched with these 8,000 men in one column across the Schuylkill over the pontoon bridge which was constructed yesterday.[54] With these troops he formed one line extending from the other side of this bridge to beyond Darby, seven miles from here, where our left wing deployed so as to cover the flank.

About 500 wagons, which we had taken along, at once began foraging behind the line. Our men constructed temporary cover as well as they could. We did not have tents with us, as we almost never did during this whole campaign.

Some rebel dragoons and a few hundred of Morgan's riflemen are swarming around us.[55] General Smallwood with 3,000 men is said to have been detached from Washington's force to Wilmington to put up redoubts there. He is also said to have orders to erect some batteries close to the bank of the Delaware River to harass our ships when they pass. I and many others hope that our General will march secretly on an evening of one of these days to slap this General Smallwood's face by means of a forced march.[56]

December 23. One of our Dragoon patrols of 20 men, sent out today, was cut off by the enemy on its way back, and intending to make their escape by a large detour, got into a swamp, resulting in 11 being taken prisoners. Some deserters who arrived yesterday and today and also other news make it certain that Washington has taken a very advantageous position in the hills near Valley Forge and that he intends to stay there during the winter. For this purpose they built huts and put up barricades and other line works in front of their camp.

We got the following news from Philadelphia that had arrived there by ship: A few hundred rebels had landed in boats on Long Island from Connecticut under the cover of a privateer; a nearby sloop of war spotted them, took the privateer, and burned and destroyed the boats so that all the rebels were cut off from their retreat and fell into our hands.[57]

December 24. Past six o'clock in the evening we heard 10 cannon shots being fired in the direction of Philadelphia. (I forgot to mention that General von Knyphausen is in command there). A little while later we heard that some hundred rebels had come down the road from Germantown with 2 cannon and that as many more had come down the road from Frankford with one cannon. They fired at our redoubt but soon retreated because their fire was answered with an intense cannonade.

December 25. Since most of the forage behind our lines had been taken away, the English General Grant was detached more to the left toward Chester with four regiments of infantry and one regiment of dragoons to cover our foraging party there. This detachment came back in the evening.

December 26. General Grey was again detached to the left with the same number of troops for the same purpose and came back in the evening.

December 27. Since noon yesterday we have had bad weather. It is said that Washington has sent 3,000 men down close to us and that he is following in person to attack us.[58] Perhaps this is one of the reasons that General Howe this morning changed our line (which was somewhat thin) by pulling back the troops, which were stationed beyond Darby a distance of about two miles.

December 28. In the morning, after the heavy artillery and other wagons had been sent to Philadelphia over the pontoon bridge, we marched over the other bridge, farther up-river, and again took a position near the city of Philadelphia. The pontoon bridge was demolished at once. By a ruse our rear guard was lucky enough to capture three officers and 37 rank and file of Morgan's riflemen.[59]

The Hessian jaegers had to march early in the morning to mask a height a bit forward of the upper bridge. After I had taken the orders to Lieutenant Colonel von Wurmb and was dashing back, I fell from my unshod horse and have, thank heaven, intact but aching bones.

December 29-December 31. During these days the troops moved into their winter quarters; they detach daily almost 1,200 men, both for the occupation of the lines and service in the town.

January 1, [*1778.*] Today all troops were assigned to their alarm positions out of town. The alarm signal is four cannon shots.

January 3. One of our dragoon patrols had a skirmish with a rebel patrol on the way to Germantown, during which they lost two officers and seven men, while we had no losses.

January 10. Colonel Abercromby was sent with 300 men of light infantry toward Germantown and as many Provincial troops were sent to Frankford. They came back in the evening without having encountered the enemy, except for some patrols, of which they brought two officers and 11 rank and file back with them.

January 14. An armed ship arrived from New York and brought all the Hessian mail, which had arrived there on a packet from England. Among them was one letter from my brother in Hannover, dated October 14, 1777, which I was happy to receive. I hope to get some more with the English letters, which according to orders, have been held in New York, for bringing them here would have been very hazardous, owing to the possibility of ice, and because of the size and weakness of the ship. This ship had indeed been attacked in the Delaware by some rebel galleys, which normally are stationed at the mouth of Christiana Creek, and it had a very narrow escape. I read with surprise in my brother's letter that a copy of my humble diary has passed through several hands and finally into very high-placed hands in London. What am I to say of this.

January 15-January 17. It is asserted that General Lee, who has been a prisoner since last year, has been freed on parole and that he went to Connecticut.[60] Many claim that Lee has instructions for peace. May heaven grant it. I wish it with all my heart, especially because this war is attended by much cruelty, which our good General Howe cannot prevent, much as he would like to.

January 18. The Queen's birthday was celebrated by a cannonade of the artillery park and all the ships at anchor here. General Howe gave a nice dinner for all English and Hessian generals and the English general staff. I remember that a year ago today I was the only one of General Howe's family who did not take part in the ceremony of receiving an order, etc. that day, for I, unfortunately, had to go to Kings Bridge, since the enemy was attacking Fort Independence and Kings Bridge.

January 19. At 11 o'clock at night, 40 dragoons were detached by a long roundabout way to seize a rebel dragoon captain by the name of Lee, who has alarmed us quite often by his boldness and who is stationed 15 miles from here.

January 20. Early in the morning this Captain Lee was indeed surprised by us; he lost two officers and eight dragoons, but he himself retreated with a few men into a massive building out of which our men could not force him, mainly because they could not stay any longer.[61]

January 21. The rebels, we are told, do not like the huts they have built in the hills of Valley Forge nor do they like the lack of rum and clothing. Hence they do not only have many sick but also much desertion far back into the country.

We have comedies here, which are performed by English officers; a ticket costs one dollar. What remains after expenses have been paid, goes to the poor. Beginning next Friday we will also have daily assemblies, without ladies, in a public house, where games can be played except those with dice. One room is reserved for chess players only. There will be a ball in this public assembly hall every Thursday, and ladies are to be invited. To defray the cost, everybody from the highest general down to the youngest ensign pays an amount equal to two days of his income. To make it clear, everyone who signs up pays in proportion to his income more or less, although the General does not get any more out of it than the youngest officer.

January 22. It is said for sure that the packet will leave tomorrow. I therefore finish with the wish that either peace will soon come from England or that at least 20,000 men will come, so that we can make peace here.

NINTH TRANSMITTAL
January 23, 1778-March 7, 1778

January 23, [*1778.*] Last night a lieutenant and six men deserted to us from Valley Forge, and this morning four of those stationed at Wilmington came over.

January 26. After we had received news that a detachment of 400 rebels had arrived at Germantown with wagons to gather the remaining provisions, and especially leather goods, etc., the 1st battalion of light infantry and two regiments of dragoons were sent there this morning. But the enemy had already left and we took nothing from them except Major Geil (the first adjutant to General Greene), who was spending some time with a beauty. It was said that there is still plenty of hay in the region of Frankford. Therefore three regiments were detached there this morning to cover our foragers and wagons, all of whom returned unmolested in the evening.

January 27. Thus, we brought almost 200 tons of hay. On the average, six deserters have come to us daily. We hear very little desertion in our army except among newly enlisted Provincial troops, who have been accepting all deserters. This caused General Howe to order that henceforth no deserter should be accepted.

February 1, [*1778.*] The packet did not leave till today because of unfavorable wind.

February 3 and 4. Toward 12 o'clock at night Simcoe's corps of Provincials marched five miles beyond Frankford and came back by another road, to the left, the next morning. The reason for this excursion was: some peasants in the region of Oxford had informed us that they intended to seize and bring in to us a rebel colonel and captain, who were using considerable force to raise militia in this area, if we would send them some 100 men. These people kept their promise by bringing the two over to us.

February 5. The second adjutant of General Howe, Major Balfour, who had been a captain together with me, was promoted to lieutenant colonel today. Reliable sources have it that General Washington has convinced Congress that General Stephen, whom they found guilty of not having performed his duty during the affair at Germantown, be discharged.[1]

February 6. A commissioner of General Burgoyne arrived today with a flag of truce. He brought several letters, among them one from the Brunswick General Riedesel to my General and one to General von Knyphausen, in which General Riedesel highly recommended a speedy exchange of the captured Brunswick officers.[2] On this occasion I got to see a list of my old friends and acquaintances of Brunswick.

February 8. This morning several small rebel detachments ruined all the mills between our lines and their position. This does not hurt us very much because we are always sure of provisions from England, while they ruin their own country by such acts.[3] The last 10 or 12 days the rebels have been deserting more than ever before. Last night two of their officers and seven rank and file came in. According to all information Washington's army at Valley Forge does not exceed 9,000 men, and is in a very bad way because of a dire need of rum, salt, and especially clothing. General Gates is meeting with Congress in York. It is also declared with assurance that there is not only friction between the members of Congress but also between Congress and General Washington.[5]

February 11. Last evening orders were given for a foraging expedition today under the command of General Erskine. An exceedingly heavy rain caused the orders to be countermanded this morning.

February 12. Whenever there is a very heavy rain we are forced to dismantle the upper bridge across the Schuylkill, by which we have communication with a command in a redoubt on the other side. The command is then relieved by some large boats. The sudden heavy rain caused us to dismantle the bridge yesterday. General Washington, who felt secure because of this, today detached General Wayne with 1,500 men and four cannon down the river about three miles beyond Darby to gather available cattle, provisions, etc.

February 14. We foraged four miles beyond Frankford under cover of three regiments. A party of our newly enlisted Provincial dragoons, who know the country very well, pushed ahead on this occasion and seized several officers and other men who are active in the rebellion, namely a few lawyers and committeemen.[6]

February 15. Upon hearing that our bridge across the Schuylkill had not yet been reconstructed, General Wayne, who had taken a position in the region of Darby, as said before, made a plan to seize our picket that was posted on the other side of the river in a weak redoubt. He attacked it at three o'clock this morning with 200 men. After a small-arms fire of about a quarter of an hour, they retreated, after they lost a few dead and several wounded; we had only a few slightly wounded.

February 16-18. The German recruits who have been distributed among the English regiments and who are very dissatisfied (for which they have good reason indeed) are now deserting in rather large numbers.

February 19. Foraging was done under the command of General Erskine. On this occasion our new dragoons not only took 34 prisoners, among them seven officers and others of distinction, but they crept so far to our flank that they were able to take a cache of clothing material, enough for 500 men, which the enemy had just been working up into uniforms.

February 21. In the evening all rebel officers, who were walking around freely on parole, as well as Captain Campbell, who was serving as General Erskine's aide, were arrested and put under heavy guard. It is said that this Captain Campbell and the captured General Irvine and also some other captured enemy colonels stationed here, have had secret correspondence with General Washington.[7] Reports agree that it was the intention of these people to seize General Howe one night and cut him down during the turmoil, in case the kidnapping should fail. Whether this is true, and whether aide Campbell (who is highly regarded in the whole army) has any such interest, I am unable to say. But I am firmly convinced that our enemy must have very good spies in our army, who know everything as soon as it transpires.

February 23. General Wayne is said to have crossed the Delaware into Jersey this side of Wilmington with 600 men to rob the country of cattle, forage, clothing and leather goods.[8]

February 24. Since General Howe has received word that 130 oxen have come across from Jersey and were being driven to Valley Forge to Washington's army under a weak cover, a detachment of English and the newly created dragoons were to go there late last evening. They managed to sneak completely around them and to drive away these 130 head of cattle.[9]

At 12 o'clock at night the two English battalions of light infantry under the command of Colonel Abercromby received orders to march at once. They were embarked on flatboats at one o'clock, and were landed at Billingsport. The intention of this operation is probably to have a slap at General Wayne, if possible.

February 25. When reports came in late this evening that 500 to 600 militia were assembled in Jersey at Haddonfield, seven miles from here, Colonel Stirling with his 42nd regiment of Highland Scots consisting of two battalions, and Simcoe's Provincial corps, were ferried across to take possession of Haddonfield.[10]

February 26. We received the news that the militia immediately left Haddonfield when they saw the approaching Scots.

February 28. A frigate arrived from New York with the English letters that had arrived with the packets of October, November, and December. Since the Hessian letters had been put on another ship at New York, we received none. The reliable news came in that the *Liverpool,* which had been sent from here to New York about three weeks ago to bring the letters safely here, was lost in a storm, but that all persons were saved.[11] Everybody, but especially

the English, are happy about the news from England that His Majesty the King will not give in, but wants to continue the war emphatically. From Jersey we have received the news that the light infantry, which had been down the Delaware as far as Salem, are on their way back without having been able to catch up with General Wayne. General Wayne had already received information about our expedition against him (as unfortunately almost always happens).

March 1, [1778.] In the afternoon the two battalions of light infantry crossed over again. Our Hessian letters arrived today.

March 2. Colonel Stirling came back from Jersey with his detachment this evening. His rear guard had been attacked by about 100 infantry and 80 dragoons under the command of General Pulaski, several of our men being wounded. But since Colonel Stirling returned at once, Pulaski's troops were completely dispersed and so our troops crossed without being molested.[12]

March 5. Several provision ships and empty transports are to leave tomorrow. I shall send this with them.

March 7. News arrived in the afternoon that 300 rebels have been in the region of Germantown since yesterday morning. Therefore a detachment of dragoons and light infantry were sent there last night. But the enemy had already left as early as 10 o'clock last night. In spite of this we captured a captain and 20 men of one of their patrols.

TENTH TRANSMITTAL
March 8, 1778-April 20, 1778

March 8, 1778. The packet sailed today.

March 11. Reliable news has it that two of our ships and one sloop of war of 10 guns have been taken at New Castle. The enemy has in this region, galleys, armed boats, and small armed vessels, which need only shallow water. They lie close to the banks and also in the smaller rivers and creeks that lead back into the country. When they see something on the ground, or unarmed merchantmen, transports, or provision ships to which they believe to be a match, they come out and take it.

March 12. Captain Campbell, the aide to General Erskine, who was recently arrested because of suspicious correspondence with the enemy, was set free today, (but without ceremony). The sentence of the court-martial says: He was acquitted because there were not enough proof and evidence to convict him. If he were completely innocent, as I personally believe him to be, this verdict of the court-martial is very harsh, because most people will now consider him to be guilty.[1]

March 13. Three English regiments and Simcoe's Free Corps, altogether 1,400 men, embarked under the command of Colonel Mawhood.[2] It is said that they will disembark farther down the Delaware in Jersey to gather provisions, of which we have been having only a scanty supply lately. In the afternoon several ships of the line and some transports with provisions arrived here from Rhode Island. They brought us the following news: Lord Admiral Howe will follow soon; the ships that had been taken by the enemy a few days ago in the region of New Castle, had been on their way to us. They were two ships loaded with hay and escorted by a sloop of 10 guns, named *Alert,* and more important, they were flying the King's flag.[3]

What hurts us, and especially me the most, is not the fact that a great number of letters for the army were thrown overboard during the affair, but that a few Hessian letters that had not had this fate and therefore fell into Washington's hands, were forwarded to us opened, and with the note on the envelope, "Letters of no consequence."

March 14-17. The rebels suffer greatly by continuous desertion. Since we have been here more than 1,500 deserters have come over, most of whom are Irishmen, who either take service on the ships or, and this is the greatest part, are sent back to their fatherland at the King's expense.

March 18. In order to keep us from getting fresh provisions from the country, the rebels have at all times, small parties on all the roads that lead to us. They seize the peasants who take all sorts of food to the market for the sake of profit. We send out daily, small and sometimes strong commands against the enemy parties in support of the peasants who bring in food (although many of them are surely spies).

For this purpose, several such detachments, made up of dragoons and light infantry, were sent out last night; one of them encountered an enemy party of which six were killed and 13 taken prisoner. Today the English had a fox hunt during which several fell off their horses. I do not like it, but the English make a great festival of it. Since an infectious disease has broken out in the local prison, where all captured rebels are locked up, the General had another large building made ready, and moved all captured officers to this new one. But before being moved, they had to promise that they would make no attempt to escape, for this was not a secure place. Nevertheless one colonel, one lieutenant colonel and one major escaped last night. Thereupon the General had all of them, some sixty, taken back to the secure prison.

March 20. In the morning my General received information that a detachment of rebels, this time regulars, had set some houses on fire two miles across the Schuylkill. The General sent there, at once, 40 men of infantry and 35 mounted Hessian jaegers. Because I received the orders for this excursion I decided to go along. Since the enemy, or rather these incendiaries, had in the meantime withdrawn, I posted the 40 men on a height two miles in front of our lines. I did this partly not to be delayed, but primarily to earn some credit for the Hessians, in case I should be lucky, because they had not been used on such occasions during the whole winter.

For a long time I looked for the enemy in vain with my mounted jaegers. We finally encountered them some nine miles from here on the road to Lancaster or rather to Valley Forge. They greeted us at first with some small-arms fire. Heaven was favorable enough to have me lose only one horse and one jaeger wounded, whereas they had several killed and one officer and 10 men taken prisoners.[4] Had they not been protected by a deep swamp, we would have captured more of them. Because this incident did not only earn for me the unreserved praise of General Howe but also raised me in the esteem of many officers, I feel abundantly rewarded. This good luck would have been of some real reward for me if I were in the English service, where the General personally takes care of all promotions.

March 21. At dawn the two battalions of English light infantry went to Germantown and took all the leather, vinegar, etc., from there and the vicinity, a total of 40 wagons. They took everything that the enemy would be picking up soon, as the General had been informed. Needless to say that the owners were remunerated.

March 22. Many deserters are still coming in.

March 23. The General received the news that Colonel Mawhood, who had been detached on the 13th of this month, has gathered much forage in the region of Salem and that he would be back today or tomorrow. He was not molested except by some militia, 30 of whom he had taken prisoners.[5]

March 24. It seems certain that an exchange of prisoners will be effected. At any rate some of our officers have already been sent back on parole, and several authorized staff officers from our and the enemy side will meet as commissioners in Germantown on the 31st of March to make final arrangements.[6] The exchange has been, and I fear will continue to be, endangered by the fact that the unreasonable enemy made it a condition that those exchanged by both sides will not serve any more. This would obviously give them a big advantage because they can at once send theirs back to till the land and can replace them by others who will serve against us. We have absolutely no way of making such substitutions.

Last night a lieutenant and six rank and file deserted to us. This lieutenant tells us that Washington's army is not in the best condition, because it has suffered not only from desertion to us but, much more, from desertion back into the provinces. Many officers are said to have resigned under various pretexts. But by the time the campaign begins, the enemy hopes to have a large army, to which the provinces of New England are expected to contribute a large contingent. Others, however, maintain that the people of New England, who are proud of their victory over Burgoyne, and fearing that we might attack them in Connecticut or Boston from Rhode Island, will remain in their provinces. Another not implausible rumor has it that the Virginians, who are also afraid for their province during the coming campaign, would call back General Washington and the Virginia troops that are serving with the enemy army.

I forgot to mention that day before yesterday, the 22nd of March, 80 Provincials or to be more exact Jersey volunteers, were ferried to Billingsport. An engineering officer is with them to throw up earthworks at Billingsport again, in which these volunteers will stay for the time being. The *Camilla,* which is still stationed down-river of Billingsport, has taken three of the armed rebel boats, which carry 4-pounders.

March 25. Thirteen deserters arrived last night, and this morning a patrol captured one officer and three men. Our army is in an especially good condition now, men and horses are big and fat. Washington is said to have sent his heavy baggage, etc., back across the Susquehanna River perhaps because he fears that General Howe might visit him at Valley Forge, since weather and roads are beginning to be good. He will now be able to march off more quickly. I think that General Washington and all his soldiers, who suffer from lack of almost everything, have gained enough honor this winter by staying throughout the winter in huts so close to us. Do not let anyone ask me why we tolerate this!

March 26. General Lee, who was walking freely around in New York on parole, has received permission from General Howe to come here, as he had requested. He arrived yesterday evening accompanied by an English officer.[7] They made the trip through Jersey with the permission of the enemy. General Howe does not want to see Lee, for which reason he has asked him not to come to public assemblies or picnics.

March 27. At noon the January packet arrived from England via New York. Under the cover of two warships, a fleet of 40 ships arrived also, laden mostly with provisions, forage, and heavy baggage, which had been left behind in New York by the troops here when the last campaign was opened.[8] Last night at one o'clock we sent out patrols made up of dragoons and infantry, each about 130 to 200 men strong, on all roads across the Schuylkill, as well as to Germantown, Frankford, etc., to push ahead seven to nine miles. They all came back at noon without having encountered any enemy forces except some small dragoon patrols.

March 28. The detachment of 1,400 men under Colonel Mawhood, which had been foraging in Jersey down-river near Salem, arrived last night with 300 tons of hay.

March 29. We had a very heavy storm this day, which tore several ships from their anchors, but caused no further damage.

March 30-April 2, [1778.] We heard that Lord Howe, who was about to sail into the Delaware, has been forced to sail out into the open sea again because of the storm on the 29th of March.

April 3. Contrary to the expectations of all of us, General Lee had a rather long conference with General Howe.

April 4. At Haddonfield in Jersey, six miles from Coopers Ferry, opposite Philadelphia, on the other side of the Delaware, 300 rebels with two cannon have been stationed again the last few days. At Coopers Ferry there is also a picket of 50 men, with sentries along the bank of the Delaware. They, but especially the officers, who were given very large and good field glasses by Washington, observe every move made on our side, and, since most of the streets lead to the Delaware, they can also survey our streets.

April 5. Last night at one o'clock, 500 light infantry were taken to the region of Billingsport in Jersey. Then, in a long round about way, they proceeded to Haddonfield, which the enemy had just left because they had received from their patrols news of our advance. But they had been in such a hurry that they forgot to advise their command at Coopers Ferry, most of whom fell into our hands, together with their field glasses, whereupon the light infantry returned via Coopers Ferry this afternoon. We captured the commanding major, two lieutenants, and 58 rank and file. One captain and some men were left on the field.

April 6. There have been conferences at Germantown on March 31st and the following days between the authorized commissioners of both sides to arrange for the exchange of prisoners. But since Germantown is not the quietest place, Newtown in Bucks County, 30 miles from here, was chosen as the site for the conference. Hence the commissioners of our side went there today, namely: Colonels O'Hara, Stephens and [Captain] Fitzpatrick, all three of the Guards.

April 8. Three of our patrols sent out today were lucky enough to encounter three weaker patrols of the enemy. From two of them we took one officer and 18 men prisoners, killing one officer and eight men. The third patrol of 14 men was completely mowed down because, as they commonly do, they had first asked for pardon and then fired at our men after they had come close.

April 9. General Howe holds the Hessian grenadiers in the greatest esteem, and, since they have been much weakened during the last two campaigns, especially at Red Bank, he asked General Knyphausen in a letter today to select good people of the regiments in New York and around here to form another grenadier battalion. Coupled with this, he asked General Knyphausen to give the command of this battalion to me.

General Knyphausen gave his full approval in spite of the fact that this command should be given to a staff officer and I was still so young a captain. My recent lucky coup with the jaegers is probably the main reason the two generals think of me so graciously and ignore other considerations. Nobody can imagine my great joy over getting the command of this battalion. I shall receive two amusettes from the English park. Now I can only hope that fortune will favor me with chances during the next campaign to do something alone, so that I may deserve the name of a soldier or else die with honor.

Since General Howe is so kind to me as his aide, I shall always have free access to headquarters. Thus, I am convinced that I will find opportunities to ask for a chance to do something with my battalion alone.

A packet from England arrived in the evening. With it I received very unpleasant news (unpleasant in several various respects) that His Serene Highness the Landgrave has taken my grenadier company away from me and has given me a musketeer company of the Landgraf regiment, which is stationed in Rhode Island. Since His Highness the Landgrave has most likely transferred me because as

an aide to the English General (an officer of the grenadiers should never willingly be absent from his unit), I have to be satisfied for the moment, especially because my gracious sovereign has already granted to me so many undeserved favors.[9]

April 14. An express frigate arrived from England, delivered dispatches for General Howe, and immediately departed to find Admiral Howe, for whom she also had dispatches. In the evening we learned that the Act of Parliament concerning nontaxation etc. of the colonies had also arrived.[10] It was immediately printed and was distributed and posted in public places this evening. Especially the English are very unhappy about the yielding of the English ministry.

We also learned the reliable news today that General Howe has been granted permission to go to England and to relinquish his command, as he had requested, and that, pending the arrival of another general, he is to hand over his command to Clinton. This news seems to have seriously depressed everyone's spirits, and those who had not thought of leaving before, do now all want to go back. Several of the most prominent ones, such as Generals Grant, Erskine, Grey, etc., are said to be applying for permission to leave.

Everybody is now expecting a ceasefire soon and certainly an early peace, which will not be favorable to England. If this should happen, the poor and unhappy people here, who have been on our side during the war, are to be pitied.

The enemy frigate *Virginia* of 30 guns, is said to have been taken by our frigate *Emerald* of 28 guns, in the mouth of Chesapeake Bay.[11] Another ship, of 20 guns, which had been chased by us, was either driven ashore or else stranded and was then set on fire by the enemy. The fleet of transports, which, according to convention, had sailed to Boston to embark Burgoyne and his corps, is said to have returned to Rhode Island, empty.

April 15. The news that General Howe will give up his command has also completely changed my plans. Hence I requested General Howe and General Knyphausen today not to have me take over the command of the battalion that has been entrusted to me and, therefore, countermand that order. This was done in spite of the fact that General Howe thought that I was acting contrary to my honor and possibly contrary to my future fortune.

Anyone who is familiar with British practice will understand that the principal one of several reasons—and General Knyphausen appreciates all of them—is the fear that the successor to General Howe will not be kindly disposed to the aide of a former commander, and that he will sacrifice him or at least see to it that he will play a very minor role. I cannot entrust to paper several other and even better reasons. But everyone can be assured that they are good ones.

It is certainly a great misfortune for me that General Howe is leaving just now. But it might be good for greater and more important things than my personal fortune and honor, and therefore I shall suffer cheerfully. Now I shall probably go to my regiment in Rhode Island as soon as General Howe leaves. How pleasant it would be if I were still in the grenadiers because they never stay behind. The Landgraf regiment will, according to all indications, continue to have quiet garrison duty in Rhode Island. Now I wish more than ever to go home.

The negotiations for the exchange of prisoners have been broken off, and our commissioners returned from Newtown yesterday. It is said that the enemy demands were too exaggerated.

April 17. Last night at 11 o'clock 160 dragoons, supported by a rear guard of 300 light infantry, were sent to Bristol on the Delaware, which is 20 miles from here (of course these are English miles of which five make one good German mile) to seize some staff officers and other officers, who went there to round up militia, according to information received by the General.

This detachment came back at noon today and brought back not only two lieutenant colonels, one major, three captains, and several rank and file, but also two sea captains who had just disembarked from the galleys, etc., which lay at anchor at Bristol. Altogether they brought back 13 officers and 46 men, and others.

Last night the frigate *Greyhound* sailed for New York with General Jones aboard.[12] He will take over General Clinton's command there, General Clinton having orders to come here.

April 18. Last night at 12 o'clock Lieutenant Colonel von Wurmb went out on an eight mile patrol with 400 jaegers across the Schuylkill bridge on the Lancaster Road. He came back at noon today without having seen anything. The common English soldiers are so angry about the Act of Parliament on nontaxation, etc., which is posted here that they tear down these proclamations during the night.

April 19. It is reported reliably that an executioner in Trenton in Jersey yesterday publicly burned the printed Act of Parliament on nontaxation.[13] If Congress thinks as these simple people do, we will not get peace although England is yielding much. Everyone maintains that Congress will accept these conditions and make peace unless they are not in their right senses.

April 20. The letters will go on the way today and therefore I have to close the packet.

ELEVENTH TRANSMITTAL
April 21, 1778-May 23, 1778

April 21, 1778. I had heard that two gentlemen of Congress and 22 sub-delegates, with other men of the topmost rebels, were staying at Dover, 42 miles beyond Wilmington down the Delaware River, 13 miles inland, to collect militia, money and food, especially cattle and flour, under the cover of 50 dragoons. I had received detailed information regarding the location of this place, its Government House, the best taverns (in which these gentlemen would supposedly lodge), and the roads that lead there, given to me by several people of that region and by two who lived at Dover.

I was so bold as to submit a plan to the General to seize these gentlemen during the night, for which purpose I asked for 100 Hessian grenadiers, as well as for two schooners or other small craft, loaded with provisions for eight or ten days. To my great sorrow I learned that the English are not in favor of such coups. I was told that it was too dangerous and no affair for me, and that further thought had to be given to it.

April 22. Yesterday the rebels patrolled with 500 men and four amusettes on the Lancaster Road as close as four miles to our lines. Had they come a little earlier, our jaeger patrol of 60 men, which had come back on this very road one hour before, probably would have fared badly.

April 23. Lord Howe finally arrived here. On his way from Rhode Island he stayed in New York for some time, and later was driven from his course by storms. The rebel militia has gathered in Jersey and apparently were about to attack Billingsport, where our Jersey volunteers had about 80 men stationed in a redoubt. But after some rifle shots they retreated when they found our men determined to defend themselves bravely.

April 24. A patrol of 150 men of our light infantry captured two officers and 52 men in the region of Chestnut Hill. Today the General reconsidered my proposition concerning Dover. Two small ships were readied and 120 Hessian grenadiers were selected to go with me. We planned to leave the next night at 12 o'clock. To my misfortune the wind became unfavorable in the afternoon, and the mis-

sion was postponed. The expedition would be undertaken the next day or the day after, but the wind remained contrary for four days, and then we received the news that these gentlemen had dispersed. I cannot describe how much this disappointment depressed me, because if my coup had been successful (and it looked like it would be), I would have distinguished myself very much, and the booty would have been larger and more important than the capture of 1,000 soldiers. Probably I will never again in my lifetime have such a good opportunity to gain honor.

Two redoubts are to be constructed about 600 paces in front of our lines on well selected, commanding heights toward Germantown. Work was started today, and working parties of 400, with 200 men to cover them, are to be sent out daily.

April 26. Our army is so well that it did not have a single death last week. Our dragoons cut down 14 men and brought in as prisoners one officer and six men of an enemy patrol that came a little bit too close today.

April 27-29. Congress has issued a proclamation, which declares as traitors, and threatens with the death penalty, all those who have any idea of treating with England in any other way than from the position of free states.[1]

April 30. News has been received that 500 militia, who had gathered from Jersey and up the Delaware under the command of General Lacey, are on their way to Washington's camp and had arrived today in the region of the Crooked Billet Tavern, 18 miles from here on the Old York Road, where they put up huts to rest a few days. Consequently 800 men, among them 100 dragoons, were sent out in the evening at six o'clock, on two roundabout roads.

May 1, [*1778.*] One of the detachments was spotted by the enemy before the second one arrived, whereupon they made a hasty retreat, which the detachment that had not arrived could have prevented. The first detachment, with the dragoons, eager for some action, attacked the enemy, who, however, fled in such haste that our infantry could not catch up with them. But the 100 dragoons assaulted so furiously that they captured 53 and left 30 killed on the field, notwithstanding the fact that the enemy was in a woods. We had only a few wounded. The encampment of huts of the enemy was set on fire and 10 wagons, which were loaded with baggage, etc., were brought in by our men, who arrived at four o'clock in the afternoon.[2]

May 3. There is dense woods a short mile from Coopers Ferry on the other side of the Delaware in Jersey. This morning at six o'clock the 55th and 63rd English regiments were ferried across with many woodcutters. They immediately started to throw up three redoubts to cover the working party. It was necessary to fill our magazines with firewood. Being short of it would be excusable only if Philadelphia were occupied by a small force that could depend on nearby sources of firewood.

May 4. General Howe reviewed the Hessians stationed here and expressed his extreme satisfaction in every way, especially by thanking them in daily orders and assuring them that he would not fail to laud them to the King. As the first flags passed the General in salute, his horse was so frightened that the General was thrown off, without, however, being injured.

May 5. Captain Hamond, who is a commodore, has been in command here during the winter while the Admiral was absent, gave a party for us today on board his ship, the *Roebuck*. There were almost 200 guests. The complete ship was superbly illuminated. There were oboists on the ship and on sloops on both sides. Dancing in two sections continued until 5 o'clock in the morning. Nine ships with 300 Englishmen and almost 200 Hessian recruits arrived today from Ireland.

May 7. This morning Allen's and Clifton's regiments of Provincials, which had been established here during the winter, but, which owing to much desertion, amounted to barely 400 men each, also crossed to Jersey at Coopers Ferry to reinforce the two English regiments stationed in redoubts there.[3] General Erskine, who might have proceeded a little bit too far reconnoitering in Jersey yesterday, was almost taken prisoner, but he escaped with the loss of four dragoons.[4] General Leslie, who commands the 63rd English regiment, also crossed to Jersey today to take command of the two English regiments, the two Provincial regiments, and a few Provincial dragoons stationed there, as well as some Jersey volunteers who were posted in redoubts at Billingsport.[5]

May 8. Last night the 2nd battalion of light infantry went up the Delaware on flatboats and four of our galleys to take or burn, if possible, the rebel galleys and other vessels in the region of Bordentown.

The new commander in chief, Clinton, arrived from New York this morning. It is now expected that General Howe will leave soon. After that I will spend a happier and quieter life again. I like General Howe, personally, but all those that have been around him with their typical English pride, make me vow never again to serve with an English general, if I can avoid it in a nice way. And since General Clinton has a Hessian brigade major, Captain [Wilhelm] von Wilmowsky with him, I hope that nobody will think of having me work with him. To be sure, the pay of the English aides is easy to pocket, but this is not a great advantage for honor's sake, unless you desire to imitate the English by having beautiful horses, etc.

The frigate *Porcupine* arrived here this morning with dispatches direct from England. Of their contents, we know only that England will doubtlessly get involved in a war with France. It is also said that Prussia is against England. If this should be true, which I hope it is not, may Heaven be gracious to my fatherland.

May 9. An enemy patrol of 400 infantry and 80 dragoons with two amusettes was in Germantown this morning, but withdrew immediately.

May 10. Our detachment of light infantry and galleys, that had gone up the Delaware on the night of May 7 to 8, came back this morning without the loss of a single man. They brought the pleasant news that they have burned all ships and other vessels, 42 in total, among them two large frigates and nine other large boats, between Bristol and four miles this side of Trenton. Except for a sloop of war, no other ships mounted any cannon. They had been carried away by the enemy, and the ships had been left behind completely unmanned.

The light infantry had landed near Bordentown, where General Pulaski had been with about 80 dragoons and where, to salute our passing galleys and boats, he had six cannon mounted on a height. The dragoons were dispersed, the cannon spiked and we burned several houses containing tents and field equipment. Some of the galleys there could not be burned because they had been sunk by the enemy a few days before.[6]

The rebels have been deserting less since they have learned of the alliance with the French, which induced General Washington to light bonfires. A few who arrived yesterday say that General Washington has sent his heavy baggage and artillery back to Lancaster, an indication that he does not want to get involved if we should finally attack him.

May 11. The packet left for England this evening.

May 12. There have been continuous celebrations in Washington's camp near Valley Forge because of their alliance with France.

May 14. Last night the enemy set on fire almost 200 cords of wood, which we had cut in front of our lines and which had been stacked up in big piles. It was ordered that all heavy baggage be packed and be ready to put aboard ships as soon as orders should be given. We were also ordered to be ready to march. A company of English artillery was embarked with their cannon to be taken to Halifax.

May 15-17. Deserters are coming in very seldom now. Thirty of the senior English officers, mostly staff officers, are making arrangements for a great celebration tomorrow in honor of General Howe. For the past two weeks they have been inviting all the worthy ladies they could find around here as well as many officers. Everyone who is invited receives an invitation, of which 780 have already been issued. On the neck out of the town a wooden hall 200 feet long and 45 feet wide, and hung with nicely painted linen, has been especially built for this occasion beside a large beautiful house, which has been luxuriously refurbished.[7]

May 18. Last night seven officers and 49 men escaped from the local prison by means of a skillfully and laboriously dug tunnel. According to our spies and other information, Washington intends to disrupt today's fete by a sudden attack. Hence, in the afternoon, small detachments of 300 men were posted three miles beyond our lines on all roads leading to us.

At half past three in the afternoon the invited guests assembled and, attended by 108 oboists, proceeded a few miles down the Delaware in three galleys and a large number of other boats, which had been decorated with flags. We passed more than 200 transports, provision and merchant ships, etc., which were all tied up in line along the city, displaying various English ship flags. The agent's ship looked especially beautiful because it flew the flags and standards of all seapowers in the world. At the top of the mainmast, it flew the large English standard with the English coat of arms embroidered on it. (I was happy to see the white horse on this occasion).[8] The warships fired a salute of 21 guns as we sailed past.

After we landed we passed through a corridor of cavalry and infantry displaying all the flags and standards of our entire corps, then we proceeded to a place arranged in the form of a square where two contingents of knights with their armor-bearers fought with lances and swords in the style of Don Quixot and Sanchopancha, their Dulcineas, sitting on elevated thrones, watching the knights who fought for them.[9]

After this, we went through a very beautiful triumphal arch to the magnificently decorated house, where tea, etc., was served. Dancing continued till nine o'clock and also gambling against a bank of 2,000 guineas. Then there were beautiful fireworks and more dancing, which lasted until 12 o'clock. Thereupon we dined in the very large luxurious hall, which was illuminated by 1,200 candles, the 108 oboists playing all that time.

There were 1030 dishes on the tables, including small ones; 480 persons were seated, the others had to stand. After supper we danced again until six o'clock in the morning. In short, everything was as splendid and magnificent as possible, and all, even those who have been in Paris and London, agree that they have never seen such a luxurious fete. The cost for it is somewhat more than 4,000 guineas, that is about 25,000 dollars.

General Washington, this evening, sent several strong detachments our way, which might have had orders to join our lines if they found them neglected. But they all retreated when they found us on guard.

May 19. General Howe received news in the afternoon that the Marquis de Lafayette, a general with our enemy and a favorite of Washington, had crossed the Schuylkill River with 3,000 men and eight cannon and had this morning taken a position at Barren Hill, about 12 miles from here in the hills extending from Chestnut Hill to Valley Forge, on our side of the Schuylkill. Therefore, Simcoe's light corps (500 men), the English light infantry (900),

BATTLE OF BRANDYWINE. *At right is a page from the von Muenchhausen diary under date of September 11, 1777. It explains the battle action at Brandywine, which had taken place but a few hours before the entry was made, as noted in the diary. The sketch map portrays all that he could observe, presumably from his post at General Howe's side. At 12 o'clock on the map, the British force can be seen moving along the road from the upper fords of the Brandywine. Dotted lines indicate the deployment of troops as they came down from Osborne's Hill to attack the "rebel batteries." Additional notations on the map read as follows: at 3 o'clock "Road to Chester which the Rebels took;" at 4 o'clock, "Chads Ford where Knyphausen crossed and attacked in the evening;" at 5 o'clock, "everything hilly;" at 7 o'clock, "morass."*

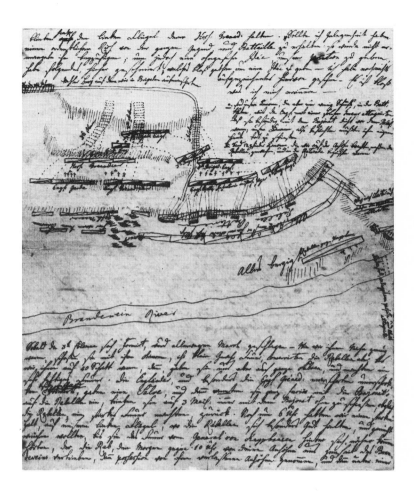

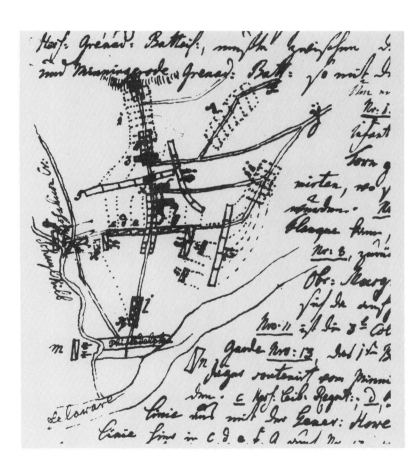

BATTLE OF GERMANTOWN. *At left is a section of a page from the von Muenchhausen diary under date of October 4, 1777. The sketch map is keyed to the text. The British force can be seen at center in two inverted letters U, on each side of Germantown Avenue, in Germantown, with protective units deployed on approaching roads. One American force can be seen coming down Germantown Avenue from the north, and, as indicated by dotted lines, deploying into battle formation. Two additional American forces can be seen coming in to attack the British right flank. These two forces entered the Germantown area via Limekiln Road.*

FIGHT FOR THE DELAWARE. *At right is a map showing the principal scene of battle on the Delaware. Fort Island, as the British called Fort Mifflin, is shown at center, separated from Carpenters and Province Islands by the "inner channel" through which the Vigilant made its way to attack Fort Island. The line across the Delaware represents the "cheveaux de frise," which actually extended only from Fort Island to Red Bank in New Jersey, or Fort Mercer, as the Americans called it.*

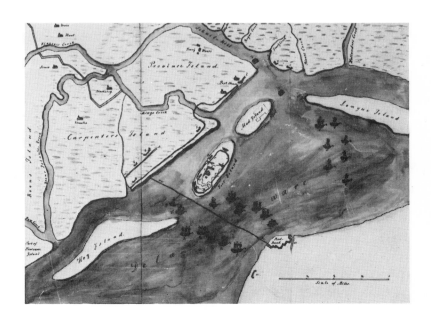

the English grenadiers (900), the Hessian grenadiers (700), the English Guards (1,000), the 1st English brigade (900), and the mounted light dragoons (400), all under the command of General Grant, set out in the evening at 10 o'clock. This column was to make an attempt to approach the right flank of the Marquis de Lafayette by various roundabout routes, thus taking a position between him and the Schuylkill, and then to attack him.[10]

May 20. This morning at six o'clock under the command of General Howe, the following troops set out: The Hessian jaegers (600), the Hessian Leib regiment and the von Donop regiment (about 1,000), two regiments of Anspachers with their grenadiers (1,100), and three English brigades, one brigade of which had detached two regiments to Jersey, (3,000). Generals Clinton and von Knyphausen were also with this column, as well as Admiral Lord Howe.

The column marched by way of Germantown to one mile this side of Chestnut Hill, where we formed into three lines close behind one another. The men were allowed to lie down to rest on their arms. The Hessian jaegers took a position on Chestnut Hill in front of us. One Hessian and two English brigades and those of the marching corps, who were on duty as guards in Philadelphia and in the line, stayed behind.

We have been expecting every moment to hear the fire of Grant's column and, should the plan succeed, to see the enemy fleeing before him, straight into our hands.

The van of Grant's corps appeared toward noon, and we heard with the greatest displeasure that Grant's vanguard was barely able to kill one French officer and seven men, and to capture five of Lafayette's rear guard, which, at the time, was wading through the Schuylkill.

Last night seven of our men deserted, two of them at the time when marching orders were given. Through these men, the Marquis de Lafayette received news of our march, whereupon he at once retreated in great haste across the river and marched back to Valley Forge. In the afternoon we returned to Philadelphia. Everyone criticised General Grant's conduct during this expedition, who, being overly cautious, moved so slowly and maneuvered so much that he gave enough time to the enemy, who had been informed of the march, to get out of the trap.

May 21. Orders were given that all the baggage and the tents are to be taken aboard ships. It was definitely decided today that I will cease to be aide to General Clinton when General Howe leaves. Captain Knight, aide to General Howe, was promoted to major today. I am now the only one of his aides, all of whom were captains with me, who is still a captain. Two of them are lieutenant colonels and the others majors.[11] The General told me that he felt sorry that it was not in his power to promote me, adding that it was my own fault because I refused to join the English service during the last winter when he repeatedly suggested it.

In the army list published by the enemy, the names of the following generals appear; *Major Generals:* Charles Lee, Philip Schuyler, Israel Putnam, Horatio Gates, William Heath, Joseph Spencer, John Sullivan, Nathanael Greene, William Earl of Stirling, Thomas Mifflin, Arthur St. Clair, Benjamin Lincoln, Benedict Arnold, Marquis de Lafayette, Robert Howe, Alexander McDougall, Baron de Kalb, Thomas Conway, *Brigadier Generals:* Thompson, Nixon, Parsons, James Clinton, Gadsden, Manyshall, McIntosh, Maxwell, Fermoy, de Borre, Knox, Nash, Poor, Glover, Patterson, Wayne, Varnum, Muhlenberg, Weedon, Woodford, George Clinton, Hand, Learned, Huntington, Pulaski, Stark.[12]

May 22. A ship arrived from St. Augustine with dispatches from the English General Prevost, who is in command there. Among the news it brought is the report that the inhabitants of South Carolina have risen in rebellion against our enemies and that 308 men have fought their way through to St. Augustine to fight for our cause. As pleasant as this news was, as unpleasant was another bit of news, namely, that several small English sloops of war and other small armed vessels that had been stationed in a river there, have been taken by the enemy. It is said to be certain that 250 savages were among several smaller reinforcements that joined Washington's forces.

May 23, [*1778.*] General von Knyphausen visited General Howe with all the Hessian staff officers to bid him farewell. It is maintained that our army will leave Philadelphia. Nobody knows why, for, counting heads, our army is twice as strong as the one of the rebels, and, with respect to courage, a hundred times as strong. Many surmise that the reason is fear of a French fleet, which could blockade the mouth of the Delaware.

The main reason for this unhappy and miserable war is the rebels in England, who govern everything there and also here, and are invincible as far as we are concerned, rather than Washington's army, which is miserable and weak in every respect. If I could presume that the English were capable of turning a clever trick, I would be inclined to believe the rumor that leaving Philadelphia was spread expressly to make Washington audacious and have him stay at Valley Forge. Then we could unexpectedly set out for Valley Forge in several columns, one of which would have to try to get around him by a forced march.

The rumor has been spreading since yesterday that several provinces, rather than allying themselves with France, are secretly considering a break with Congress and to negotiate separately with England for good conditions. Whether this is true I am unable to say.

I finish here, since the packet will be closed tonight, and, as is said, General Howe will leave tomorrow for sure.[13]

Fr. Ernst von Muenchhausen

BIBLIOGRAPHY

Short Titles

AA   *American Archives*, Peter Force, ed., Washington, D. C., 1837-1853.

AHR   *Journal of The Society for Army Historical Research*, London.

Am. M   *American Maps and Map Makers of the Revolution*, Peter J. Guthorn, Monmouth Beach, N.J., 1966.

Andre   *Major Andre's Journal...June 1777 to November 1778*, Tarrytown, N.Y., 1930.

Army List *A List of the General and Field Officers, as they rank in the Army....*, London, vols. 1776-1779.

Baur.   *Revolution in America*, Bernhard A. Uhlendorf, translator and annotator, New Brunswick, N.J., 1957.

Boudinot *Journal of Historical Recollections...During the Revolutionary War*, Elias Boudinot, Philadelphia, 1894.

Br. Jnl.   British Journal 1776-1778, anonymous Finestone Collection #409, American Philosophical Society Library, Philadelphia, Pa.

Br. M   *British Maps of the American Revolution*, Peter J. Guthorn, Monmouth Beach, N.J., 1972.

Brun   *Guide to the Manuscripts in the William L. Clements Library*, Christian Brun, Ann Arbor, Mich., 1959.

Buettner   *Narrative of Johann Carl Buettner in the American Revolution*, New York, N.Y., n. d.

Chapelle   *The History of the American Sailing Navy*, Howard I. Chapelle, New York, N.Y., MCMXLIX.

Chastellux   *Travels in North America....*, Marquis De Chastellux, Howard C. Rice Jr., ed., Chapel Hill, N.C., 1963.

Clinton   *The American Rebellion Sir Henry Clinton's Narrative of his Campaigns 1775-1782*, William B. Willcox, ed., New Haven, Ct., 1954.

Clowes   *The Royal Navy*, William Laird Clowes, London, 1899.

Cont. Jnl.   *Continental Journal and Weekly Advertiser*, Boston.

Delaware   *Fight For The Delaware 1777*, Samuel S. Smith, Monmouth Beach, N.J., 1970.

Ewald   Captain Johann Ewald Journal, 4 ms. vols., Library of His Highness Friedrich Ferdinand, Prince of Schleswig-Holstein, Gluksburg/Ostee, Germany.

Glyn   Diary of Ensign Thomas Glyn April 14, 1776-August 17, 1777, Princeton University, Special Collections.

Gruber   *The Howe Brothers and the American Revolution*, Ira D. Gruber, New York, N.Y., 1972.

Hall   *The History of the Civil War in America*, vol. I, "by an Officer of the Army," London, 1780. Note: Vol. 2 was never published. The author is said to have been either Capt. William Cornwallis Hall of the 28th regiment or Capt. John Hall of the 46th regiment.

Hamilton   *The Works of Alexander Hamilton*, John Cabot Lodge, ed., New York, N.Y., 1904.

Heitman   *Historical Register of Officers of the Continental Army....*, Francis B. Heitman, 1914.

Heusser   Journal of the fusilier regiment von alt Lossberg... 1776-1783, Georg Ludwig Christian Heusser, translated by Robert Oakley Slagle for his doctoral thesis at The American University, Washington, D. C., 1965.

HSP   Historical Society of Pennsylvania, Philadelphia, Pa.

Historical Mag.   *The Historical Magazine*, vol. VII, Second Series, No. 2, [1870].

Hunter   Diary of Andrew Hunter, July 22-November 24, 1776 & June 28-October 1, 1779, Princeton University, Special Collections.

HV   *The Hessian View Of America 1776-1783*, Ernst Kipping, Monmouth Beach, N.J., 1971.

JCC   *Journals of the Continental Congress*, 1907 ed.

KP   *The Kemble Papers, 1773-1789*, 2 vols., New York Historical Society, New York, N.Y., 1874, 1875.

Loc. cit.   Local citation

LP   *The Lee Papers*, 4 vols., New York Historical Society, New York, N.Y., 1871-1874.

Mack.   *Diary of Frederick Mackenzie*, Cambridge, Mass., MCMXXX.

Martin   *Private Yankee Doodle*, Joseph Plumb Martin, George F. Scheer, ed., 1962. First published as *A Narrative of Some of the Adventurers, Dangers, and Sufferings of a Revolutionary Soldier....*, Hollowell, Me., 1830.

MC&H   *Military Collector and Historian*, Journal of the Company of Military Historians, Washington, D.C.

Mont.   *The Montresor Journals*, New York Historical Society, New York, N.Y., 1882.

Moore   *Diary of the American Revolution from Newspapers and Original Documents*, Frank Moore, New York, N.Y., 1860.

Morris   *Margaret Morris Her Journal....*, John W. Jackson, ed., Philadelphia, Pa., 1949.

Narrative   *The Narrative of Lieut. Gen. Sir William Howe, & c.* Published in the *Monthly Review*, 1780; republished in *Sir Billy Howe*, Bellamy Partridge, New York, N.Y., 1936.

NHH   Nieders. Hauptstaatsarchiv, Hannover, Germany.

NJA   *New Jersey Archives*, Trenton, N.J.

Pa. A   *Pennsylvania Archives*, Harrisburg, Pa.

Pa. Mag.   *The Pennsylvania Magazine of History and Biography*, Philadelphia, Pa.

Parsons   *Life and Letters of Samuel Holden Parsons*, Charles S. Hall, New York, N.Y., 1968.

Pickering   *The Life of Timothy Pickering*, Octavius Pickering, Boston, 1867.

PNJHS   *Proceedings of the New Jersey Historical Society*, Newark, N.J.

Princeton   *The Battle of Princeton*, Samuel S. Smith, Monmouth Beach, N.J., 1967.

Pr. Lib.   Princeton University Library, Map Dept., Princeton, N.J.

PRO   Public Record Office, London, England.

Prov. Gaz.   *Providence Gazette*, Providence, R.I.

Robertson   *Archibald Robertson...His Diaries and Sketches in America 1762-1780*, H. M. Lydenberg, ed., New York, N.Y., 1930.

Sabine   *The American Loyalists*, Lorenzo Sabine, Boston, Ma., 1847.

Schlieffen   Schlieffen, Martin Ernst, Freiherr von, Von den Hessen, ihren Fursten und Schreyern, from the French (Des Hessois en Amerique,) in: *Nachricht von einigen Hausern des Geschlechts der von Schlieffen*, vol. II, Berlin 1830, p.157.

Searle   *The American Journal of Amborse Searle 1776-1778*, E. H. Tatum, Jr., ed., San Marino, Calif., 1940.

Sullivan   *The Military Services...of Major-General John Sullivan....*, Thomas C. Amory, Boston, Ma., 1868.

Trenton   *The Battle of Trenton*, Samuel S. Smith, Monmouth Beach, N.J., 1965.

VF   *Valley Forge Crucible of Victory*, John F. Reed, Monmouth Beach, N.J., 1969.

von Jung.   Von Jungkenn Papers, 7 vols., William L. Clements Library, Ann Arbor, Mich.

Wilkinson   *Memoirs of My Own Times*, James Wilkinson, 1816.

WP   Washington Papers, Manuscript Division, Library of Congress, Washington, D. C. (See *Index to the George Washington Papers*, Washington, D. C., 1964).

WW   *The Writings of Washington*, John D. Fitzpatrick, ed., 39 vols., Washington, D.C.

ANNOTATIONS

FIRST TRANSMITTAL
November 17, 1776-December 26, 1776

1. A scheduled embarkation of the Leib (or de Corps) regiment to which Capt. von Muenchhausen belonged, was to be made from New York City, with the destination Pelham, in Westchester County, New York. Here the Leib regiment was to join other units that had moved up the East River in flatboats on the 17th, preparatory to the invasion of Rhode Island under Lt. Gen. Henry Clinton.

2. King's bridge was located on the crossing of the now-obliterated Spuyten Duyvil Creek at the north base of Marble Hill, west of the present line of Broadway and just south of West 230th St., New York City. Ft. Knyphausen was located at what is now Fort Washington Avenue and West 183rd St., the highest ground on Manhattan Island.

No previous or "last letter" has been found. It was presumably written to Capt. von Muenchhausen's brother Wilhelm August Friedrich in Hannover to whom the diary published here was also addressed.

3. The march was probably from White Plains, New York, where the regiment earlier had been engaged, and the place of arrival was on the outskirts of the City of New York, then at about Chambers Street.

4. British field headquarters on the 18th, as indicated in Howe's orders, was at "DeLancey's Mill." *(KP 1:411)* This mill was located north of the city on the Bronx River in what is now Bronx Park, close to the crossing of 180th Street.

5. As noted in a letter to his mother, Capt. von Muenchhausen purchased two horses soon after arriving in America. It was not required that a grenadier captain be mounted, but if he wished to have a horse, and could afford to pay for his mount, he was permitted to do so. Capt. von Muenchhausen's second horse was undoubtedly ridden by his servant, Ludwig. After becoming aide to Gen. Howe, von Muenchhausen noted that Ludwig "has good food and drinks in the kitchen of a general and furthermore, I give him one guinea per month...for this I ask him to take care of my belongings, washing etc. .. but he is indolent and spends too much time with girls." *(NHH 52:III:29)*

6. Lt. Gen. Leopold von Heister, commander of all German troops under Gen. Howe, spoke French as well as German, having been in French service early in his career. Gen. Howe spoke only English. From Muenchhausen's remark it would appear that, prior to Muenchhausen's appointment, Howe had no one on his staff who could translate his orders directly into German. Capt. von Muenchhausen spoke English, French and German.

7. This was probably Maj. Carl von Wurmb who in 1776, held a post in the Leib regiment. He may have been the same Maj. Wurmb referred to by Maj. Baurmeister in his letter of 11.27.76, "Major von Wurmb is again taking part in the expedition with his regiment. He has been very ill." *(Baur.53)*

8. The composition of this corps was "Two Companies Chasseurs, 1st. and 2d. Light Infantry, 1st. and 2d. Grenadiers, 2 Battalions of Guards, 33d. Regiment, and 42d. Regiment, 3 Battalions of Hessian Grenadiers, 100 Men of Rogers's, without Arms, two Engineers, with twelve Carpenters and three Guides." *(KP 1:411)* "Rogers's" was Rogers' Corps later to become Wemys' Corps, and eventually the Queen's Rangers.

9. For the location of Forts Lee and Constitution in relation to the Hudson River and existing roads, see a contemporary map of the installations. *(Brun 519)* There was another Fort Constitution on the Hudson, opposite New Windsor, see *(Am. M)*.

10. Gen. Washington wrote to Gen. Charles Lee on the 21st, "Yesterday morning, the Enemy landed a large body of troops, below Dobbs Ferry, and advanced very rapidly to the fort call'd by your name; I immediately went over, & as the fort was not tenable on this side, & we in a narrow neck of land, the passes out of which, the enemy were attempting to seize, directed the troops consisting of Beal's, Heard's the remainder of Ewing's brigades, & some other parts of broken regiments, to move over to the West side of Hackensac river...." *(LP 2:295)* These were the brigades of Brig. Gen. Reazin Beall of Maryland militia, Brig. Gen. Nathaniel Heard of New Jersey militia, and Brig. Gen. James Ewing of Pennsylvania militia, all a part of Brig. Gen. Hugh Mercer's "Flying Camp."

Gen. Washington, at his headquarters at Hackensack, had received intelligence of the landing at "10 a.m." *(AA 5:3:781)* Accompanied by Maj. Gen. Israel Putnam, Washington immediately departed for Fort Lee, where Maj. Gen. Nathanael Greene was in command. Greene also had received word of the landing at "about 10 o'clock." *(Hunter 11.22.76)* Greene immediately began preparing for an evacuation of the fort, based on the reputed size of the British force that had landed. The colonel who was left in command of the fort may have been Col. David Brearley of the New Jersey militia. Andrew Hunter, who was in the fort, said, "The enemy soon took possession of Fort Lee and had nearly taken a number of our men. Col. Brearley... having set the rout of the Troops had nearly gone into the enemy camp...." *(Hunter 11.20.76)*

11. Curator of the museum of The New York Historical Society, Richard J. Koke, who is a student of New York in the Revolution, states as follows in regard to British headquarters in New York during the war. "British headquarters, after the occupation of New York in September 1776, was established, pretty much, in the Kennedy Mansion at the foot of Broadway opposite Bowling Green—on the west side at what is now No. 1 Broadway. A tablet marks the site. The Kennedy place can be said to be, more or less, the official city headquarters during the entire British occupation from 1776-83. However, immediately on the British landing on Manhattan Island on September 15, Howe obviously established his headquarters in the Beekman Mansion (erected 1763), which stood near Turtle Bay at what is now First Avenue and 51st Street. A memorandum by John Hannah, a gardener at the Beekman estate during the entire period of the American Revolution, states that Sir William Howe occupied the Beekman House from September 15, 1776 for a period of 7½ months, which would bring his occupancy to April 20, 1777." It is not known to which of Howe's New York headquarters Capt. von Muenchhausen reported, whether it was to Kennedy's, Beekman's, or to field headquarters at De Lancey's Mill.

12. "General Howe after having visited Fort Lee went to New York to his Quarters there." *(Robertson 113)*

13. This was about three hours later than Howe's usual dinner time. Muenchhausen noted in a letter to his mother, "General Howe stands much for cleanliness and properness. I have to put on a clean linen shirt in the morning. At about five to six or seven o'clock in the evening we, as well as the General, change clothes, and we all go to dinner." *(NHH 52:III:29)*

14. "Admiral Howe" was Richard Howe, General William Howe's older brother. Admiral Howe, in addition to being commander of naval forces in American waters, was commander in chief on American station, thus outranking his brother. "Lord Hotham" was Commodore William Hotham who participated in the 1776 landing on Staten Island under Admiral Howe. "Commodore Parker" was Peter Parker who came from England with a contingent in 1776 and, enroute to New York, participated in the

ill-fated attack on Charleston, S. C. "Generals Clinton and Lord Percy" were Lieutenant General Henry Clinton, second in command under General Howe and Lieutenant General Hugh Percy, next in command, the latter sharing that rank order with Lieutenant General Charles Cornwallis. "Governor Tryon" was Major General William Tryon who had been royal governor of New York prior to the war.

15. This was the British 4th brigade consisting of the 17th, 46th, 55th and 40th regiments, with Maj. Gen. James Grant in command.

16. These were the Rall, Knyphausen and old Lossberg regiments, with Col. Johann Gottlieb Rall in command.

17. "The 1st Battalion and Light Infantry and Light Dragoon advanced to Amboy. Donop's Corps to Woodbridge, and the Reserves and Guards to Elizabeth Town. The 4th Brigade remain'd at Newark." *(Robertson 114)*

18. This route via the Bergen Peninsula was the personal route of Cornwallis, not the route taken by the main army, which marched in a more direct route from Hackensack to New Brunswick. Cornwallis undoubtedly took a route close to the water so that he could be more readily in touch with Gen. Howe, who was at New York. "Bootbridge" means boat bridge in German; its location has not been identified.

19. Although the Americans believed the British movement in force into New Jersey was the beginning of a drive toward Philadelphia, the British, as noted in officers' diaries, viewed it merely as a move to provide suitable winter quarters. On the day following the landing, one British officer noted, "Quarters for a considerable part of the Army will now probably be taken in Jersey. At least we may stretch as far as Brunswick, which will include an extensive tract of Country, and afford quarters and supplies for a large force." *(Mack. 113)*

20. Gen. Lee had crossed the Hudson River from Peekskill, N.Y. with a large force on 12.2.76. He had with him Col. John Glover's brigade of 1259 men, Col. Paul Sargent's brigade of 862 men, and Col. Daniel Hitchcock's brigade of 822 men, a total of 2943 men. *(AA 5:3:1402)* British intelligence accurately estimated the force at "five and twenty hundred or three thousand." *(KP 1:102)*

21. Muenchhausen's Leib regiment had been stationed on Staten Island much of the time since its arrival from Germany. Their redoubts there, some of them within view of Amboy in New Jersey, were as follows: "at Amboy Ferry [and] between Amboy Ferry and the Old Blazing Star [Ferry]." *(Baur. 33)* The first mentioned was on the height near the present Tottenville and the second was near what is now Kreischerville.

22. One Brunswick mentioned here is New Brunswick, New Jersey, and the other is the city of Brunswick (Braunschweig), capital of the German Duchy of Brunswick in which service Muenchhausen had been prior to his volunteering his services to the Landgrave of Hesse-Cassel. The proper name of the school was Collegium Carolinum founded in 1745 by Duke Carl of Brunswick. It is now named Technical University Carolo-Wilhelmina.

23. One hour to the right was "to [Boundbrook] Bondbrook." *(Robertson 115)*

24. One of these officers was "Colonel [Stephen] Moylan." *(AA 5:3:1070)* He was a Pennsylvanian, but not by birth, having been born in Ireland.

25. One reason for changing plans to advance beyond Brunswick was that "General Howe became possessed of a letter...written by General Washington to the Board of War, in which he had given an exact account when the time of service of all our battalions would expire, and his apprehensions that the men would not reinlist without first going home to see their families and friends." *(AA 5:3:1326)* Another reason for advancing

beyond Brunswick was that, almost as soon as Cornwallis had landed in Jersey, "Loyalists arrived at Headquarters who assured the commanding general that Washington and his army were in wretched condition; if the campaign were continued the enemy would disperse and break up." *(Ewald)* Among those Loyalists were "several distinguished men from Pennsylvania who urgently requested General Howe to attack General Washington as forcefully as possible....Some of these men especially Mr. [Joseph] Galloway, became so angry about the delay of the British that he shouted that it was obvious they did not want to finish the war." *(ibid)*

26. The force that was withdrawing in front of the British advance was two brigades under Brig. Gen. Lord Stirling and Brig. Gen. Adam Stephen, with Stirling in command. Their strength was "1,200 men." *(WW 6:331)*. These troops had been left behind mainly to protect Gen. Lee's flank in his expected march south to join Gen. Washington.

27. This was the College of New Jersey, now Princeton University. The building undoubtedly was Nassau Hall, although Muenchhausen's window count is somewhat off.

28. This was a stone abutment bridge over Stony Brook, south of Princeton, on what is now Stockton Street.

29. The "plain" was in the general area of the Trent House, now a museum, located on South Warren Street, Trenton. The "wooded valley" was the valley formed by the banks of Assunpink Creek, which flows into the Delaware River near the Trent House.

30. The American crossing was near the "plain," at the foot of what is now Ferry Street, Trenton.

31. It was on the Pennsylvania shore, opposite Ferry Street, that the Americans had placed their "strong batteries."

32. In search of boats or a usable ferry, Cornwallis had marched north as far as Coryell's Ferry, which crossed the Delaware from what is now Lambertville, N.J. to New Hope, Pa.

33. Gen. Washington had been suspicious that if the enemy found no boats at Trenton, they would try to cross higher up, so he sent a 400-man regiment under Col. Nicholas Haussegger to Coryell's Ferry. Their objective was to hold off any attempted crossing as long as possible, to allow Washington to "bring our cannon up and play upon them." *(WW 6:339)* Haussegger's regiment was made up of Pennsylvania and Maryland Germans. They were fresh, newly arrived troops.

34. He was Lt. Col. James Paterson of the 63rd regiment, appointed adjutant general 4.18.76. *(KP 1:339)*

35. Lee had advanced from Peekskill, New York, to Morristown, New Jersey, where he established headquarters, and wrote Washington, then at Trenton, that it was his opinion that the best way to stop the British was by "attacking their rear." *(LP 2:338)*

36. Having crossed over the Delaware on the 4th and 5th, the American force was now deployed along the west side of the Delaware, with corps headquartered from south to north as follows: Col. John Cadwalader at Bristol; Brig. Gen. James Ewing at Hoops Mill on Biles Creek, south of present Morrisville; Brig. Gen. Philemon Dickinson at Yardley's Ferry, now Yardley; Brig. Gen. Hugh Mercer, at or near Scudder's Falls, north of present Yardley; Brig. Gen. Adam Stephen at McKonkey's Ferry, now Washington Crossing; Brig. Gen. William Alexander (Lord Stirling) at Thompson-Neely House near present Brownsburg, all in Pennsylvania. Gen. Washington's headquarters was in what is now Morrisville, at Thomas Barclay's "summer seat" until he moved on the 14th to William Keith's house, 10 miles north, on Jericho Creek.

37. This force advanced south as far as Burlington, N.J. American

Commo. Thomas Seymour reported that "four or five hundred of the Enemy had entered the town." (WW 6:355) The presence of "the Gentlemen of the [row] gallies" under the command of Seymour were a constant threat to a Hessian approach to the Delaware in search of boats or a suitable ferry. (Morris 42)

38. Congress retired to Baltimore, Maryland.

39. Muenchhausen is obviously referring to hanging members of Congress, if caught.

40. On the morning of the 13th, Lt. Col. William Harcourt of the 16th dragoons departed his camp on the west bank of the Millstone River, north of the present Millstone, N.J. He and his men rode about two miles north, then crossed over to the east bank of the Millstone, and headed for the bridge over the Raritan River at Bound Brook. After crossing the bridge, he proceeded north over what is now King George Road in the direction of Basking Ridge. His route is clearly marked on a contemporary American map made by Maj. John Clark, aide to Gen. Greene, dated Morristown Feb. 11, 1777. (Pr. Lib.)

41. The French colonel was Sieur Gaiault de Boisbertrand.

42. The cannon were to be used at Burlington against the American row galleys, which were giving the Hessians so much trouble in the Delaware.

43. The turnover was accomplished at Brunswick.

44. These regiments were probably the 7th and 26th British regiments, the 7th being sent to New Bridge, and the 26th to Hackensack.

45. In the absence of Cornwallis, the Jersey command fell to Maj. Gen. James Grant.

46. No record has been found as to where Gen. Howe had been on this day; it is presumed that it was somewhere in Westchester County, New York, where control of the territory was much in question.

47. The Delaware did freeze up at Trenton, in mid-January. Margaret Morris noted in her diary on January 15, 1777, at Burlington, "I was a good deal affected this Evening on seeing the Hearse in which General Mercer's Body was conveyed over the River on the Ice to be buryd at Philada." (Morris 66)

48. One of the escaping officers was Capt. Heinrich Boeking. (Trenton 26) The other officer may have been Ens. Heinrich Zimmermann. Both were commanding troop details to the south of Trenton when the attack began. For maps of the area and battle action see (Trenton).

SECOND TRANSMITTAL
December 27, 1776-February 14, 1777

1. Gen. Cornwallis was planning to return to England for the winter, aboard the Bristol, scheduled to leave New York on December 27. Because of the disaster at Trenton on the 26th, Cornwallis was ordered to return to Jersey and to resume his command there, which had been turned over to Gen. Grant.

2. The force left at Princeton consisted of 859 men. They were the bulk of the British 4th brigade consisting of the 17th, 40th and 55th regiments plus some mounted and dismounted dragoons of the 16th regiments, all under the command of Lt. Col. Charles Mawhood. (Princeton 36)

3. The force that Cornwallis was pursuing consisted of "six pieces of artillery under Captain [Thomas] Forest, [Col. Edward] Hand's riflemen, a Virginia Corps under Colonel Charles Scott and the German battalion of [Col. Nicholas] Haussegger." (Wilkinson 1:135) This force had been under the command of Brig. Gen. Roche de Fermoy, but about noon, command was taken

over by Col. Hand. Their strength was approximately 1,000 men. (Princeton 11)

4. The "etc." meant the British 2nd brigade consisting of the 5th, 28th, 35th, and 49th regiments, together with a detachment of the 16th dragoons, who on the march south, had been left at Maidenhead, now Lawrenceville. This force was under Brig. Gen. Alexander Leslie.

5. At Trenton, Washington formed his line south of Assunpink Creek. This creek had but one bridge over it in the area, and Washington was well positioned to defend it. The creek was fordable only in one place in its lower reaches, and that was near the bridge. Back of Washington's line there was an elevation upon which he had placed several cannon that could be played very effectively on the bridge and the ford, should an attempted crossing be made.
be made.

6. As night fell on January 1, Washington had in camp at Trenton, and available for duty, as follows: a combined brigade of 1,400 men from the New England brigades of Glover, Sargent, and St. Clair, with St. Clair in command; a combined brigade of 325 men from the brigades of Mercer and Stirling, with Mercer in command; 400 men of Stephen's brigade; 600 men of Ewing's brigade; and 610 men of Roche de Fermoy's brigade, totaling 3335 men. An additional 2647 men arrived just in time to make the march. These were the Pennsylvania militia brigades of Cadwalader and Mifflin. (Princeton 34,35) Both the regulars and the newly arrived militia marched over the same road to Princeton.

7. The regiments that had set out in march to Trenton from Princeton were the 17th and 55th, although the 55th was just getting under way. The dismounted dragoons of the 16th regiment were with the 55th. They were escorting a wagon train of provisions. A detachment of mounted 16th dragoons accompanied the 17th regiment. The 40th regiment stayed behind to guard Princeton.

8. There were two separate actions. The 17th regiment and the mounted dragoons occupied and defended the hill located where the battle monuments stand on the present Mercer St., Princeton. The 55th regiment and the dismounted dragoons took a position back of Frog Hollow along present Alexander St. to help the 40th regiment defend the Princeton garrison. For maps and details of these engagements see (Princeton).

9. The official count of British casualties was 18 killed, 58 wounded, 200 missing or captured, total 276 (KP 1:115). General Washington said, shortly after the battle, that "Our losses in Slain is 6 or 7 Officers and about 25 or 30 Privates, the Number of Wounded is not ascertained." (WW 6:481) No further American report has been found.

10. Cornwallis' force marched all night enroute to Brunswick. They "arrived at Day Break on the 4th at the Heights above Brunswick." (Glyn 39) They waited "for several hours" in this position on the southern outskirts of the town, expecting an attack from the Americans. (ibid) When it did not come, the British entered the town. The next day, the 5th, Cornwallis deployed his force on the north side of the Raritan "with their right at Amboy and their left at Brunswick." (PNJHS 70:136) To consolidate his force further, the troops that had been strung out in several cantonments in Jersey north of the main force, were called down to Elizabethtown where they assembled under the command of Maj. Gen. Vaughan. (KP 1:106)

11. This engagement was the so-called "Second Battle of Trenton." There were heavy casualties on both sides in this running engagement, which lasted several hours. The claim that the Americans lost 400 men seems rather high, although there was much bitter hand-to-hand fighting. For details of this battle see

(Princeton 13 et seq.).

12. As the Americans approached the battlefield, Mercer's brigade was the farthest from Princeton, which could be interpreted as being the "rear guard," although it would be more properly called the left column.

13. Brig. Gen. Hugh Mercer 1725-1777, surgeon and apothecary of Fredericksburg, Va., was a friend and long time military associate of Gen. Washington. He had been promoted to brigadier in 1776, to command the so-called "Flying Camp." When this force was depleted by expiring enlistments at the end of 1776, Mercer was given command of a brigade consisting of remnants of his own Flying Camp and other enlistment depleted brigades.

14. At Rhode Island were a "Detachment of Royal Artillery, and 17th Light Dragoons, 3d. Battalion Light Infantry, 3d. Battalion Grenadiers, 3d. and 5th. Brigades British, and two Brigades Hessian (Losberg's and Schmidt's)...." *(KP 1:418)* The 3rd brigade of British were the 37, 52, 38, 10; the 5th were the 22, 43, 54, 63. The two Hessian brigades consisted of the Leib, Prinz Carl, Ditfourth, Landgraf, Huyne, Buenau.

15. From Elizabethtown, the British had sent out a reconnaissance party in the direction of Springfield, headed by Lt. Mesnard of the 17th dragoons, with about 12 of his light horse, plus the Waldeckers. When they were attacked by the Americans "the Waldeckers, in attempting their Retreat up the Hill, found their passage stopped, and retreated from the Rebels to a House, where they sustained some fire, but were in the end all taken prisoners." *(KP 1:106)*

16. On the 5th, Gen. Washington had written to Maj. Gen. William Heath, in command of American forces in the New York Highlands: "The Enemy are in great consternation, and as the Panick affords us a favourable Opportunity to drive them out of the Jerseys...you should move down towards New York with a considerable force, as if you had designs upon the City...the Enemy will be reduced to the Necessity of withdrawing a considerable part of their force from the Jerseys, if not the whole, to secure the City." *(WW 6:472)*

17. Ft. Independence was located about two miles northeast of Kings Bridge in the "y" of a road, one branch of which ran north, and the other east, to East Chester. For maps showing the fort location and its general form, see *(Br. M 130/24, 130/43)*. In modern terms of reference the fort was located at the edge of the hilltop west of what is now Jerome Reservoir in the Borough of the Bronx, on a site now traversed by Giles Place and nearby Sedgwick Avenue.

18. One of the "Free Corps" was the Loyalist unit known as Rogers' Rangers. The other "Free Corps" consisted of two small companies referred to as "The New York Companies" or the "Independent Companies." These two companies were later designated the "New York Volunteers". Muenchhausen uses the term "Free Corps" to refer to any non regular army unit of volunteers, either Loyalist or Patriot.

19. Lt. Col. Stephen Kemble stated that, "About ten this Morning [January 18] the Rebels appeared in number about 2,500 before Fort Independence, under the command of General Wooster, and Summoned it to Surrender, offering the Hessians the best terms; Rogers and New York Companies to surrender at discretion, as most of them were supposed to be Americans; a denial; some Cannon Shot exchanged, and the Rebels retired as far as Cortland's house, which they have plundered, and where they remain on the 22nd." *(KP 1:108)* General Wooster was Brig. Gen. David Wooster, who commanded a force under Maj. Gen. William Heath.

20. Although the diary was written in German, this sentence was in French, "Je crois ou plutot je soupçonne que mon General suivra bientôt, et que nous aurons bientôt quelque affaire."

THIRD TRANSMITTAL
February 15, 1777-April 17, 1777

1. This was Brig. Gen. Montfort Brown, former governor of the Bahamas.

2. These were the 600 Scots who, as noted in Capt. Muenchhausen's entry on June 8, 1777, "came from England and landed in Boston not knowing that we had already left that place."

3. Brig. Gen. Brown commanded several Loyalist regiments, one was the regiment in which he held a colonelcy, the Prince of Wales American regiment. This regiment consisted of about one fourth of Brown's strength during the attempted raid.

4. This was Jacob Morris, son of the prominent New Yorker, Lewis Morris, signer of the Declaration of Independence. The appointment was made by Gen. Lee, and information thereof sent from Lee's headquarters in New York to Washington at Cambridge on 3.3.76. In part, Lee said "I have...appointed one of the sons of Lewis Morris, to whom I was under sort of engagement." *(LP 1:343,344)*

Jacob Morris became ill after Lee's expedition to Charleston, S.C., in June 1776, and he was not with Lee at the time Lee was captured. Regarding the visit to Lee in captivity, Lee wrote to Gen. Washington that "I am extremely glad Morris is so far recovered that there is a probability of his leaving Philadelphia, where I left him (as I thought) in a very bad way from his effects of his Southern Expedition." *(LP 2:359)* Lee added, "You will much oblige me therefore by sending Morris to New York the instant he joins you. General Howe will I make no doubt transmit a passport for him by the same flag of truce with this letter." *(ibid)*

Shortly after Capt. Morris' return from visiting Lee, he refused an advancement to major in the 5th New York regiment. Some officers reputed the "refusal to General Lee's persuasion," which Morris denied. *(LP 2:369)*

5. As late as 5.3.77 Gen. Washington informed Congress that "The desertions from our Army of late, have been very Considerable. Gen. Howe's proclamation and the bounty allowed to those who carry their Arms, have had an unhappy influence on too many of the Soldiers...." *(WW 8:8)*

6. On 3.10.77, Lt. Col. Alexander Hamilton aide to Gen. Washington noted in a letter to Brig. Gen. Alexander McDougall that "He [Washington] has been very much indisposed for three or four days past, insomuch that his attention to business is pronounced by the Doctors to be very improper..." *(WP 3.10 AH/AMcD)* His ailment is said to have been a "quinsy sore throat," which had been ailing him for several weeks, beginning shortly after he attended the funeral of Col. Jacob Ford in January. *(Loc. cit.)*

7. This was Capt. Archibald Campbell of the New York Volunteers. Kemble noted in his journal, "Captain Campbell's New York Company attacked a party of Rebels in Wards House; Killed between 30 and 40 and took 20 and odd Prisoners, but on entering the house was Killed himself with four or five Men." *(KP 1:111)*

8. This was Lt. Col. John Bird of the British 15th regiment.

9. Brig. Gen. Alexander McDougall, in his report to Washington after the encounter, said that the enemy reached Peekskill at noon. At 1 o'clock, about 500 men in eight flatboats landed at Lents Cove, on the south side of the bay, with four pieces of artillery drawn by sailors. Seeing his force was out numbered, McDougall withdrew toward the Highlands after destroying whatever stores he

could handle before being overpowered. *(WP 3.29 AMc/GW)*

10. Lee's 1764 visit to Germany was undoubtedly made while enroute from England to be in Polish service. The record shows that Lee was in Germany again in 1770 on his return from Poland. For some details of his service as a major general under Polish King Poniatowski, see his letter dated "Vienna, Decr. 24th 1769." *(LP 1:88 et seq.)*

11. St-Luc-Lucan has not been identified. Carleton was British Maj. Gen. Guy Carleton, governor of Quebec.

12. This would indicate that Capt. von Muenchhausen was one of the sources of British headquarters news assembled by Maj. (then captain) Carl Leopold Baurmeister, acting adjutant general of German forces in America, who was at German headquarters. Baurmeister would consolidate all the important news, mostly of German interest, and write letter reports to Baron von Jungkenn, Lord High Chamberlain and Minister of State. These Baurmeister Letters have been published under the title *Revolution in America,* Bernhard A. Uhlendorf ed., New Brunswick, 1957.

13. Within a few days of the pontoon bridges being sent to Amboy, John Mercereau, one of Washington's spies, informed Washington of their arrival there. Mercereau even gave some of their dimensions. Washington suspected that they might be for use in crossing the Delaware, and he requested Mercereau to go at once to the Delaware River in the neighborhood of Coryell's Ferry, now New Hope, Pa. and Lambertville, N. J., to measure the width of the river there, and somewhat above there, to determine whether the pontoon bridges could be used for crossing anywhere in that area. *(WW 7:481)*

14. This was Maj. Gen. Benjamin Lincoln.

15. Gen. Lincoln noted that I "lost one of my aid-de-camps protem," while returning to the place first attacked to recover Lincoln's papers and baggage, all of which eventually fell into enemy hands. *(Cont. Jnl. 4.24.77)*

16. Washington in his report to the Board of War on 4.14.77, admitted only to the loss of "two pieces of Artillery and with them Lieuts. [William] Ferguson and [Charles] Turnbull with about twenty men of Colo. [Thomas] Proctors Regiment..." *(WW 7:411)* All were from Proctor's Pennsylvania Artillery battalion, designated the 4th Continental artillery.

17. Col. Elias Boudinot said that Cornwallis planned the attack because "a certain Farmer...who lived in the midst of our [the American] Camp had communicated to Lord Cornwallis our Countersign...." *(Boudinot 66)* For two accounts of this engagement, one British and one American, see *(2 NJA 1:339;342,343)*.

FOURTH TRANSMITTAL
April 18, 1777-May 22, 1777

1. The six English regiments were the 4th, 15th, 23rd, 27th, 44th, and 64th. Maj. Gen. William Tryon was in command, and Brig. Gen. James Agnew was second in command. Brig. Gen. William Erskine was next in command. The Provincials were actually "One hundred Men from 57th. Regiment and one hundred and fifty Provincials of Lieut. Col. Bayard's Corps." *(KP 1:114)* Bayard was John Bayard of the King's Orange Rangers.

2. An American account of what appears to be this action is found in *(2 NJA 1:360,361)*.

3. These men were Brig. Gen. Benedict Arnold and Maj. Gen. David Wooster. Wooster was commander of Connecticut continental troops. Arnold, also a continental officer, had been visiting his sister at New Haven, and had hurried to the scene, whereupon he took over command of Brig. Gen. Gold Selleck Sillman's Connecticut militia troops.

4. Gen. Wooster died May 2, 1777 as a result of wounds received at Ridgefield on April 27, according to Heitman.

5. The *Empress of Russia* was renamed the *Vigilant* when she was converted to a battery ship. In her converted condition she carried "Seven 24-pounders on each side of her main deck and three 6-pounders on each side of her quarter deck, with two spare ports for moving guns from one side to the other." *(PRO/CO 5:127/22-27)* The *Britannia* is described in detail by Capt. von Muenchhausen under date of 7.17.77.

6. This was probably the horse given to Capt. von Muenchhausen by Gen. Howe on 12.8.76, after Muenchhausen's horse had his leg shot away by American cannon fire.

7. For British and American accounts of this engagement see *(2 NJA 1:378-379,383-386)*.

8. At British headquarters in New York, it had been expected that Maj. Gen. Guy Carleton would join Lt. Gen. John Burgoyne in his 1777 invasion of the United States from Canada, via Lake Champlain. Carleton, however, did not participate, upon receiving instructions from England late in March, to remain in Canada with a substantial force. The rumor that Crown Point had been taken was indeed false. The Burgoyne force did not even enter Lake Champlain until the third week in June, and did not reach Crown Point until June 27.

FIFTH TRANSMITTAL
May 23, 1777-June 8, 1777

1. As of this date there remained in Rhode Island the British 22nd, 43rd and 54th, plus the Hessian regiments Landgraf, Ditfourth, Huyne and Buenau. *(PRO-CO 5/94:1:212)*

2. He was Borries Hilmar von Muenchhausen. The father and grandfather of this diarist were also named Borries von Muenchhausen. However, this was a frequently used Muenchhausen given name, and there appears to have been no close relationship between the two Muenchhausens serving in America.

3. Gen. Count Kielmansegg seems to have been a member of the Royal Court in Hannover.

4. This raid was authorized by Gen. Washington on the 25th, when he suggested to Brig. Gen. Samuel Holden Parsons, "I would even (under the Information given in your Letter) go further, and consent to an Expedition immediately to Long Island...." *(WW 8:125)*

5. The American troops at Bound Brook were under the command of Maj. Gen. Benjamin Lincoln. Bound Brook was not being evacuated, as thought by the British; it involved merely a switching of units from one command to another to conform with General Orders of May 22, outlining a completed rearrangement of the army. At about the same time, American headquarters was being moved from Morristown to Middlebrook, which probably confused the enemy further.

6. Grant's reconnaissance force consisted of the "1st Battalion of Light Infantry with a party of the 16th Light Dragoons." *(Glyn 50)*

7. Ens. Glyn of the Guards said that when the firing, coming from the direction of Princeton, was heard at Brunswick, the brigade of Guards was ordered to march to Grant's assistance. Upon their arrival at the point of fire, they formed in the rear of the light infantry. The Americans "advanced with two pieces of Cannon & began to cannonade us when we were ordered to lay down, & being covered by the ground, no loss ensued except Major General Grant having his Horse shot dead under him...." *(Glyn 51 verso)*

8. Capt. Friedrich Henrich Lorey commanded a company of mounted Hessian jaegers. One of his exploits, possibly the one being referred to by Muenchhausen, was when a few days past Lorey "suc-

ceeded in posting himself in an ambush between Princeton and Bonhamtown and surprised a troop of the enemy, falling upon them so suddenly that six of their most prominent men asked for pardon..." *(Baur. 87)*

9. The County of Anspach-Bayreuth was one of the six German territories making subsidiary treaties with Great Britain. Col. Friedrich Ludwig Albrecht von Eyb was in overall command of both Anspach-Bayreuth regiments. The first regiment was designated the Eyb regiment and the 2nd was designated the Voit regiment for Col. Friedrich August Valentin Voit von Salzburg. For a scholarly article on the troops of Anspach-Bayreuth see *(MC&H XIX:2:48)*.

10. Rheinfels was a Hessian town and fort on the right bank of the Rhine, halfway between Wiesbaden and Koblenz. From here Hessian troops bound for America were sent down the Rhine on barges to Holland, where they boarded English transports.

11. Their exact strength was 1305 men. *(PRO-CO 5/94:1:212)*

12. This is a reference to the Seven Years' War (1756-63), in which Anspach took part along with other German territories.

13. Apparently word had not been received as of this date that Carleton had not gone on the expedition with Burgoyne. The Brunswick troops, who had been under Carleton, however, were with Burgoyne.

14. This was Lt. Col. John Campbell.

15. This was Brig.-Col. James Webster.

16. This was Col. Carl Emil Ulrich von Donop.

17. In contrast, as of 5.20.77, Gen. Washington's continental army of foot regiments with him in New Jersey amounted to "8,188 men." *(WW 8:Opp 170)* To this total should be added artillery continentals amounting to "1,370 men." *(WW 10:279)* Four dragoon continental regiments consisting of approximately 1,000 men complete the continental man-count. *(WW 9:156)* To this figure should be added an approximate 2,000 New Jersey militia, which could be utilized. This brings the total force, available to General Washington at the beginning of this campaign to approximately 12,588 men. According to Capt. von Muenchhausen's count the British had 14,900 men in Jersey.

SIXTH TRANSMITTAL
June 8, 1777-August 31, 1777

1. This was a reference to the First Watchung Mountain, which lay back of Bound Brook. The encampment of the main American army, at this point in time, was at a place called Middlebrook, which also was the name of a stream that runs through a gap in the mountain and joins the Raritan River on the southern outskirts of what is now the city of Bound Brook.

2. Maj. Carl Leopold Baurmeister was acting adjutant general for Hessian forces in America.

3. From Piscataway, Lorey and Muenchhausen rode north to Ambrose Brook where the road swung left, and followed the brook toward the village of Bound Brook.

4. At this point in time, the four continental dragoon regiments were as follows: the 1st was commanded by Col. Theodorick Bland, and 2nd by Col. Elisha Sheldon, the 3rd by Lt. Col. George Baylor and the 4th by Col. Stephen Moylan. When Washington's body guard unit was reorganized on May 1, 1777, a mounted unit was included, and taken chiefly from the 3rd dragoons. Prior to May 1, dragoons were detached from dragoon units to serve with the commander in chief.

5. The order of march was as follows: "1st Division: Lt. Gen. Cornwallis & Maj. Gen. Grant, Hessian and Anspach Jaegers, Two Battalions Light Infantry, Two Medium 12-pounders, British Grenadiers with their Guns, 33rd and 42nd Regiments, Two Howit-

zers and two sixes, 5th, 49th, 52nd, 37th, four 6-pounders, Hessian Grenadiers, Queen's dragoons. 2nd Division: Lt. Gen. Heister, Maj. Gens. Stirn, Vaughan, & Grey, Brig. Gens. Agnew & Leslie to march by the left, four Companys of Light Infantry, Light Company and Guards, and Ferguson's Rifle men, 4 grasshoppers, 1st Brigade with two 12-pounders and two 6-pounders, Stirn's Brigade, 2nd & 4th Brigades, two 6-pounders to each Brigade, 3rd & 1st Brigade, two 6-pounders to each Battalion [Brigade?], 17th Dragoons." *(Br. Jnl.)*

6. Sullivan had not yet assembled the division he would command during the 1777 campaign. The troops at Princeton presently under Sullivan were "The Troops from Maryland, the lower Counties (on Delaware) and Hazen's Regiment, together with the Artillery Company, and light horse now at that Place." *(WW 8:62,63)* The force there totaled 1500 plus.

7. Maj. André said the "misunderstandings" were that "From the Orders it appeared that the First Division was to form in column of march on the Princeton Road at 11 o'clock in the evening, but with respect to the Second Division, altho' it was expressed they were to strike tents, no place of rendezvous was appointed, nor were they directed to form in column, tho' the order to march was given. General De Heister had understood he was included in the Order given to the First Division to assemble on the Princeton Road, and purposed bringing up his column in the rear of Lord Cornwallis's. General Grey, on the other hand, abiding by the letter of the Order, thought we were to remain on our ground till further Orders should be received." *(Andre 26)*

8. It would have made no difference if the British had not had a mix-up in orders regarding their march, for Sullivan had already been warned of the probable intentions of the British, and he "had Changed his Post to Rocky hill, an Event which took place only the Evening before, and which it is presumed, they [the British] were not well advised ·of when they left Brunswick." *(WW 8:244)* Then on the 14th Sullivan was ordered to march to "Fleming Town [Flemington] as soon as possible," more easily to form a junction with the main army, if necessary. *(WW 8:248)*

9. On June 13, Washington had ordered that Col. Daniel Morgan and his "Corps of Rangers newly formed...are to take Post at Van Veghten Bridge and watch, with very small Scouting Parties...the Enemys left Flank, and particularly the Roads leading from Brunswick towards Millstone, Princeton & ca. In case of any Movement of the Enemy you are Instantly to fall upon their Flanks and gall them as much as possible, taking especial care not to be surrounded, or have your retreat to the Army cut off." *(WW 8:236)*

10. "Cornwallis pass'd the Millstone at Schenck's bridge...." *(Robertson 136)* The Jno. Clark Junr. map of February 11, 1777, shows "Peter Schenck's Mill and Bridge" near what is now Blackwell's Mills, two miles south of the Hillsborough Bridge. *(AM.M 12/1)*

11. The small force that was engaging Cornwallis here was a detachment of Col. Morgan's corps. After the engagement Morgan was pursued up the west side of the Millstone River as far as Van Ests Mill, which lay about two miles north of Hillsborough. Regarding this encounter Lt. Col. Tench Tilghman wrote that the enemy moved north along the Millstone as far as Van Ests Mill. They had some skirmishing with Colo. Morgan's Riflemen and "have halted and taken post upon a high piece of Ground." *(WW 8:249 note)* Van Ests Mill is also shown on the Clark map, noted in the preceding annotation.

12. On the 15th, Sullivan was ordered to move closer to the enemy into "the Sowrland Hills; in this Situation you will have it in your power to harass the Rear and left Flank of the Enemy, while we

oppose them upon their Front and Right." *(WW 8:251)* The Sourland Hills were back of Hopewell, N.J., stretching several miles southwest and northeast.

13. Lt. Col. Stephen Kemble noted this dissatisfaction in his journal as follows: "Find from the general tenor of Officers Conversation that they are not well pleased with Affairs, but they often speak without thought. Asserted by several that Guides offered to Conduct General Howe by a Road where he might Attack the Rebels in their Entrenchments to advantage, but that he took no Notice of it, this may be without foundation as well as the former, and the General is the best judge of his own Actions." *(KP 1:124)*

One officer wrote, "If I am not mistaken, Lieutenant Colonel Mawhood offered, with a brigade, and a battalion of light infantry, to attempt forcing one of the debouchées, or openings, that led to their camp, which might have brought on something general; but the proposal was over-ruled and rejected...." *(Hall 279)*

14. To Chevalier d' Anmours, Gen. Washington wrote on June 20, 1777, "I have received your favour of the 6th. Instant, transmitting me your observations on the State of American Affairs, and the part that France is interested by the motives of good policy to act in consequence of it.... An immediate declaration of War against Britain, in all probability, could not fail to extricate us from our difficulties." *(WW 8:265,266)* The receipt of this letter appears to be sufficient reason for having the bonfire.

15. A British manuscript map titled "Sketch of Brunswick" shows a bridge across the Raritan River labeled "A log bridge built by the army 1777." *(Br. M 57/25)*

16. The force that opposed Gen. Howe was "Morgans Rifle Corp; they fought, it seems, a considerable time within the distance of, from twenty, to forty yards; and from the concurring Acct. of several of the Officers, more than a hundred of them [the enemy] must have fallen." *(WW 8:295,296)*

17. The strong force "some way off" may have been any one of "several Brigades that were ordered upon that Service," not one of which arrived in time to support Morgan. *(WW 8:296)*

18. Privy Councellor von Muenchhausen was Capt. Muenchhausen's uncle Friedrich Ernst, at the Court of the Duke of Brunswick. War Councellor von Muenchhausen was Capt. Muenchhausen's brother, William August Friedrich, at the court of Hannover.

19. On June 20, three days prior to Muenchhausen's diary entry on the 21st, Gen. Washington wrote to the Congress enclosing extracts from a letter from Col. Henry Jackson to Gen. Knox, informing Knox of "two brigs" capturing Hessians. *(WW 8:271)*

20. The Landgrave of Hesse Cassel released Gen. von Heister, officially, due to his age and ill health, but the true reason was different. Heister was a stiff and completely militarily minded general who was not accustomed to diplomatic bargaining with British commanders. The cautious report of Lord Suffolk on the misunderstanding between Howe and von Heister was climaxed in a letter to Hessian Minister Baron Schlieffen of January 25, 1777,"... Il faut absolument que Heister soit rappelé. Le Roi est determiné...." [It is absolutely necessary that Heister be recalled. The King is determined.] *(Schlieffen)*

Leopold von Heister was born in Homberg, Hessia in 1716. After first entering French service, he changed to Hessian service and was promoted to lieutenant in 1739, captain in 1745, and major in 1754. In 1763 he became a major general and was promoted to lieutenant general in 1772. In 1775 he was awarded nobility "von," prior to becoming commander in chief of the Hessian forces in America. Von Heister died in Cassel on October 19, 1777, shortly after returning to Germany from America.

Gen. von Knyphausen was Wilhelm Knyphausen, Baron Innkaussen and Knyphausen, born in 1716, at Lutzburg in East Friesland, and educated at the Berlin Gymnasium. He served in the Seven Years' War as a major of grenadiers and was promoted to lieutenant colonel in 1760. In 1775 he attained the rank of lieutenant general and came to America as second in command to General von Heister.

21. On the 24th, Washington gave orders to advance to "Lord Stirling's Division and some other Troops lower down in the Neighbourhood of Metuchen Meeting House." *(WW 8:298)* Thomas Conway had been given a brigade on May 19, 1777, just a few days prior to this, and his brigade became a part of Stirling's division at that time. The Short-hills are a part of a narrow band of rolling hills running northwest from Amboy toward the First Watchung Mountain, and skirting the south edge of the present Ash Swamp Park.

22. On June 24 "The [American] army marched to Quibbletown [New Market], about five miles from its encampment, and halted; the intelligence respecting Howe's situation not being such as to warrant our proceeding to Amboy, where in a plain country, he might attack with his whole force." *(Pickering 144)*

23. The light infantry was in the Cornwallis column or division, thus indicating that this action was between Cornwallis and the Americans. *(Br. Jnl.)*

24. The force that Cornwallis met was Stirling's division, which consisted of Brig. Gen. Thomas Conway's brigade and Brig. Gen. William Maxwell's brigade totaling "1798 men." *(WW 8:opp. 170)*

25. In their fight, Gen. Cornwallis formed a line of battle against Gen. Stirling consisting of "the 1st light infantry, 1st British grenadiers, 1st, 2d, 3d Hessian Grenadiers; 1st battalion of guards, Hessian chasseurs [jaegers], and the Queen's Ranger," a total of nearly 5,000 men. *(Moore 449)*

26. An American account of this engagement follows: "He [Cornwallis] met with Lord Stirling's party early in the morning, a smart engagement ensued, and our men stood their ground manfully for a considerable time; but the amazing superiority of numbers obliged them to retreat, and the enemy having flanked them, they lost two pieces of cannon, with a number of men.... It is a pity that this party [Stirling's] could not have been properly reinforced without hazarding a general battle." *(2 NJA 1:415,416)*

As indicated in the American account, there was some criticism of General Washington's action in this engagement. When the fight with Stirling began near Oak Tree, Washington, with his main army, was two or three miles away, at Quibbletown. At this point in time, Washington decided that it was "absolutely necessary, that we should move our force from the low Grounds, to occupy the Heights" at Middlebrook. *(WW 8:307,308)*

After reentering the passes that led to the heights, Washington ordered Brig. Gen. Charles Scott to take a body of light troops to hang on the enemy's "Flank and to watch their Motions." *(ibid)* According to Lt. Col. Alexander Hamilton, aide to Gen. Washington, "Lord Stirling's party...after a smart skirmish with the enemy's main body, made their retreat good to Westfield, and ascended the pass of mountains back of Scotch Plains." *(Hamilton 9:78)*

27. These redoubts are shown on map *(Br. M 130/43)*.

28. After Clinton's successful invasion of Rhode Island, he turned over the Rhode Island command to Lt. Gen. Hugh Percy and took advantage of permission, given him earlier by Gen. Howe, to return to England for a short visit. Upon his arrival there in March, he was knighted by the King, and subsequently he held

high level consultations on the progress and future plans for prosecuting the war. He then returned to New York aboard the *Liverpool*.

29. Howe's proclamation was dated November 30, 1776, and it offered that anyone, within sixty days, who would swear to obey the King and remain at peace, could return to their homes without molestation or penalties. For a detailed account of the particulars of this proclamation and surrounding circumstances, see *(Gruber 146 et seq.).*

30. This is probably a reference to the attack, in March 1777, on Ft. McIntosh, located on the Satilla River, which borders Georgia and Florida. An undocumented account states that Capt. Richard Winn of the South Carolina Rangers was in command there with but 50 men. When news came to American Maj. Gen. Robert Howe, at Charleston, that Capt. Winn was under attack, Howe sent Lt. Col. Francis Marion to his rescue with a detachment of 105 men. Marion did not arrive in time, and the fort was overrun by a force of Tories and Indians sent there from St. Augustine by Maj. Gen. Augustine Prevost.

31. Gen. Howe's orders stated, "Major Gardiner, of the 45th. Regiment, Aid-de-Camp to the Commander in Chief, is appointed to do duty as Major to the 2d. Battalion Grenadiers till further Orders. Major Fox, of 49th. Regiment, Aid-de-Camp to the Commander in Chief, is to do duty with his Regiment till further orders." *(KP 1:470,471)*

32. Gen. Clinton was the principal cause of this delay. His argument given to Gen. Howe, as later related, was as follows: "I stated the probable risks and delays it [a Philadelphia campaign] would be exposed to from the sickness and southerly winds generally prevalent in that climate in the summer months, and with all deference suggested the many great and superior advantages to be derived at the present moment from a cooperation of his whole force with General Burgoyne on the River Hudson. And I took the liberty at the same time to say that it was highly probable, the instant the fleet was decidedly gone to sea, Mr. Washington would move with everything he could collect either against General Burgoyne or me and crush the one or the other, as neither would be very capable of withstanding such superior forces unless timely intelligence should fortunately bring the fleet back to our relief." *(Clinton 61,62)*

33. Maj. Gen. Richard Prescott's captors were Maj. William Barton of Stanton's Rhode Island State regiment, with a detachment of his men. The raiding party came from Tiverton, R. I. The aide who was captured with Prescott was Maj. William Barrington. For the capture of Prescott, Barton was presented with a sword by a resolve of the Continental Congress.

34. The letter Howe received from Burgoyne on the 15th was dated July 2, and it informed Howe that he was emplacing guns preparatory to taking Ticonderoga. However, the messenger who brought the letter, stated that he learned, after he had started out for New York, that Ticonderoga had fallen. On the 15th, Howe's Deputy Adjutant General Kemble entered in his journal, "The Commander in Chief received a Letter this day from General Burgoyne, who had just opened his Batteries against Ticonderoga. He says he heard [from the messenger] the place was taken, but does not alledge it as a fact. Accounts are likewise to be credited that Mr. Washington had removed towards the North River, and that part of his Troops were some days since in Pompton, [N.J.], but that is not to be depended upon. If he quits and goes up to oppose Mr. Burgoyne, we shall Attack him in the Rear, in all probability, or why the delay in our Movement from this." *(KP 1:125)*

35. Washington had remained at Morristown with the bulk of his army until July 10, when he moved north to Pompton Plains, N.J.

Here, he remained until the 14th, when his force marched to Van Aulen's eight miles from Pompton Plains. The next day he advanced farther north to the Clove, in Orange County, N.Y. His route was more inland than noted by Muenchhausen.

36. Capt. William Cornwallis was six years younger than his brother. He had been a member of Parliament from Eye prior to the war, and resumed his seat in 1782. He was a distinguished naval officer, and was known in the navy as "Billy Blue."

37. The fleet consisted of "two hundred and sixty seven sails." *(PRO-Adm. 1/487:37)*

38. Howe's artillery was under the command of Brig. Gen. Samuel Cleaveland. If Cleaveland's artillery, which embarked for Philadelphia was the same as it was in the recent Jersey engagements, it consisted of ten 24-pounders, eight heavy 12-pounders, twelve light 12-pounders, thirty 6-pounders, fourteen 3-pounders, four 8 inch, six 5½ inch, four 13 inch, two 8 inch, six 5½ inch. *(PRO-CO 5/94: Pt. 1:212)* His artillery detachment consisted of "33 officers and 385 men." *(ibid)*

39. Capt. von Muenchhausen sailed aboard the *Britannia* as noted in a letter to his mother dated "August 9, 1777 On board the Ship *Britannia*." *(NHH:52:III:29)*

40. Captain of the *Nonsuch* was Walter Griffith.

41. Bremerlehe is now a small fishing port on the lower Weser River between Bremen and Bremerhaven. It served as a major port in the 18th century. Most of the Hessian troops marched from Cassel to Karlshafen on the upper Weser River, where they boarded flatboats that took them to Bremerlehe to board English transports there.

42. Captain of the *Repulse* was Henry Davis.

43. This story is not true according to English reports. The British frigate *Fox* was taken off Boston while under full sail. A two-day running battle ensued, with the *Fox* finally being overpowered by the American ships *Boston* and *Hancock*. For full British details of the encounter see *(Clowes IV: 5 et seq.).*

44. Capt. Andrew Snape Hamond was commander of a flotilla of ships guarding the entrance to the Delaware. He had, in 1770, been captain of Admiral Howe's flagship, the *Barfleur*, and he was held in great respect by the Howe brothers.

A group of Loyalists also came aboard the *Eagle* and informed the Admiral and Capt. Hamond about "the state of the river and the chain, the cheveaux de frise & c." *(Pa. Mag. 18:183 note)* The Howe brothers were told that the Americans had placed these obstacles in the river to wreck any British ships attempting to cross them. After a long conference, it was decided that a landing in the Delaware would be abandoned in favor of a landing in the Chesapeake, which was, according to reports, free of obstacles.

45. This entry indicates that both Howe brothers were, at this point in the voyage, on the Admiral's flagship the *Eagle,* and from subsequent entries, Gen. Howe continued to sail up the Chesapeake with his brother.

46. Howe issued a proclamation on August 27 offering protection to all who would surrender their arms. For details of this proclamation and the circumstance surrounding its issuance see *(Gruber 238,239).*

47. This was Ft. Mifflin on Mud Island.

48. For a map showing the location of the sunken ships, chains and cheveaux de frise see *(Delaware 35)*. Cheveaux de frise were large coffers or boxes, some 63 feet long by 40 feet wide. Fifteen- to twenty-inch squared pine logs formed the frames of these coffers, which were lined on the sides and bottom with planking. Inside these coffers were secured heavy poles with iron-tipped spikes. The poles extended out from the top of the coffers at an angle of approximately 45 degrees. When completed on shore,

these boxes were towed out into the Delaware to strategic spots. Here they were filled with rock and sunk to the bottom, the spikes being slightly under water at low tide, where they could tear the bottom out of 18th century wooden ships.

49. Although brander means fireship in German, Muenchhausen refers to both branders and fireships, which would indicate that there was some difference between the two. A fireship is usually a hulk that is set afire to be carried by the tide or the flow of the river up against an enemy vessel to set it afire.

50. The British renamed the *Hancock,* the *Iris. (Chapelle 73)* Chapelle says the captain of the Hancock was Joseph Manley. *(Chapelle 73)* Clowes say his name was John Manley *(Clowes IV: 5)*

51. The three British ships were the 44-gun *Rainbow,* the 18-gun brig *Victor,* later to be joined by the 32-gun frigate *Flora. (Clowes IV: 6,7)*

52. This was undoubtedly the Rappahannock River, for the next day they were off the Potomac River.

53. This was probably off Cove Point, Md.

54. Sharp's Island, located 3½ miles S SW of Black Walnut Point, which is the extreme tip of Tilghman's Island, is no longer in existence. Early deeds show the island to have surveyed-out at about 700 acres. As of 1944 the island had eroded down to seventy acres. According to a local citation, it was finally reduced to a shoal visible only at mean low tide, during World War II, when it was used for air bombing practice.

55. It is said that 18th century red often had a purple cast to it. Muenchhausen did not mention seeing an emblem in the corner of the flag as authorized by Continental Congress on June 14, 1777, just two months prior to this date. Their resolution read "Resolved, That the flag of the United States be thirteen stripes, alternate red and white: that the union be thirteen stars, white in a blue field, representing a new constellation." *(JCC 8:464)*

56. The depth of the hold of the *Roebuck* was 16 ft. 4 in., which was standard measurement for 44-gun 5th rate ships. Muenchhausen's reference "her especially shallow draft" might imply that the *Roebuck* had been purposely lightened to accomplish her work in the shallow Delaware, where she had been on station.

57. Capt. Montresor noted in his journal on this date, "At seven this morning I attended Sir Wm. Howe and Lord Howe with my armed Schooner, an armed Sloop and a Galley to the mouths of the Rivers Rappahannock and the Elk and Turkey Point, the different Boats attending, sounding the Channel." Montresor meant the Susquehannah rather than the Rappahannock. *(Mont. 441)*

58. The reason for no disembarkment on the 24th was probably the weather. Capt. Montresor noted "A hard squall with very heavy rain and sharp lightning and thunder which continued from eight till 12 this night [the 23rd] and the whole night [was] distressingly hot and close." *(Mont. 441,442)*

59. Montresor noted that the landing was made on Turkey Point "at the Ferry House called Elk Ferry in the Province of Maryland." *(Mont. 442)* There is no town presently at this location, although there are a few houses at the water's edge. The grading of the old access road to the Ferry is plainly visible from a paralleling road, and piling stumps of the old ferry slip remain.

60. On Sunday the 24th the American army had marched through Philadelphia and had advanced to Darby. On the 25th, "The army marched through Chester to Naaman's Creek." *(Pickering 152)* "The General went with all the horse, save Sheldon's to reconnoitre." *(ibid)* Upon his return on the 26th, he wrote to Congress, "I this Morning returned from the Head of Elk, which I left last night." *(WW 9:136)*

61. Washington noted in his letter to Congress that it was from "Iron Hill and Grey's Hill" that he observed the enemy on the 27th. *(WW 9:137)* In this reconnoitering mission, Gen. Washington appears to have used a map made for him that day and signed "Laid down at 200 ft in an inch the 27th day of August An. Dom. 1777, Jacob Broom Survr. N. Castle Coy." *(PHS)* The map has numerous notation on it in the hand of Gen. Washington. It is a very crude map showing virtually straight lines for roads, showing no elevation, and showing only a few of the water courses in the area, all of this suggesting that, at this stage in the campaign, Washington was not very well informed on the state of the terrain on which he might be called upon to fight.

62. In Washington's letter to Congress on the 25th he voiced concern regarding these supplies. He said, "There are a great quantity of Public and private Stores at the Head of Elk, which I am afraid will fall into the Enemy's hands, if they advance quickly...." *(WW 9:132)*

63. While Adm. Howe and General Grey were in camp it was arranged that, because Howe was about to make a movement to his right, or east, from the Head of Elk, Gen. Knyphausen should send a force under Gen. Grey across Elk River "to Cecil Court-house tomorrow, and that they may move in time for him to take a post one mile or two beyond the Court-house on the road to Christien [Christiana] Bridge." *(Andre 39)* This would protect Howe's flank as he moved to his right. The balance of the Knyphausen force was to "cross to the same place on Sunday," the 31st. *(ibid)*

64. Washington reported on the 30th that "24 British prisoners arrived, taken yesterday by Captn. Lee of the Light Horse." *(WW 9:148)*

65. On the 30th Washington wrote to the President of Congress, "I was reconnoitering the Country and different Roads all Yesterday and am setting out on the same business again." *(WW 9:148)*

66. An amusette, translated as "plaything" in French, was a very small field cannon invented by Marshal Saxe. Weight of the ball was approximately 500 German grams, which is about 550 U.S. grams, or about a 1¼ -pounder.

SEVENTH TRANSMITTAL
September 1, 1777-October 26, 1777

1. This inaccurate figure as to Washington's strength, received from three captured enlisted men, this same day will be revised downward considerably by information gained from more reliable sources.

2. This strong patrol was "200 Rangers of Wemys's Corps." *(Mont. 445)*

3. Commander of the corps was the French Marquis de La Roueire. The marquis, having served in the French Garde du Corps as a lieutenant, was commissioned a lieutenant colonel in the American army on May 10, 1777. In American service the marquis used the name Charles Armand-Tuffin. On May 19, 1777, Armand-Tuffin was authorized to raise a "Partisan Corps" with the suggestion that he try to raise his quota from those who spoke French, but if that was impossible, he could recruit others "not exceeding 200." *(WW 8:91)* Apparently he was unable to recruit sufficient men. Thus, on June 11, 1777, "Col. De-La Rouerie is appointed to the command of the Corps, heretofore under Major Ottendorf." *(WW 8:226)* Ottendorf was Nicholas Dietrich Baron Ottendoeff, major of three companies raised in Pennsylvania.

4. Heitman spells the name Uechritz, and gives his name and record as follows: "Uechritz, Louis Augustus de Baron. Lieutenant

of Ottendorf's Battalion 29th April, 1777; taken prisoner at the Head of Elk, 2d September 1777; exchanged 1780; Captain Armand's Partisan Corps 1781, and served to the close of the war. Name also spelled Uttricht."

5. In addition to the approximately 10,000 continentals with Washington in June (see note under 6.8.77), the following troops had been added to Washington's army: 1st and 2nd North Carolina brigade under Brig. Gen. Nash, totaling "1079 men." *(WW 10:279)* Maj. Gen. John Armstrong's Pennsylvania militia division had also joined Washington. Armstrong two brigades under Brig. Gens. Potter and Irvine totaled "2973 men." *(1 Pa A 5:595)* This gave Washington a strength of approximately 14,000 men, against Howe's approximately 16,000 men, as per Muenchhausen's entry 7.18.77.

6. The two French Generals were probably Maj. Gen. Marquis de Lafayette and Maj. Gen. Philip Charles Jean Baptiste du Coudray. Muenchhausen's remark would suggest that he thought Armand to be a German, which he was not. The other colonel may have been Col. Henry Leonard Philip Baron de Arendt.

7. If there were three brigades on this advance, the designation of the third is not known. One was Brig. Gen. Conway's and one was Brig. Gen. William Maxwell's brigade. Maj. Gen. Stirling's two brigades totaled "1,798 men" as of 5.20.77 *(WW 8: opp.170)*

8. In addition to Coudray's apparent disagreement with Washington over tactics at the Head of Elk, Coudray previously had a disagreement with Washington over Billingsport, which Coudray considered as the proper place to defend the Delaware instead of at Fort Mifflin and Fort Mercer. *(Pa. Mag. 18:181)* Coudray would be drowned while crossing the Schuylkill on September 15, 1777.

9. This was Lt. Henry Haldane, listed as one of the officers killed during the day's action, indicating that Haldane did not survive the operation. *(Mont. 446)*

10. Gen. Washington noted that after the engagement here, the Americans, under Gen. Maxwell, retreated to "White Clay Creek." *(WW 9:173)*

11. "Half-moons" were probably lutes. "Other (wind) instruments" might refer to flutes. The word wind, in parentheses, is as in the manuscript.

12. This was not the force of Col. Armand-Tuffin, which had been encountered the day before yesterday, but was a newly organized force under the command of Brig. Gen. William Maxwell. It had been organized in Washington's Additional After Orders of 8.28.77, as follows: "A corps of Light Infantry is to be formed, to consist of one Field Officer, two Captains, six Subalterns, eight Serjeants and 100 Rank and File from each brigade." *(WW 9:145)* These were taken only from "Greene's and Steven's [Stephen's] Division." *(WW 9:153)*

From Headquarters at Wilmington on 9.2.77, Gen. Washington had written Col. Armand-Tuffin, "Sir: I have a complaint lodged against your Corps by a number of reputable Inhabitants in the Neighbourhood of Elk. As I find that your men cannot be restrained from committing Violences while in the Country, I desire you will immediately march them to this town." *(WW 9:166,167)*

13. On the 4th, British headquarters was located at "Aiken's Tavern," now Glasgow, Del. *(KP 1:485)*

14. For several accounts of this attack, which took place August 22, see *(2 NJA 1:457 et seq.; KP 1:127-130).*

15. Washington's letter to Howe, dated September 5, read as follows: "Sir, I did myself the Honor to write you on the 16th. of July upon the subject of an Exchange of Major General Prescot for Major General Lee. As I can only attribute your Silence upon a Matter so personally interesting to both of those Gentlemen to your having received my former Letter, I am induced to transmit you a duplicate of it, to which I beg leave to request an Answer. I Have the Honor etc." *(WW 9:186)* The letter to Howe was sent by a flag of truce from an advance post of Gen. Maxwell, who had instructions to "Let some decent [well groomed] Officer go with the flag." *(WW 9:182)*

16. On the 6th, official documents show the British "Camp at Pencadar." *(KP 1:487)* This was undoubtedly "Pencader [Presbyterian] Mtg." shown on a contemporary map as being directly across the road from "Aikens Tav." where headquarters had been since the 3rd. *(Brun 521)*

17. Howe's orders of 9.8.77 show the spelling of the headquarters as "Nicholl's House." *(KP 1:489)* Capt. Montresor, on the 9th, refers to "Head Quarters at Nichols's House Mill Creek Hundred." *(Mont. 448)*

18. Timothy Pickering, adjutant general to Washington, noted in his journal on September 9, "Left Newport in the morning before daylight, and marched to Chad's Ford; crossed it, and encamped on the east side of the Brandywine." *(Pickering 154)* It would appear that in this day's march Washington used a map made by Jacob Broom dated "the 27th day of August An. Dom. 1777." Washington made several notations on the map regarding the road to Chad's Ford. *(HSP)*

19. Capt. Montresor said that the Cornwallis column marched "from Head Quarters at Nichols's House Mill Creek Hundred by a bye road to Hokesson Meeting House." *(Mont. 448)* This Quaker Meeting house is on the northwest outskirts of the present village of Hokesson. The route of both British columns were to be joined, according to prearrangement, a short distance before reaching Kennett Square, at New Garden Meeting, in the present village of New Garden.

20. Welch's Tavern was situated at the present Longwood, two miles east of Kennett Square.

21. As Capt. Muenchhausen noted, it was the original plan that Howe's division "would be able to catch up with General Knyphausen before he reached New Garden." Now, since it was learned that Knyphausen had already passed New Garden, the Howe force marched over a more direct road to Kennett Square.

22. This information was received "at five this evening," while Muenchhausen was on his mission to deliver orders to Knyphausen. *(Mont. 449)* In addition to sending his baggage to Chester, it was learned that Washington "had moved heavy Artillery to the Turks Head." *(ibid)* This was a sure sign to Howe that Washington was preparing to make a stand. The Turks Head was the name of a tavern located in present city of West Chester, which was about four miles from where it is known Washington placed his heavy cannon. At that time, however, Turks Head may also have referred to the general area.

23. The four Hessian regiments were "Leib Regiment, Donop's, Mirbach's and the Combined Battalion." *(Baur. 107)* The two English brigades were the "1st and 2nd." *(ibid)* The dragoons were of the "16th regiment." *(ibid)* The Provincials were "one battalion of Queen's Rangers." *(ibid)* The English chasseurs were "Captain Ferguson's British Riflemen." *(ibid)*

24. The two brigades of English infantry were the "3rd and 4th." *(Baur. 107)* The two squadrons of dragoons were of the "16th Regiment of Dragoons." *(ibid)* Howe described his artillery as "four light 12-pounders and the artillery of the birgades." *(PRO-CO 5/94 p639.no.68)*

25. The only American record of any contact with this large flanking force of the British army, this early in the day, was

reported as follows: "Sept. 11, 1777, Great Valley Road Eleven o'clock a.m. Dear General, A large body of the enemy from every account 5000 with 16 or 18 field pieces, marched along this road just now. This road leads to Taylor's and Jeffries fords on the Brandywine... we are close to their rear with about 70 men. Capt. Simpson lay in ambush with 20 men, and gave them three rounds within a small distance, in which two of his men were wounded one mortally. I believe Genl. Howe is with this party as Joseph Galloway is here known by the inhabitants with many of whom he spoke, and told them that Genl. Howe is with him. Yours, James Ross Lieut. Col. D. P. Regt." *(WP 9.11 Ross/GW)*

Ross' intelligence, unfortunately for the Americans, was not acted upon because of contradicting and, what was considered, more reliable information received by Gen. Sullivan from Maj. Spear of the militia who had just come down from the fords of the Brandywine and reported that he "heard nothing of the enemy above the forks of the Brandywine and is confident that they are not in that quarter." *(WP 9.11 Sul/GW)*

26. The crossing of the two forks of the Brandywine were at "Trumbull's Ford and at Jefferies' Ford." *(Mont. 449)*

27. Arrived at "an open clear height [Osborne's hill] at ½ past two." *(Mont. 449)*

28. As the troops rested on Osborne's Hill "Sir William Howe with the most cheerful countenance conversed with his Officers and invited several to a slight refreshment provided on the Grass." *(Br. Jnl)*

29. Gen. Sullivan said that "At half past two, I received orders to march with my division,—to join with, and take command of, that and others [Stephen's and Stirling's divisions] to oppose the enemy...." *(Sullivan 49)* Stephen's and Stirling's division earlier had been ordered to move away from the Brandywine toward the Birmingham Meetinghouse hill to meet the surprise attack of the British on their flank.

30. This penetration was "to the very height overlooking the 4-gun battery of the Rebels at Chad's Ford." *(Andre 46)*

31. Knyphausen's order of crossing was as follows, according to his official report dated 10.21.77, "The 4th and 5th Regiment in Front; The 2nd Battn. of the 71st, ...Then Captain Ferguson's Riflemen, the Queen's Rangers, the 23rd Regiment, the Remainder of the 1st & 2nd Brigade, Light Dragoons, & Major General Stirn's Brigade, which closed the whole." *(AHR I X:35)*

32. Howe's column consisted of 7,966 men and Knyphausen's column consisted of 6,429 men based on Muenchhausen's statement of the composition of each column, and his statement of the strengths of each unit. Washington's reference to his 8,000 men conforms with his return of five continental divisions totaling 8,188. *(WW 8:opp. 170)* However, he had additional miscellaneous continentals such as artillery, dragoons and Nash's North Carolina brigade totaling about 3,500 men. *(WW 10:279,398,opp.246)* Further he had with him 2,973 of Armstrong's Pa. militia. *(1PaA5:595)* This made a grand total for the British of 14,395 men, and for the Americans 14,661 men, almost a standoff as far as numbers were concerned.

33. Sixty three British officers were killed or wounded in the engagement. For a complete list of casualties see *(PRO-CO 5/94 pg.660 Enc.1)*. For British and Hessian return of losses by regiment see *(KP 1:135-137)*.

34. For a complete list of ordnance taken from the Americans see *(PRO-CO 5/94 pg. 660 Enc.2)*.

35. This was Col. Johann August von Loos who had been colonel of the von Lossberg regiment, which had been part of the Rall Brigade captured at Trenton on 12.26.76 and from which was formed the Combined Battalion out of the remnants of the brigade. In America he served mostly in a brigade command capacity.

36. "Each regiment had given three wagons for the transport of the invalids." *(Baur. 113)* At the same time, "350 prisoners" taken at Brandywine, were escorted to Wilmington. *(Heusser 41)*

37. Governor John McKinley was taken to Philadelphia when that city was captured by the British. When Philadelphia was evacuated in May 1778, McKinley was taken to New York, where he was paroled in August 1778, in exchange for Governor William Franklin, former colonial governor of New Jersey.

38. The location of British headquarters is plainly shown on the manuscript map made in 1777 by Hessian officer S. W. Werner. *(Br.M 132/22)* In modern terms of reference the headquarters was located on Harvey Road, near the headwaters of Harvey Run. There is a marker outside the house at this location, but it is said that it is not the 18th century headquarters house.

39. The army under Howe "marched toward Lancaster by way of the Turk's head, Goshen Meeting and the sign of the Boot on the Downingtown road." *(Mont. 452,453)* Cornwallis' and Howe's columns joined "at Goshen Meeting." *(Br. Jnl.)* This Quaker meeting is located on the southeast quarter of the junction of Chester Road (Pa. Hwy. 352) and the Paoli Pike, which runs from West Chester to Paoli. The Middle Road to Lancaster, which was the objective of the British march, was the Swedes Ford Road.

40. Cornwallis' march toward Goshen was up the east side of Chester Creek as indicated on Capt. Muenchhausen's sketch map of the march, and shown also on another contemporary British map. *(Br. M 132/2)*

41. This was the so-called "Battle of the Clouds." Col. Pickering said of the action as follows: "About nine in the morning we were informed that the enemy were advancing towards us. The troops got under arms, and the baggage was sent off. An advance party of the enemy attacked our picket, just posted (about 300 strong), who shamefully fled at the first fire. About this time it began to rain. General Scott, with his brigade, was ordered to advance to attack this party of the enemy, or skirmish with another expected in our front. The rain increased. It was now discovered that the ground on which the army was drawn up for battle, particularly the ground where the park of artillery was posted, was not well chosen ....So, after some hesitation, the orders were given to retire to better ground in our rear. While this was performing, the rain poured down vehemently; and by the time the whole had gained their new ground, the arms were absolutely unfit for action." *(Pickering 159)*

42. This was Col. Carl Emil von Donop who had organized the Hessian grenadier regiments and the jaeger corps before coming to America, where he served mostly in a brigade command capacity.

43. "The Head Quarters is at the sign of the Boot in the Township of Goshen and within ½ mile of the Township of W. Whiteland. The Boot is within 5 miles of Downing Town." *(Mont. 453)* "The Boot [is] three miles from White Horse." *(Mont. 454)*

44. Washington had moved from "White Horse Taverns" to "Yellow Springs" and from there to "Reading furnace." *(WW9:230,231,235)* From Reading Furnace, Washington "crossed over the Schuylkill at Parker's Ford, and marched down to Trap." *(Pickering 161)*

45. After halting an hour at White Horse "the whole army moved on towards Philadelphia, until we arrived at Randel Malins, being 2½ miles further. There we struck off (the roads forking) on the Swedes Ford Road to Treduffrin, one mile beyond Howell's Tavern, being 4½ miles to that Tavern and encamped one mile further, making

5½ miles more, in all this day, Eleven miles. Lord Cornwallis's column continuing the Philadelphia Main [Conestoga] Road, ...running only one Mile from this Camp, where his Lordship formed a junction [with us] and camped." *(Mont. 454)*

46. "Genl. Wayne, with the Division under his Command, is in the rear of the Enemy, and will be joined tomorrow or next day, I expect, by Genl. Smallwood and Colo. Gist with their Corps." *(WW 9:238)* Wayne's Division consisted of the 1st and 2nd Pennsylvania continental brigades, totaling 1640 men.

47. The force of about 2,000 men consisted of "the 40th and 55th Regiments, under Colonel Musgrave, and the 2d Battalion Light Infantry, the 42d, 44th Regiments under General Grey" with Grey in overall command. *(Andre 49)*

48. The next morning after the Paoli rout, "General Howe sent a troop of dragoons to the place of encounter, with orders to destroy all the enemy's abandoned muskets, which numbered about one thousand. The wounded were taken to nearby houses." *(Baur. 115)*

49. This information probably came from a troop return picked up by the British the day after the Paoli encounter. It may have been a return of the 2nd Pa. brigade, which on Jan. 1, 1778, numbered 685 men. *(WW 10:opp.246)*

50. Capt. Patrick Ferguson commander of the English riflemen had been wounded at Brandywine, and because their number had been so reduced, orders on September 13 read, "The British Riflemen are to join the Light Companies of the Regiments to which they respectively belong." *(KP 1:495)*

51. Washington's movement toward Reading could have been prompted in part by a British feint at seven in the morning, when "Sir Wm. Erskine with the mounted and dismounted [German] chasseurs, one squadron of the 16th Dragoons and part of the 2nd Light Infantry patrolled up the Pottsgrove [Pottstown] road which leads to Reading." *(Mont. 456)*

52. Muenchhausen apparently did not know that the name of the ford six miles above Fatland Ford was Gordon's Ford, although he knew the ford existed. He thought that Fatland and Gordon's Ford were the same as indicated by his remark "Fatland Ford, or more commonly called Gordon's Ford..." Because of this, he is somewhat mixed up in his ford references. So as not to confuse the reader, we have corrected his text in this regard.

53. Norrington House was the former home of Isaac Norris for whom Norristown was named. The occupant of the house at the time Howe made his headquarters there was Col. John Bull. *(Loc. cit.)*

54. Howe said "the Army encamped on the 23rd with its left to the Schuylkill, and the right upon the Monatomy Road, having Stony Run in front." *(PRO-CO 5/94 p.639 No 68)*

55. Regarding the incident at Swede's Ford, Gen. Howe noted, "The 2nd Battalion of Light Infantry was detached to Swede's Ford, which a small party of the Enemy immediately quitted." *(PRO-CO 5/94 p.639 No 68)*

56. Howe made "his Head Quarters at Stenton near Germantown." *(Mont. 460)*

57. A later report indicated that the men captured at Frankford were not Commo. Thomas Seymour and Col., now Gen. James Potter but "a Colonel, a principal Commissary, a captain of a Frigate, and a Captain of Light Horse, and two or three of his men." *(Mont. 458)*

58. The three Allen brothers were John, Andrew and William, sons of William Allen, Chief Justice of Pennsylvania. The chief justice had gone to England at the outbreak of war and died there in 1780. All three sons put themselves under the protection of General Howe in December 1776, at Trenton, and went to New York where they resided until Howe came to Philadelphia in 1778. The family home was known as Mt. Airy on the northern outskirts of Germantown.

59. John Penn was lieutenant governor and grandson of William Penn founder of the province. Although taken prisoner and held on parole, Lieutenant Governor Penn was never found guilty of any overt act against the American cause.

60. On his march into the city, Cornwallis was "accompanied by Enoch Story, Jos. Galloway, Andw. Allen, William Allen and others." *(Pa Mag. 1:7)*

61. Cheveaux de frise are described in note under date August 6, 1777. The fortified island was Fort Mifflin, on Mud Island.

62. The other frigate was the *Montgomery*. For a detailed account of this encounter see *(Delaware 7)*.

63. On the 28th Gen. Washington in his general orders congratulated the northern army under Gen. Gates for their initial victory over Gen. Burgoyne at Saratoga on 9.19.77. *(WW 9:276,277)*

64. The order of American march was "Genl. Sullivan's division leading, followed by Lincoln's [now Wayne's], McDougall's, Greene's [divisions]; these form the first line; then the park of artillery, then the second line in this order, Stirling's division, Nash's [brigade], Stephen's [division]." *(WW 9:297)*

65. The original was first published in the *Pennsylvania Evening Post* of July 10, 1777, and reprinted in *(Moore 453)*. Muenchhausen's text differs slightly from the account printed in Moore.

66. This was Henry E. Lutterlough deputy quartermaster-general of the continental army. The German spelling of his name was Lutterloh. Reichell has not been identified.

67. Washington "Having received intelligence, thro' Two intercepted Letters, that Genl. Howe had detached a part of his force for the purpose of reducing Billingsport and the Forts on Delaware," decided this was the time to attack. *(WW 9:308)*

Washington's plan called for the following: "The Divisions of Sullivan and Wayne, flanked by Conway's Brigade, were to enter the Town by way of Chestnut Hill [Germantown Avenue], while Genl. Armstrong, with the Pennsylvania Militia should fall down Manatawny [Ridge] Road by Vandeerings Mill and get upon the Enemy's Left and Rear. The Divisions of Green and Stephen, flanked by McDougal's Brigade, were to enter by taking a circuit by way of the Lime Kiln Road at the Market House and attack their Right wing, and the Militia of Maryland and Jersey under Generals Smallwood and Foreman were to march by the old York road and fall upon the rear of their Right. Lord Stirling with Nash and Maxwell's Brigades was to form a Corps de Reserve." *(WW 9:309)* The reserves were "commanded by Major-General Lord Stirling." *(Sullivan 58)* Sullivan commanded his wing and Greene commanded his.

68. "It was so foggy on this morning that one could hardly see fifty paces." *(Baur. 119)*

69. The 40th and 5th regiments were part of the 2nd Brigade. Commander of the 40th was Lt. Col. Thomas Musgrave. Commander of the 5th was Lt. Col. William Walcott, who would be wounded this day, and would die November 16, 1777. *(KP 1:544)*

70. It was the Chew House that was occupied by Musgrave, who "for upwards of an hour resisted the efforts of the Enemy, who in vain brought several pieces of cannon upon them and attempted to storm the house." *(Andre 55)*

71. "The 37th and 15th Regiments were moved from the 4th and 3rd Brigades [respectively] across German Town to the left of the 5th and 55th." *(Andre 55)* "On the left and on the West side of German Town the 4th and 3rd Brigades and Hessians moved forward from their Encampment in a direction parallel with the

Village." (Andre 56)

Musgrave was finally relieved by "Major General Grey at the head of three Battalions of the 3rd Brigade, turning his front to the village, and Brigadier General Agnew, who covered Major General Grey's left with the 4th Brigade...was done with great slaughter. The 5th and 55 Regiments, [of the 2nd Brigade], from the right, engaging them at the same time on the other side of the village, completed the defeat of the enemy in this quarter." (PRO-CO 5/94 p.639 No.68)

72. In defending the British right wing "the Light Infantry, being well supported by the 4th Regiment, sustained the Enemy's attack with such determined bravery, that they could not make the least impression on them." (PRO-CO 5/94 p.639 No.68) When the enemy gave way on this front, they were "pursued thro' a strong country between four and five miles." (ibid)

73. "Lord Cornwallis came up as the Rebels had retired, and took command of the left wing." (Andre 56) Cornwallis had with him "two Battalions British and one Hessian Grenadiers, with a squadron of Dragoons, and his Lordship getting to German Town just as the enemy had been forced out of the village." (PRO-CO 5/94 p.639 No. 68) They "had run most of the way to German Town." (ibid)

74. Brig. Gen. James Agnew was commander of the 4th brigade of British foot. One of the colonels killed was Lt. Col. John Bird of the British 15th regiment. (Baur. 121) For a regimental return of killed, wounded, and missing at Germantown see (KP 1:137; PRO-CO 5/94 pg. 667,668).

75. Gen. Washington wrote on October 8 that "Our losses will amount, in killed and wounded, to upwards of three hundred." (WW 9:330) On that same day Washington wrote another letter stating, "our killed and wounded amount to near four hundred." (WW 9:331) By the 18th Washington wrote, "Our losses in the late action was, in killed, wounded, and Missing, about 1,000." (WW 9:398)

American officers who were killed during the battle, or died from their wounds, were "Brigadier General [Francis] Nash of the North Carolina troops...Major [Edward] Sherburne of Portsmouth, aide-de-camp to General Sullivan...and Major White (an American, married, I think, in England)." (Pickering 176) John White, volunteer aide de camp to Gen. Sullivan, appointed September 27, 1777, died October 10, 1777 of wounds received at Germantown.

76. Friedrich Christian Arnold, Baron von Jungkenn, Muentzer von Mohrenstamm, was Lord High Chamberlain and Minister of State in Cassel.

77. The chain of redoubts was built across the narrow part of the Philadelphia peninsula formed by the Schuylkill and Delaware Rivers. The redoubts, as shown on British maps, were roughly between what is now Callowhill and Spring Garden Streets, except that they were somewhat irregularly placed to take advantage of the terrain. (Br. M 132/6)

78. The man was "Martin Hurly, Private Grenadier of the 44th Regiment." (KP 1:512)

79. The battery was "at the N. Side of the mouth of Schuylkill," near what is now Franklin Delano Roosevelt Park. (Mont. 463)

80. The British and Hessians consistently refused to use names given to forts by the Americans, in this case Ft. Mifflin. This fort was designed and built on Mud Island in 1771 under the direction of Capt. John Montresor of the British Engineers. (Mont. 417) When war came, the Americans took over the installation and named it Ft. Mifflin for Maj. Gen. Thomas Mifflin of Pennsylvania.

81. Chain shot consisted of two solid round shot linked together by a forged chain. When fired, they made a screeching noise.

82. Capt. von Muenchhausen's sovereign, the Landgrave of Hesse-Cassel, personally approved all patents of his officers, and he signed the appropriate orders as prepared by the war-ministry. The date of the patent was 6.13.77.

83. The American landing force consisted of "Major Ballard...with 100 men." (Historical Mag. 87) Ballard was Maj. Robert Ballard of Virginia, third in command at Ft. Mifflin.

84. Maj. John Vatass was tried for his conduct on this date, which led to his retirement from the army.

85. The Americans reported that one captain, two lieutenants, one ensign, and 56 privates of the 10th were captured. The captain had a broken arm, and he was immediately paroled so he could have medical attention. The two lieutenants were taken to Ft. Mifflin, where they dined with Col. Samuel Smith, the commander there. "One Ensign and 56 Privates...were immediately sent over to Red Bank [Fort Mercer]. (1 Pa.A 5:663)

86. This alarm was caused by American deserters who came into camp and said that "General Washington was again approaching with his army to attack." (Baur. 123)

87. Carpenters Island, to the south of Province Island, was separated from Province Island by a small tidal stream. The island is now a part of the Philadelphia airport.

88. Muenchhausen spells the name Stamford. A Hessian return lists him as Capt. Ludwig Friedrich von Stanforth. (HV 40)

89. Washington's headquarters on the 14th was "Towamensing" near the present Kulpsville, Pa. (WW 9:368)

90. Here again the British and Hessians refuse to call the fort by its American name. Ft. Mercer at Red Bank, now National Park, was begun April 16, 1777, by the Pennsylvania militia as part of the protection of Philadelphia. On October 16, 1777, the command of the fort was taken over by continental forces, and work began on reducing the size of the fort. This work was under the direction of Capt. Thomas Antoine Mauduit, a French volunteer. The fort was named in honor of Brig. Gen. Hugh Mercer, who was mortally wounded at the Battle of Princeton, January 3, 1777.

91. A fire raft, as distinguished from a fireship or brander described in a note under date of 8.6.77, and was a bundle of logs tied together and soaked with flammable material.

92. This undoubtedly was caused by receipt of the news of the second and final victory over Burgoyne at Saratoga on 10.7.77.

93. These were fused, exploding balls.

94. Red Hot shot were balls, which, before firing, had been heated in a blacksmith's forge to glowing red. These were fired from the British "howitzers." (Mont. 467)

95. The regiments were the "2nd Light Infantry, the 33rd, 64th, and 44th Regiments" under General Grey; and the "1st Light Infantry, 5th, 23d, 42d and 55th Regiments" under General Grant, with Grant in over-all command. (Andre 59)

96. On the 17th, Washington's headquarters was at "Peter Wentz's" near the present Center Square. (WW 9:391)

97. The bridge was built "at Gray's Ferry," presently Gray's Ferry Avenue. (Baur. 125)

98. Howe said that the reason for moving his camp into Philadelphia from Germantown was "to expedite the reduction of Mud-Island, which had proved more difficult than was at first supposed." (Narrative) Upon his arrival in Philadelphia, Howe occupied the home of General John Cadwalader on Second Street below Spruce, and later moved to the home of Governor Richard Penn in Market Street between Fifth and Sixth. (Loc. cit.)

99. These provisions included "a hundred wagons of ammunition and a train of heavy artillery with 18 pieces." (Baur. 125)

100. Montresor noted the "Wind at North" on the 22nd, which

would have been unfavorable for coming up-river. *(Mont. 469)*

101. These men were Col. Carl Emil Ulrich von Donop, commander of the force; Lt. Col. Friedrich Ludwig Christoph von Minnigerode, commander of the von Minnigerode grenadier battalion; Lt. Col. Ernst Rudolph von Schieck, commander of the Mirbach regiment of infantry. For details of the action see *(Delaware 20-23).*

102. The assault from the ships on the Minnigerode battalion was "in the flank and in the back having hit them continuously with outstanding effect." *(von Jung. 7:5)* The most devastating fire came from the American row galleys who were so close-in that they could communicate with the fort "by means of speaking tubes." *(Buettner 52)*

103. These two regiments were "the 1st Light Infantry and the 27th Regiment." *(Robertson 153)*

104. The *Augusta* was set afire either by American cannon fire or by an accident aboard the *Augusta*. No one ever pinpointed the cause of the fire, which was discovered by Robert Reed when "about 11 a.m. the Master [of the *Augusta,* Reed] went to the cabin and found the ship to be on fire." *(PRO-Adm. 1:5308:3)* The *Merlin,* which had gone aground earlier, could not be gotten off, and she was set afire, by orders.

105. The orders read "The Commander in Chief returns his thanks to Col. Donop and all the Officers and Men of the Hessian Detachment under his Command, for their Gallant and Spirited attempt in the attack of the Evening of the 22d. Instant, which, though not attended with the success it merited, reflects great honour and credit upon them." *(KP 1:524,525)*

106. He was "English body-surgeon Grand." *(von Jung. 7:5)*

107. Hessian surgeons who were sent over to Red Bank were "Regiment-surgeon Pausch and Regiment-surgeon Goechter." *(von Jung. 7:5)*

108. Lt. Col. Balthasar Brethauer had been lieutenant colonel of the Rall regiment, and was one of the officers captured during the Battle of Trenton, and later exchanged. Brethauer did not command a regiment that took part in the attack on Fort Mercer at Red Bank, thus, it is assumed that he was on Col. von Donop's staff.

109. Seth Pomeroy died 2.19.77; Steel may be Archibald Steele, deputy quarter master general; Hern may be Nathaniel Heard or Edward Hand; Stephenson probably is Adam Stephen; Crofts is a mystery; Andrew Lewis resigned 4.15.77.

EIGHTH TRANSMITTAL
October 27, 1777-January 22, 1778

1. These were men from the 71st regiment plus "about 100 Marines from the Fleet." *(Robertson 154)*

2. These men were Col. Christopher Greene, not brigadier general as noted by Muenchhausen, Capt. Israel Putnam, Jr., aide to Brig. Gen. James Varnum and Maj. Mauduit du Plessis.

3. The officer sent from Burgoyne carried a letter to General Howe dated October 20, 1777. The letter covered Burgoyne's operations from the 13th to the surrender on the 17th. Included also were details of the surrender negotiations with General Gates. For details see *(KP 1:534 et seq.).*

4. The words United States of America are underlined in the manuscript.

5. Gen. Washington had asked Brig. Gen. James Potter of the Pennsylvania militia to "harass the parties of the enemy on Province Island in such a manner as to produce a great Diversion in favor of Fort Mifflin." *(WW 9:392)*

6. Washington reported to Congress that there was "an attack made by Genl. Varnum, with a 12 and an 18 pounder fixed near Red Bank, [upon] the Enemy's Ships. He thinks he damaged the *Somerset* of 64 Guns considerably, as she got on ground and was for some time exposed to his fire." *(WW 10:22)*

7. These troops were "the 7th, 26th, 63d Regiments, two Battalions of Anspach, about 300 Jaegers, 4 to 500 Convalescents and recruits, and the 17th Regiment of Light Dragoons and 70 of the Guards." *(Robertson 154)*

8. Orders were "to fire 80 rounds each gun" per day. *(Mont. 474)*

9. Casimir Pulaski had been made brigadier general and chief of continental dragoons September 15, 1777.

10. Three of the British ships involved were "the *Isis,* a galley and sloop." *(Mont. 475)*

11. On this day Gen. Washington noted "The weight of the Enemy's Fire upon Fort Mifflin has made such an impression upon the works that I think it more than probable that the Garrison will soon be obliged to evacuate it totally, altho' I have directed them to keep up a show of possession as long as possible." *(WW 10:59)*

12. Because of obstructions, placed in the main channel of the Delaware River by the Americans, it was not possible for the British warships to get within range of Ft. Mifflin. After soundings were made in the inner channel of the river between Ft. Mifflin and Carpenters and Province Islands, it was decided to reduce the weight of the battery ship *Vigilant* for an attempt to get her through. When lightened, she drew only "11½ feet," although she would be carrying one "24-pounder, nine 2 pdr, six 4 pdr." *(Andre 64; Mont. 519)*

13. The sloop was the *Fury,* a converted "Horse sloop." *(PRO-Adm. 51:4224:2)*

14. These British ships were the "*Isis, Somerset, Roebuck, Liverpool* [and] *Pearl.*" *(Mont. 476)* For the exact location of the *Vigilant* and other British ships, as well as the channel through which the American ships tried to pass in order to attack the *Vigilant,* see a contemporary British naval map of the action in *(Delaware 35).*

15. Ft. Mifflin had a masonry wall facing down-river, also facing the main channel of the Delaware. On the up-river side, and on the side facing the British batteries on Carpenters and Province Islands, the fort was made of wood. The "log houses" were blockhouses built into the corners of the wooden section of the fort.

16. On the 15th, the fort commander "at seven o'clock in the evening...sent over [to Jersey] all the garrison except 40 men." *(Prov. Gaz. 3.14.78)* During the next few hours some cannon were spiked. Ten cannon were loaded onto a scow and sent toward Jersey, but the scow sank in crossing. Then "a little after 2 a.m." the Americans set fire to the fort and the last of the garrison rowed over to Jersey "in three batteaux." *(WP 11.16 Var/GW; Martin 90)*

17. The French major was Francois Louis Fleury who was second in command of the fort during most of the siege. Lt. Col. Samuel Smith was officially in command of the fort. Col. Smith, however, had left the fort on the 11th because of an injury. Senior officer in the fort on the 15th was Maj. Simeon Thayer who had arrived with replacements on the night of 12/13, and Thayer's majority predated Fleury's.

18. The American navy in the Delaware, particularly the larger vessels, were stationed off Fort Mercer at Red Bank, a distance of about a mile and a quarter from British positions on Carpenters and Province Islands. The masts of the American vessels were easily visible to the British, and any ship movement could be detected.

Gloucester was just up-stream of Red Bank, at the mouth of Big Timber Creek.

19. The English regiments were the "7th, 26th, and 63d Regiments." *(Robertson 154)*

20. After Burgoyne's surrender at Saratoga on October 17, Maj. Gen. Horatio Gates sent Col. Daniel Morgan's corps south to join Gen. Washington. Then, on November 10, Gates sent Brig. Gen. John Glover's and Brig. Gen. John Paterson's brigades south. Morgan's corps had "552 officers and men fit for duty." *(WP 10.17 Gates ret.)* Paterson's and Glover's brigades had "963 and 1176 men present and fit for duty." *(ibid)*

21. Maj. Gen. Horatio Gates was not with either force.

22. One American brigade was sent to New Jersey by Gen. Washington on the 19th, that of Brig. Gen. Jedediah Huntington, totaling "1200 men." *(1 Pa A 6:28)* On the following day Gen. Washington sent Maj. Gen. Nathanael Greene's division consisting of the brigades of Brig. Gen. Peter Muhlenberg and Brig. Gen. George Weedon, totaling "2000 men." *(ibid)*

23. On the night of 19th the American naval officers held a council of war aboard the sloop *Speedwell,* off Red Bank. It was the unanimous decision that "in the Morning flood...of the 20th...to go up the Western Channel, [but] be prepared with combustible matter so as to be set instantly on fire and consumed, should the wind on said Morning flood not be such as to render their passage practicable." *1 Pa. A 6:21)* On the 20th, there was "no wind blowing," resulting in the destruction of the two American ships. *(1 Pa. A 6:28)*

24. The British frigate was the captured American frigate, *Delaware.* It was stationed in the Delaware north of Philadelphia, at Kensington.

25. At three o'clock in the morning on the 20th, "13 galleys [moved up-river] close up under Cooper's Ferry," now Camden, N. J. *(1 Pa. A 6:28)* On the morning of the 21st, before daylight, "the Brig *Convention*...the schooner *Delaware*...with six shallops" attempted to run past the now British commanded American frigate *Delaware.* *(2 NJA 1:496)* All got by "except the [schooner] *Delaware* and one shallop, which were ran aground and set on fire." *(ibid)* Not having enough wind for the balance of the fleet to attempt the passage, "the Brig *Andria Doria,* xebecks *Repulse* and *Champion,* the sloops *Race-horse* and *Champion,* with two floating batteries and three fire-ships were accordingly set on fire and destroyed." *(ibid)*

26. The "small passage through the Cheveaux de Frise" consisted of "two strong piers," which were just under water at low tide. *(Searle 264)* These piers were on each side of the main channel. Strung across the channel from each pier was a chain, which could be removed for passage of American boats. During the later stages of the assault on Ft. Mifflin, when no more traffic through the passage was advisable, a "Hulk boat" was sunk in the channel, just behind the piers. *(1 Pa. A 5. opp.720)*

27. On October 15, Capt. John Graves Simcoe of the 40th regiment was "appointed to Command the Corps of Queen's Rangers with Provincial Rank of Major, in the room of Major Wemys who returns to his duty as Aid-de Camp to Maj. Gen. Robertson." *(KP 1:519)*

28. The jaegers were protecting the rear of "Lord Cornwallis's Corps at Gloucester." *(Andre 66)*

29. Gen. Greene gave an American account of this action as follows: "The Marquis [Lafayette] with about 400 Militia and the rifle corps of Morgan" attacked the enemy picket at evening on the 25th. They "kill'd about 20 & wounded many more & took about 20 prisoners." After the enterprise, Lafayette said that he was "charmed with the spirited behavior of the Militia & Rifle

corps—they drove the enemy about half a mile and kept the ground until dark." *(WP 11.26 Gre/GW)*

30. "Lord Cornwallis, having sent over his baggage and cattle, [on the 26th] crossed from Gloucester" on the 27th. *(Andre 66)* They landed at "Gloucester Point in Pennsylvania." *(Mont. 479)*

31. Maj. Andre said there were three British vessels involved, "the *Vigilant,* a galley and an armed Schooner." *(Andre 63)*

32. Lord Cornwallis returned to Philadelphia "this ev'g. and brought over 400 head of cattle from the Jerseys." *(Pa. Mag. 1:31)*

33. Pennypack Creek enters the Delaware just below the present North Philadelphia Airport.

34. The reason for the cancellation, or postponement, was undoubtedly the arrival of the fleet of 27 ships which carried, in addition to provisions, the "17th Dragoons, 7th., 26th., and 63d. Regiments, Recruits and Convalescents of the Army making about 4,000." *(KP 1:142)*

35. The British force marched in two divisions, but in one column, as follows: In the van under Lt. Gen. Cornwallis, 2 batts. light infantry, chasseurs (dismounted jaegers), 2 batts. Br. grenadiers, 2 batts. Hessian grenadiers, 4th Br. brigade, 2 squadrons 16th dragoons, 2 medium 12-pounders, 2 howitzers. In the second division under Lt. Gen. von Knyphausen, regt. Du Corps (Leib), regt. Donop, 1st Br. brigade, 2 light 12-pounders, 2 batts. Guards, 1 squadron 16th dragoons, 5th regt., 27th regt., 2 light 12-pounders, 26th regt., 7th regt., 3rd Br. brigade, 2 squadrons 17th dragoons, hospital wagons, rum wagons, empty wagons, 2nd batt. 71st regt., mounted jaegers, 1 squadron 17th dragoons, Queen's rangers to flank the right of the wagons. *(Robertson 158; Baur. 134,135)*

36. "Morgan's rifle Corps is to form upon the left of the Maryland Militia [covering the army's right flank] and Webbs Regiment upon the right of the Pensa. Militia [covering the army's left flank]. These Corps, and the Militia (who are to act in detachment, and not in a solid or compact body) are to skirmish with, and harass the Enemy as much as possible, taking especial care to gain their flanks and rear if possible." *(WW 10:138,139)* Between these two flanks, the first and second lines of the entire army were posted. See arrangement of troops. *(WW 10: Opp.138).*

37. Eleven miles from Philadelphia is Erdenheim, then called Ness Tavern as indicated on a then current American military map of the area. *(Am. M 51D5)* The mill that was taken was on the Wissahickon near the junction of Cricket Road and Valley Green (or Blue Bell) Road, in Flourtown. *(Loc. cit.)*

38. The church was St. Thomas Episcopal, near the junction of Skippack Turnpike and Bethlehem Turnpike.

39. This was Brig. Gen. James Irvine of the Pennsylvania militia. His British opposition was "the 2d Battalion Light Infantry." *(Robertson 159)* In the skirmish, Brig. Gen. Irvine was "wounded, thrown from his Horse and taken Prisoner." *(WW 10:145)*

40. The next night Muenchhausen was to gain more reliable information from an American officer who deserted to the British. The officer would inform Howe that Washington's force totaled only, "eleven thousand two hundred fit for duty," which was almost the exact strength of Howe's force. *(Baur. 138)*

41. The march was "by Cheltenham and Jenkins Town." *(Andre 68)*

42. Grey's English Brigade was the "3d Brigade." Grey's column "turned off from the grand Column into White Church Road," now Church Road. *(Andre 68)*

43. "The grand Column proceeded as far as Abingdon [Abing-

ton] and there also turned to the left and came near Edge Hill, where Sir William Howe halted." *(Andre 68)*

44. The van was composed of "the 1st battalion of light infantry and the 33rd regiment." *(Hall 370,371)*

45. The troops they engaged were "Colo. [Daniel] Morgan and his Corps, and also by the Maryland Militia under Colo. [Mordecai] Gist." *(WW 10:143)* They were operating under orders as outlined in note dated 10.5.77. The Americans lost "Twenty Seven Men in Morgans Corps in killed and wounded, besides Major [Joseph] Morris, a Brave and gallant Officer, who is among the latter. Of the Maryland Militia, there were also Sixteen or Seventeen wounded." *(WW 10:143,144)* The British lost "four officers and thirty men killed and wounded." *(Hall 370, 371)*

46. Howe's force followed the Americans to "within ½ a mile of Sandy Run where they remain'd some time, then the whole were ordered back to Edgehill." *(Robertson 160)*

47. The main body of the Army returned via "the old York Road." The Grey force also took the York Road falling into it "at Shoemaker's Mill," at present Elkins Park. *(Andre 70)*

48. These were ships being sent in compliance with Article #2 of the Burgoyne Surrender Convention, signed at Saratoga. It read "A free passage to be granted to the Army under Lieut. Gen. Burgoyne to Great Britain, on condition of not serving again in North America during the Present Contest, and the Port of Boston is assigned for the Entry of Transports to receive the Troops, whenever Gen. Howe shall so order." *(KP 1:536,537)* This article, eventually, would not be honored by the Americans.

49. In Howe's letter to Germain dated July 7, 1777, he noted that the war is "now upon a far different scale with respect to the increased powers and strength of the enemy, than it was last campaign....a corps of 10,000 Russians, effective fighting men, might insure the success of the war to Great-Britian in another campaign...." *(Narrative)*

As far back as 1775, when Britain was negotiating with the Germans regarding the furnishing of auxiliary forces, there were rumors that similar Russian treaties were being negotiated. No treaties came out of these negotiations with Czarina Katharina II (the Great), although there was continued speculation in the field.

50. Muenchhausen had anticipated this move in his journal entry of 11.30.77. The force consisted of the "Light Infantry, Grenadiers, Guards, 23d, 28th, 49th, 27th and 33rd—100 [Hessian] Chasseurs and Lengerke's Battalion and the 16th and 17th Dragoons." *(Andre 71)*

51. "A Bridge of Waggons made across the Schuylkill last Night consisting of 36 waggons, with a Bridge of Rails between each." *(Pa. Mag. 21:305)* It would appear that Washington was pleased with the result of Potter's efforts on the 11th, for in General Orders the next day he noted "The Commander in Chief, with great pleasure, expresses his approbation, of the behaviour of the Pennsylvania Militia yesterday, under Genl. Potter, in the vigorous opposition they made to a body of the enemy on the other side Schuylkill." *(WW 10:151)*

52. On the 12th, Washington had moved his headquarters to "Swede's Ford;" by the 14th Washington had reached "Gulph Creek," where he was at the time of Muenchhausen's entry in his diary. *(WW 10:150,152)* Washington would not reach Valley Forge until the 20th.

53. Adm. Howe's destination was Newport, Rhode Island. He arrived there January 2, 1778.

54. The only troops left in Philadelphia were "Eight English battalions, the Queen's Rangers, one officer and twenty-four English dragoons, and Stirn's and Woellwarth's brigades...under General von Knyphausen." *(Baur. 148)*

55. Gen. Potter of the Pennsylvania militia and Col. Morgan's Corps were working in concert in the area to disrupt British foraging parties. They were under no specific orders from Gen. Washington. He merely told Gen. Potter, "The mode [of harassment] I leave intirely to Colo. Morgan and yourself." *(WW 10:182)*

56. On this day Washington warned Smallwood to be on the alert, and he requested him to report on the "progress you make in fortifying yourself." *(WW 10:183)* From this it can be assumed that Smallwood was not directly participating with Morgan and Potter in trying to disrupt the enemy. Smallwood's orders of the 19th had been "to March immediately for Wilmington, and take post there. You are not to delay a moment in putting the place in the best posture of defence...." *(WW 10:171)*

57. This was an attack under the command of Brig. Gen. Samuel Parsons in which Col. Samuel Webb, commanding one of three detachments, embarked from Connecticut and was caught in rough water on the sound, whereupon four officers and 20 men of his continentals, plus 40 militia men, were captured by a British sloop of war. For details of this encounter see *(Parsons 134)*.

58. Washington had planned an attack on the relatively small garrison remaining in Philadelphia while Howe was across the Schuylkill foraging with 8,000 of his troops. There would be an attempt first to take possession of the two floating bridges then "cut them loose from the West Shore." *(WW 10:203)* After accomplishing this, Washington could easily handle the Philadelphia garrison without worrying about the 8,000 British south of the Schuylkill. By the 27th however, Washington had abandoned the plan because his intelligence people had told him that the Philadelphia force "can be so easily and readily reinforced from the main body as to render any attempt upon them abortive." *(WW 10:213)* In fact, by that date, Howe had learned of the planned attack, and had already sent some troops back into the city.

59. The ruse was accomplished by "a Dragoon who personated a Rebel horseman." *(Andre 73)*

60. Lee was placed "out on parole at New York" by Gen. Clinton on 12.27.77. *(LP 2:375,376)*

61. Capt. Henry Lee's report to Gen. Washington presented a somewhat different story. Lee said he "obliged the party consisting of 200, disgracefully to retire after repeated but fruitless attempts to force their way into the house, leaving two killed and four wounded without receiving any other damage on his part than having his Lieutenant Mr. [William] Lindsay slightly wounded unless any of his out-patroles should have been unfortunately Surrounded and taken which is not yet known." *(WW 10:321)* As indicated by Muenchhausen, further investigation by Lee would reveal that there were additional casualties.

NINTH TRANSMITTAL
January 23, 1777-March 7, 1778

1. Maj. Gen. Adam Stephen was dismissed from the American army on November 20, 1777.

2. Friedrich Adolph, Freiherr von Riedesel, a Brunswicker, was major general in command of German auxiliary troops in Canada under British Maj. Gen. John Burgoyne. Riedesel and British Maj. Gen. William Philips were not exchanged until October 13, 1780, for American Maj. Gen. Benjamin Lincoln, who had been captured at Charleston, May 12, 1780.

3. On February 1, 1778, Washington had written to Maj. John Jamison, "You are therefore, in concert with Genl. Lacey to fix upon a certain time and attempt to disable all the Mills upon Pen-

nepack, Frankfort, and Wissahicken Creeks...." (WW 10:413)

4. The Continental Congress had moved from Philadelphia to York, Pennsylvania in September 1777 as the British stood at the fords of the Schuylkill near Valley Forge, threatening to take Philadelphia, the capital.

5. In a letter written by Lt. Col. Tench Tilghman dated February 2, 1778, he noted "Our Enemies have already heard of and exult at [the continuing] appearance of division and faction among ourselves.... If the General's conduct [was in any provable way] reprehensible let those who think so...make the charge and call him to account publickly before that body [Congress]...." (VF 31)

6. These were the Pennsylvania dragoons under the command of Capt. Richard Hovenden. (KP 1:576; Sabine 1:546) As of 3.24.78, Hovenden had "91 effectives and 85 fit for duty." (PRO-CO 5:7:447)

7. These men were British Capt. Alexander Campbell and American Brig. Gen. James Irvine.

8. Gen. Wayne was gathering cattle in Jersey, but was taking no chances in having them taken by the British. He drove them, as instructed to do, across "the Delaware at Coryell's Ferry [Lambertville, N.J. and New Hope, Pa.] and then keep higher up the Country before they strike across. They should fall in with Schuylkill, at Potts Grove and cross the River there." (WW 10:524)

9. This was a herd of cattle "coming from New England....Some of the disaffected in Bucks County, gave information of them and a party of light Horse pushed up 20 miles and carried them off." (WW 10:524)

10. The militia was that of "Col. [Joseph] Ellis who commanded a detachment of militia at Haddonfield." (2 NJA 2:91)

11. "The Liverpool Frigate on Shore on Long Island; little prospect of her being saved, unless got off before Yesterday [2.11.78], as the Wind has been very hard from the Sea, with a Snow Storm [at New York]." (KP 1:148)

12. The day before the engagement with Pulaski, Gen. Washington had sent an express to Pulaski in New Jersey to "afford General Wayne all the assistance in your power, and the rather as the Service in which he is engaged is of great importance." (WW 11:7) Wayne continued to be engaged in securing cattle for Washington's army, but now was equally interested in preventing Stirling and his 42nd regiment from getting cattle for their commissariat.

TENTH TRANSMITTAL
March 8, 1778-April 20, 1778

1. The day after Capt. Alexander Campbell was acquitted, "Mary Figis, Spinster, Tried by the General Court Martial... for Willful and Corrupt perjury on the Trial of Capt. Alexander Campbell is found guilty of the Crime laid to her charge...to be put in the pillory for half an hour, and to be imprisoned for Six Months." (KP 1:561)

2. The three English regiments under Col. Charles Mawhood were "the 17th, 27th and 46th." (Mont. 482)

3. The two ships carrying hay were the Katy and the Mermaid. For an American account of this enterprise, see (2NJA 2:118,119). An English account states that the Alert was retaken by the Experiment, and that the date of the encounter was March 7. (Mont. 481)

4. Baurmeister says: "At Gulph Ferry Mill, fifteen miles from here, is a strong enemy outpost detached from Valley Forge. On the night of the 19th-20th this post sent out a party of sixty men, who crept up close to the Schuylkill opposite the 10th Redoubt,

where they collected some cattle and set fires. The wing adjutant, Captain von Munchhausen, with forty mounted Hessian jaegers under Lieutenant Mertz was so fortunate as to catch up with this party the following morning just before they reached Black Horse. He captured one officer and ten men and killed and wounded several more. The rest of the rebels were lucky to be able to hide behind a swamp. The Jaegers had only one horse killed." (Baur 157)

5. For American accounts of Mawhood's foraging trip, known in American annals as "The Attack on Quintin's and Hancock's Bridge," see (2 NJA 2:144,145; 168-170). For a British account see (Robertson 164-166).

6. These men were Lt. Col. Charles O'Hara, Lt. Col. Humphrey Stephens, and Capt. Richard Fitzpatrick, for the British. (KP 1:564) Representing the Americans were Col. William Grayson, Lt. Col. Robert Hanson Harrison and Lt. Col. Elias Boudinot. (WW 11:213)

7. Gen. Lee was accompanied to Philadelphia by two men, as noted in Joshua Loring's letter to Elias Boudinot of 3.18.78, as follows: "I am to acknowledge the receipt of yours of 8th Inst. inclosing a Pass for Major Williams & myself to go to Phila. with General Lee." (LP 2:380) Logan was commissary of prisoners for the British and Boudinot his counterpart for the Americans. The English officer was Major Griffith Williams. He was "former commander of Burgoyne's artillery. (Baur. 159)

8. The ships were under the convoy of the Thames, a 32-gun ship, and the Daphne, a 20-gun ship.

9. Capt. Muenchhausen did not know that behind Gen. Howe's move to provide a regiment for him was the fact that on April 9, the very day Howe proposed the subject to Gen. von Knyphausen, Howe had received word that the King had given Howe leave to return to England. Further, the Landgrave of Hesse Cassel, probably had no knowledge that Howe had requested of his King permission to be relieved of his command. Undoubtedly the Landgrave's action was taken on the assumption that Howe would be continuing in service and that Muenchhausen would remain his aide, under which conditions it was decided by the Landgrave that it would be better for Muenchhausen to be transferred technically from a grenadier or line regiment, to a garrison regiment. However, with Howe's now impending departure, Muenchhausen was faced with the problem of actually having to serve in a garrison regiment rather than his preferred and former grenadier regiment.

10. This was the Conciliatory Resolution passed by Parliament on February 20.

11. The Virginia carried 28 guns, and was built in 1776, at Baltimore. The Conquerer also was involved in the capture of the Virginia. (Chapelle 65-67)

12. "General Daniel Jones succeeded to the Command of York Island and Posts depending...." arriving there May 3, 1778. (KP 1:150)

13. These were handbills distributed by Gen. Howe, a quantity of which was also sent to Gen. Washington, which he did not distribute.

ELEVENTH TRANSMITTAL
April 21, 1778-May 23, 1778

1. This oath of allegiance, authorized by Congress, was included in Washington's General Orders of May 7, 1778, together with a schedule for administrating the oath, by division, brigade and corps. (WW 11:361)

2. This was the so-called action at Crooked Billet, now Hatboro, Pa. Brig. Gen. John Lacey of the Pennsylvania militia gives his ac-

count in *(1 Pa. A. 6:470,471)*.

3. Allen's Provincials were also known as the "Pennsylvania Loyalists" or The "Pennsylvania Volunteers." Their commander was Col. William Allen of Philadelphia. For his biography see *(Sabine 1:157)*. Clifton's Provincials were also known as the "Roman Catholic Volunteers" later becoming absorbed by the "Volunteers of Ireland." Their commander was Lt. Col. Alfred Clifton.

4. Gen. Erskine, who was quartermaster-general, was in Jersey surveying the area for possible places to cut wood. Capt. Robertson noted, "Went with Sir William To Cooper's Ferry in the Jersey's, to reconnoitre a Proper Place for taking post to secure the cutting of fire wood." *(Robertson 171)*

5. Capt. von Muenchhausen was mistaken regarding the regiment in which Leslie was a colonel. He was colonel of the 64th. *(KP 1:329)*

6. For other details of this expedition see *(Robertson 172; Mont. 490; 2 NJA 2:217,218; WW 11:378,379; New York Gazette, 8.24.78 No. 1401)*.

7. The beautiful home was the Wharton Mansion. *(Loc. cit.)*

8. The white horse was the heraldic emblem of the Dukes of Brunswick, later Kings of Hannover. The House of Hannover succeeded to the British throne in 1714 with the Elector Georg von Hannover, who became King George I. of Britain.

9. Don Quixote, Sancho Panza and Dulcinea were characters in the Cervantes Don Quixote.

10. The first part of the route was "out the Frankford road then turned [westward] at Oxford...." *(Chastellux 1:171)* The rest of the route was via "White march [Whitemarsh] and Plymouth meeting quite in his [Lafayette's] Rear." *(Robertson 172)*

11. The two aides who attained the rank of lieutenant colonel were Maj. Cornelius Cuyler who was made lieutenant colonel of the 55th regiment 10.7.77, and Capt. (late major) Nesbett Balfour who was made lieutenant colonel of the 23rd regiment 1.31.78. Capt. William Gardiner was made major 7.14.77, and Capt. Henry Fox was made major on the same date.

12. The name Manyshall does not appear in army lists consulted.

13. John Montresor entered in his journal "Sunday 24th. At ½ past one this afternoon his Excellency Sir Wm. Howe took his Departure from this city for England, to the great regret of this Army. Wind Southerly and fresh." *(Mont. 493)*

APPENDIX

BRITISH GENERAL STAFF
UNDER GENERAL WILLIAM HOWE

Brig. Gen. James Paterson, adjutant general
Brig. Gen. William Erskine, quartermaster general
Brig. Gen. Samuel Cleaveland, aide de camp
Brig. Gen. James Agnew, aide de camp
Brig. Gen. Alexander Leslie, aide de camp

BRITISH LINE GENERAL OFFICERS
UNDER GENERAL WILLIAM HOWE

Lt. Gen. Henry Clinton	Maj. Gen. Augustine Prevost
Lt. Gen. Charles Cornwallis	Maj. Gen. James Robertson
Lt. Gen. Hugh Percy	Maj. Gen. William Tryon
Maj. Gen. James Grant	Maj. Gen. John Vaughan
Maj. Gen. Charles Grey	Maj. Gen. Thomas Wilson
Maj. Gen. Valentine Jones	Brig. Gen. Edward Matthew
Maj. Gen. Robert Pigot	Brig. Gen. James Pattison
Maj. Gen. Richard Prescott	Brig. Gen. Francis Smith

Note. The ranks of the above general officers were temporary and applicable in America only, including that of Gen. Howe. Staff general officers often performed line duties during campaigns.

HEADQUARTERS STAFF OFFICERS
UNDER GENERAL WILLIAM HOWE

Capt. Robert Mc Kenzie, secretary to the general
Maj. Cornelius Cuyler, aide
Maj. Stephen Kemble, deputy adjutant general
Capt. Henry Bruen, deputy quartermaster general
Capt. John Montresor, chief engineer
Capt. Nesbitt Balfour, aide
Capt. Henry Fox, aide
Capt. William Gardiner, aide
Capt. Henry Knight, aide
Capt. Friedrich von Muenchhausen, aide

BRITISH REGIMENTS
UNDER GENERAL WILLIAM HOWE (1)

4th / The King's Own (2)	356
Col. Studholme Hodgson 11.7.68 (3)	
Lt. Col. Henry Blunt 11.24.75 (4)	
Lt. Col. James Ogilvie 6.4.77	
5th / The Northumberland	307
Col. Hugh Percy 11.7.68	
Lt. Col. William Walcott 1.31.74 (5)	
Lt. Col. William Meadows 11.16.77 (27)	
6th (see note 6)	
7th / The Royal Fuzileers (7)	307
Col. Richard Prescott 11.12.74	
Lt. Col. Alured Clarke 3.10.77 (26)	
10th / The North Lincolnshire	312
Col. Edward Sandford 1.14.63	
Lt. Col. Francis Smith 2.13.62 (8)	
14th (see note 9)	
15th / The Yorkshire East Riding	367
Col. Richard Cavan 9.7.75	
Lt. Col. John Bird 1.13.76 (10)	
Lt. Col. John Maxwell 10.5.77 (15)	
Lt. Col. Joseph Stopford 1.31.78	
16th / The Buckinghamshire (11)	
Col. James Gisborne 3.4.76	
Col. James Robertson 5.14.78	
Lt. Col. Alexander Dickson 1.11.76	
17th / The Leicestershire	233
Col. Robert Monckton 10.25.59	
Lt. Col. Charles Mawhood 10.26.75	
18th (see note 12)	
22nd / The Cheshire	431
Col. Thomas Gage 3.29.62	
Lt. Col. John Campbell 6.24.75	
23rd / The Royal Welsh Fuzileers	353
Col. William Howe 5.11.75	
Lt. Col. Benjamin Bernard 8.28.71	
Lt. Col. William Blakeney 1.30.78	
Lt. Col. Nesbitt Balfour 1.31.78	
26th / Cameronians (13)	341
Col. Adam Gordon 12.27.75	
Lt. Col. Dudley Templer 9.7.68 (14)	
Lt. Col. Charles Stuart 10.26.77	
27th / Inniskilling	324
Col. Eyre Massey 2.19.73	

Lt. Col. John Maxwell 10.26.75 (15)
Lt. Col. William Murray 10.5.77 (16)
Lt. Col. Edward Mitchell 11.3.77 (25)

28th / The North Gloucestershire — 286
Col. Thomas Earle 7.15.73
Col. Charles Grey 3.4.77
Lt. Col. Robert Prescott 9.8.75

33rd / The 1st Yorkshire West Riding — 368
Col. Charles Cornwallis 3.21.66
Lt. Col. James Webster 4.9.74

35th / The Dorsetshire — 315
Col. H. Fletcher Campbell 8.10.64
Lt. Col. Robert Carr 3.5.75 (17)
Lt. Col. James Cockburne 10.30.76

37th / The North Hampshire — 308
Col. Eyre Coote 2.19.73
Lt. Col. Robert Abercromby 11.30.75

38th / The 1st Staffordshire — 314
Col. Robert Pigot 12.11.75 (18)
Lt. Col. William Butler 8.1.75

40th / The 2nd Somersetshire — 300
Col. Robert Hamilton 3.20.70
Lt. Col. James Grant 7.26.60 (18)
Lt. Col. Thomas Musgrave 8.28.76

42nd / The Royal Highland — 597
Col. John Murray 4.25.45
Lt. Col. Thomas Stirling 9.7.71
Lt. Col. William Murray (15)

43rd / The Monmouthshire — 380
Col. George Cary 9.26.66
Lt. Col. George Clerk 2.8.75 (19)
Lt. Col. James Marsh 8.28.76

44th / The East Essex — 312
Col. James Abercromby 3.13.56
Col. James Agnew 4.4.76 (20)
Lt. Col. Henry Hope 10.5.77

45th / The 1st Nottinghamshire — 393
Col. William Haviland 6.1.67
Lt. Col. Henry Monckton 7.25.71

46th / The South Devonshire — 312
Col. John Vaughan 5.11.75
Lt. Col. Enoch Markham 5.11.75

47th (see note 21)

49th / The Hertfordshire — 335
Col. Alexander Maitland 5.25.68
Lt. Col. Henry Calder 7.12.73

50th (see note 22)

52nd / The Oxfordshire — 253
Col. John Clavering 4.1.62
Col. Cyrus Trapaud 5.14.78
Lt. Col. Valentine Jones 3.4.60 (23)
Lt. Col. Mungo Campbell 6.15.76 (24)
Lt. Col. Edward Mitchell 10.7.77 (25)
Lt. Col. Christopher French 11.3.77

54th / The West Norfolk — 440
Col. Moriscoe Frederick 4.30.70
Lt. Col. Alured Clarke 10.26.75 (26)
Lt. Col. Andrew Bruce 3.10.77

55th / The Westmoreland — 261
Col. Robert Pigot 9.7.75 (18)
Col. James Grant 12.11.75
Lt. Col. William Meadows 9.22.75 (27)
Lt. Col. Cornelius Cuyler 11.16.77

57th / The West Middlesex — 420
Col. John Irwine 11.4.67
Lt. Col. John Campbell 5.1.73

59th (see note 28)

60th (see note 29)

63rd / The West Suffolk — 450
Col. Francis Grant 11.5.68
Lt. Col. James Paterson 6.15.63 (30)

64th / The 2nd Staffordshire — 395
Col. John Pomeroy 1.1.66
Col. Alexander Leslie 10.19.75 (31)

65th (see note 32)

71st [1st battalion] (33) — all batts. 992
Col. Simon Fraser 10.25.75
Lt. Col. William Erskine 11.23.75 (34)

71st [2nd battalion]
Col. Simon Fraser 10.25.75
Lt. Col. Archibald Campbell 11.23.75

1st Light Infantry (35) — all batts. 1130
Maj. Thomas Musgrave (36)
Lt. Col. Robert Abercromby

2nd Light Infantry (35)
Maj. John Maitland

1st Grenadiers (35) — all batts. 1080
Lt. Col. William Meadows

2nd Grenadiers (35)
Lt. Col. Henry Monckton

1st Guards (37) — all batts. 887
Lt. Col. [Henry] Trelawny

2nd Guards (37)
Lt. Col. [James] Ogilvie

16th Light Dragoons (38) — 353
Col. John Burgoyne 3.18.63
Lt. Col. William Harcourt 6.24.68

17th Light Dragoons (38) — 384
Col. George Preston 11.9.70
Lt. Col. Samuel Birch 4.24.73

Royal Artillery (39) — 597
Brig. Gen. Samuel Cleaveland 4.4.76
Brig. Gen. James Pattison

1st & 2nd Marines (see note 40)

Ferguson's Rifles (41) — 130
Capt. Patrick Ferguson 9.1.68

Total — 15,323

PROVINCIAL GENERAL OFFICERS
UNDER GENERAL WILLIAM HOWE

Brig. Gen. Oliver De Lancey
Brig. Gen. Montfort Brown
Brig. Gen. Cortland Skinner

PROVINCIAL REGIMENTS
UNDER GENERAL WILLIAM HOWE (42)
New York Units

New York Volunteers (43) — 206
Capt. Archibald Campbell (44)
Capt. Alexander Grant (45)
Lt. Col. George Turnbull (46)

1st battalion De Lancey's (47) — 235
Brig. Gen. Oliver De Lancey (48)
Lt. Col. John Harris Cruger

2nd battalion De Lancey's — 181
Col. George Brewerton

Lt. Col. Stephen De Lancey	
3rd battalion De Lancey's	157
Col. Gabriel Ludlow	
Lt. Col. Richard Hewlett	
Prince of Wales American Regiment (49)	292
Brig. Gen. Montfort Brown	
Lt. Col. Thomas Pattinson	
King's American Regiment (50)	337
Col. Edmund Fanning (51)	
Lt. Col. George Campbell	
King's Orange Rangers (52)	173
Lt. Col. John Bayard	
Loyal American Regiment (53)	166
Col. Beverley Robinson	
Lt. Col. George Turnbull (54)	
Lt. Col. Beverly Robinson Jr.	

New Jersey Units

1st New Jersey Volunteers (55)	51
Lt. Col. Elisha Lawrence (56)	
2nd New Jersey Volunteers	144
Lt. Col. John Morris	
3rd New Jersey Volunteers	126
Lt. Col. Edward Vaughan Dongan (57)	
Lt. Col. Isaac Allen	
4th New Jersey Volunteers	207
Lt. Col. Abraham Van Buskirk	
5th New Jersey Volunteers	139
Lt. Col. Joseph Barton	
6th New Jersey Volunteers	94
Lt. Col. Isaac Allen (58)	
West New Jersey Volunteers (59)	est. 50
Lt. Col. John Vandyke	

Miscellaneous Units

Queen's American Rangers (60)	398
Lt. Col. Robert Rogers (61)	
Lt. Col. Christopher French (61)	
Maj. James Wemys (62)	
Maj. John Graves Simcoe	
Pennsylvania Loyalists (63)	120
Lt. Col. William Allen	
Maryland Loyalists (64)	189
Lt. Col. James Chalmers	
Roman Catholic Volunteers (65)	174
Lt. Col. Alfred Clifton	
Guides and Pioneers (66)	124
Col. Beverley Robinson	
Maj. Samuel Holland	
Independent Companies (67)	48
Lt. Col. Timothy Hierlihy	
Pennsylvania Light Dragoons (68)	102
1st Troop Philadelphia Light Dragoons (69)	
Capt. Richard Hovenden	
Chester County Troop Light Dragoons (70)	
Capt. Jacob James	
Bucks County Troop Light Dragoons (71)	
Capt. Thomas Sandford	
Total	3,713

HESSIAN HEADQUARTERS STAFF
UNDER GENERAL VON KNYPHAUSEN (72)

Maj. Gen. [Johann Daniel] Stirn
[Col. Henrich Julius] von Kospoth (73)
[Lt. Col. Johann] von Cochenhausen, quartermaster general
Maj. [Carl Leopold] Baurmeister, acting adjutant general
[Capt. Carl Ludwig] Marquard, aide
[Capt. Ernst Friedrich] von Westerhagen, aide
[1st Lt. Joachim Hieronimus von] Bassewitz, aide
[Lt. Col. William] Faucitt, aide (74)
Capt. [George] Beckwith, aide extraordinary (75)
[Capt. Henry] Phipps, aide (76)

HESSIAN LINE OFFICERS
UNDER GENERAL VON KNYPHAUSEN

Maj. Gen. Carl von Bose
Maj. Gen. Johann Christoph von Huyne
Maj. Gen. Friedrich Wilhelm von Lossberg
Maj. Gen. Werner von Mirbach
Maj. Gen. Martin Conrad Schmidt

Note. The ranks of the above general officers were temporary and applicable in America only. Staff general officers often performed line duties during campaigns.

HESSIAN REGIMENTS
UNDER GENERAL VON KNYPHAUSEN

Buenau Infantry	480
Col. Rudolph von Buenau (77)	
Lt. Col. Johann Adam Scheffer	
Combined regiment (later Woellwarth)	467
Col. Wolfgang Friedrich von Woellwarth	
Capt. Wilhelm von Wilmowsky (78)	
Lt. Col. Balthasar Brethauer (79)	
Ditfourth Fuzileer	540
Col. Carl von Bose (80)	
Col. Max von Westerhagen	
Lt. Col. Ferdinand Henrich von Schuler	
Donop Infantry	544
Col. David Ephriam von Gosen	
Lt. Col. Carl Philip Heymell (81)	
Lt. Col. Erasmus Ernst Hinthe	
Huyne Infantry	434
Col. Johann Christoph von Huyne	
Lt. Col. Hubert Frantz Kurtz	
Landgraf Infantry	431
Col. Henrich Julius von Kospoth	
Lt. Col. Carl Christian von Ramrodt	
Leib Infantry (Du Corps)	598
Col. Friedrich Wilhelm von Wurmb	
Lt. Col. Otto von Linsing	
Mirbach Fuzileer	553
Col. Justus Henrich von Block	
Lt. Col. Justus Henrich von Schieck (82)	
Lt. Col. Hans Friedrich Biesenrodt	
Prince Carl Infantry	569
Col. Johann Wilhelm Schreiber	
Lt. Col. Wilhelm von Loewenstein	

Prince Hereditary Fuzileer (Erbprinz)	449
Col. Carl Wilhelm von Hackenberg	
Lt. Col. Johann von Cochenhausen	
Stein Infantry	316
Col. Franz Erdmann Carl von Stein	
Lt. Col. Arnold Schlemmer	
Truembach Infantry	535
Col. Ernst von Bischhausen	
Lt. Col. Borries Hilmar von Muenchhausen	
Wissenbach Infantry	356
Lt. Col. Friedrich Porbeck (83)	
Lt. Col. Carl Kitzel	
Koehler Grenadier (84)	397
Lt. Col. Johann Christoph Koehler	
Lengerke Grenadier	440
Lt. Col. George Emanuel Lengerke	
Linsing Grenadier	437
Lt. Col. Christian von Linsing	
Minnigerode Grenadier	430
Lt. Col. Friedrich Ludwig von Minnigerode	
Jaeger Rifle Corps	293
Lt. Col. Ludwig Johann Adolph von Wurmb	
Artillery Corps (85)	655
Total	8,924

MISCELLANEOUS GERMAN REGIMENTS
UNDER GENERAL VON KNYPHAUSEN

1st Anspach-Bayreuth	548
Col. Friedrich Ludwig Albrecht von Eyb	
2nd Anspach-Bayreuth	539
Col. Friedrich August Valentin Vort von Salzburg	
Anspach-Bayreuth Jaeger Corps (86)	218
Waldeck	407
Col. Johann Friedrich von Hanxleben	
Total	1,712
Grand total troops under General William Howe (87)	29,672

VARIOUS BRITISH BRIGADING
UNDER GENERAL WILLIAM HOWE

BOSTON 1.21.76 *(KP1 :298,299)*
Robertson: 38,43,44,1st & 2nd Marines
Pigot: Musgrave lt. inf., Wemys grs.,17,45,55
Jones: 5,22*,35,52,65
Grant: 4,40,47,49,Agnew grs.
Smith: Clarke lt. inf., 10,22*,63
*One of these, as printed, is probably 23.

HALIFAX 5.15.76 *(KP1 :355)*
2nd / Pigot:5,49,35
6th / Agnew:23,64,44
5th / Smith:43,63,22
1st / Robertson:27,45,4
4th / Grant:17,55,40
3rd / Jones:38,52,10

NEW YORK 8.16.76 *(Glyn 6)*
1st / Robertson:15,45,27,4
5th / Smith:43,63,54,22
4th / Grant:17,46,55,40
3rd / Jones:37,52,38,10
6th / Agnew:23,57,64,44
2nd / Pigot:5,35,49,28

NEW JERSEY 5.8.77 *(PRO-CO5 :94:212)*
Matthew:Guards,lt. inf,grs.
1st / Vaughan: 4,23,38,49
2nd / Grant:10,27,40,52
3rd / Grey:15,33,44,55
4th / Agnew:17,37,46,64
5th / Leslie:71
Reserve:42

NEW BRUNSWICK 6.12.77 *(Br. Jnl.)*
1st / Trelawny:1st Gds.,23,40 (88)
2nd / Agnew:4,15,44
3rd / Markham:10,27,46 (89)
4th / Mawhood:17,38,64 (90)
Stirling:33,42 (91)
Calder:5,49,52,37 (92)

ENROUTE TO PHILADELPHIA 7.18.77 *(Muench.)*
1st / Vaughan:4,23,28,49
2nd / Grant:5,10,27,40,55
3rd / Grey:15,17,42,44
4th / Agnew:33,37,46,64
5th / Leslie:71,Ferguson rifles

VARIOUS HESSIAN BRIGADING
UNDER GENERAL WILLIAM HOWE

STATEN ISLAND 1776 *(HV 39)*
Mirbach / Block, Mirbach, Donop, Wutgenau, Prince Hereditary
Stirn / Linsing, Leib, Prince Carl, Ditfourth, Truembach
Lossberg / Koehler, Huyne, Stein, Knyphausen
Schmidt / Minnigerode, Lossberg, Rall, Buenau

NEW JERSEY 5.8.77 *(PRO-CO5 :94:212)*
Donop / Linsing, Minnigerode, Lengerke, Koehler (93)
Stirn / Leib, Mirbach, Donop, Combined
Bischhausen / Prince Charles, Truembach, Stein, Wissenbach, Prince Hereditary (94)
Lossberg / Landgraf, Ditfourth, Huyne, Buenau

ENROUTE TO PHILADELPHIA 7.18.77 *(Muench.)*
Donop / Linsing, Minnigerode, Lengerke
Stirn / Leib, Mirbach, Donop
Loos / Combined, Hessian Jaegers, Anspach-Bayreuth Jaegers (95)

APPENDIX NOTES

(1) Unless otherwise noted, the material in this appendix is taken from three primary sources: *A List of the General and Field Officers, as they Rank in the Army....*London 1776-1783; *Kemble Papers,* being the journal of Maj. Stephen Kemble, adjutant general

of the British army in America and Gen. Howe's Order Book, published in two volumes by The New York Historical Society 1874-1875; British and German troop return of men fit for duty, Public Record Office, London, dated 5.8.77. *(PRO-CO 5:94:212)* Only those regiments or units that served in America under Gen. Howe from 1776-1778 are covered in this appendix, and only for that period. Neither Gen. Gage's nor Gen. Clinton's periods of command are covered. The date given after an officer's name is the date he attained that rank in the regiment.

(2) Before 1751 British regiments were named for commanding colonels of regiments. In 1751, King George II gave all British regiments number designations, which system prevailed throughout the period of the American Revolution. It was not until after the Revolution, in 1782, that regiments were given county names. In the 1783 Army List, numerical designations were retained, but the county affiliations were added in parentheses.

(3) Although Hodgson was colonel of the 4th regiment, which was the highest regimental rank attainable, he was, at the same time, a lieutenant general in the army. Thus, he held two ranks, his regimental rank and his army rank. Although being colonel of 4th regiment, there was no requirement that Hodgson must be with his regiment or even in the same theater of operation. In fact Hodgson did not even come to America with his regiment. However, those regimental colonels who did come to America, and whose regiments also came, did not serve with their regiments, but served in various brigade, division or headquarters posts, completely apart from their regiments.

(4) Actual field command of a British regiment generally was held by a lieutenant colonel. The listing here of a second regimental lieutenant colonel indicates that the first one was either promoted, retired, seriously wounded, killed, or on extended duty. For example, Lt. Col. George Maddison retired, and was replaced by Lt. Col. Blunt. Blunt in turn was replaced by Lt. Col. James Ogilvie when Blunt carried Gen. Howe's letter of July 7, 1776 to Lord Germain at Whitehall, which extended voyage called for a replacement. In some cases, a lieutenant colonel was not immediately, or in the exceptional case ever, replaced, leaving regimental field command of the regiment to the ranking major. This was the case in the 10th regiment where Maj. John Vatass commanded that regiment after Lt. Col. Francis Smith was made brigadier general.

(5) Walcott died of wounds 11.16.77.

(6) The 6th arrived from the West Indies and was drafted 12.5.76.

(7) Prescott was lieutenant colonel of this regiment prior to becoming its colonel. The bulk of the 7th was captured during the invasion of Canada in 1775; the balance was left in Canada and drafted by the 4th; prisoners were exchanged before the end of 1776, and regiment reinstated in the line at New York, rebuilt to strength, and arrived at Philadelphia 11.18.77.

(8) Smith was made brigadier general by 1.21.76, and the command of the 10th was left with Maj. John Vatass. The regiment was greatly depleted during the Philadelphia campaign resulting in the regiment being drafted 10.25.78.

(9) The 14th was at St. Augustine, Illinois and New Providence in 1774; part was in Virginia and the back country in 1775, where many were cut off; a few men got to Boston and Halifax, then held by the British; those who reached British sanctuary were drafted at New York 12.5.75. Another part of the regiment, which had been at St. Augustine, was drafted in 7.77.

(10) Bird died of wounds received at Germantown 10.4.77.

(11) Return of troops not shown on Howe's report of 5.8.77, as the regiment had departed for Pensacola, Fla., 1.20.77. Total as of 5.1.1780 return was 284. *(PRO-CO 5:99:254)*

(12) The 18th was in Philadelphia and inland in 1774; in 1775, five companies were in New York and two were in Illinois; in 1775, three companies went to Boston and were incorporated into units there 12.3.75.

(13) The 26th was captured during the invasion of Canada in 1775; prisoners were exchanged before the end of 1776; regiment rebuilt to strength in 1777. British Army Lists for 1783, 1784, and 1785 do not show a county name for the 26th. It first appears in the 1786 list as "Cameronians."

(14) Lt. Col. Templer retired 10.26.77, probably about the time the regiment was being rebuilt.

(15) Maxwell transferred from the 27th to the 15th, 10.8.77, and Murray of the 42nd took his place in the 27th.

(16) Murray deceased 11.3.77.

(17) Carr died of wounds 10.30.76.

(18) Grant made colonel of the 55th 12.11.75, replacing Col. Pigot who became colonel of the 38th. Pigot and Grant made major generals 5.12.76.

(19) Clerk became barrack master general 6.4.76.

(20) Agnew was lieutenant colonel of this regiment prior to becoming its colonel. This was the date his colonelcy became official as noted in the *Kemble Papers*. Agnew became major general 5.11.76.

(21) The 47th was in New York in 1774; to Boston in 1774; to Canada in 1776.

(22) The 50th arrived at Staten Island 11.8.76 and was drafted.

(23) Jones made brigadier general 5.12.76.

(24) Campbell lost in attack on Forts Montgomery and Clinton 10.77.

(25) Mitchell transferred to 27th 10.13.77.

(26) Clarke transferred to 7th 3.10.77.

(27) Meadows transferred to 5th 11.16.77.

(28) The 59th in Nova Scotia and Newfoundland in 1774; to Boston in 1774; incorporated into corps at Boston 12.3.75.

(29) The 1st and 2nd battalions of the 60th were raised in America; the 3rd and 4th in England; in 1776 three companies were in South Carolina with detachment at St. Augustine; 1777 detachments at Pensacola, and St. Augustine; 1778 detachments at Charleston, St. Augustine, and in Georgia; detachments also in Jamaica, St. Vincents and Antigua during 1776, 1777, 1778.

(30) Paterson made adjutant general of the army 4.18.76.

(31) Leslie made brigadier general and aide to Gen. Howe 4.4.76 at Halifax. He had been lieutenant colonel of this regiment prior to becoming its colonel.

(32) The 65th at Boston 1776; drafted at Halifax 5.22.76.

(33) The 71st was disbanded at the end of the war. The 2nd battalion ended its service in 1783 and the 1st battalion in 1784. A 3rd battalion of the 71st was formed during the war and was shown on Ens. Glyn's order of battle dated 8.16.76. Capt. Muenchhausen also mentions the 3rd battalion in his diary entry 12.9.77. Little is known of its action. A Hessian diary under date of 9.14.77 states "Colonel [Alexander] McDonald and his three Scottish battalions took possession of Wilmington...." *(Heusser)*

(34) Erskine listed as brigadier general in a return 8.16.76; made quartermaster general 10.7.76.

(35) A standard British regiment of foot consisted of 10 companies, two of which were called "flank companies," one being a light infantry company and the other a grenadier company. In 1776 at Boston, a few light infantry companies were formed into two units, referred to as "Musgrave's and Clarke's light infantry." At the same time some grenadier companies were formed into units, referred to as "Wemys' and Agnew's grenadiers." On 5.14.76 at Halifax, 18 light infantry companies were formed into two battalions with Maj. Musgrave and Maj.

Dundass commanding the 1st battalion and Maj. Maitland and Maj. Strausbenzee commanding the 2nd. At the same time, 22 grenadier companies were formed into two battalions with Lt. Col. Meadows and Maj. Mitchell commanding the 1st battalion and Lt. Col. Monckton and Maj. Stuart commanding the 2nd.

As early as 10.15.76 an additional light infantry and an additional grenadier battalion were formed. The 3rd light infantry was commanded by Maj. Johnson, and the 3rd grenadier battalion was commanded by Maj. Marsh and Maj. Stuart. These additional battalions of light infantry and grenadiers are mentioned in Maj. Kemble's orders of 10.16.76 and in Ens. Glyn's order of battle of 8.16.76, but little is heard of these units after that. Ens. Glyn shows four grenadier battalions, the 1st commanded by Lt. Col. Meadows and Maj. Mitchell, the 2nd by Lt. Col. Monckton and Maj. Dilkes, the 3rd by Maj. Marsh and the 4th by Honble. Maj. Stuart. According to Kemble, the 3rd battalion light infantry and the 3rd battalion grenadiers departed with Gen. Clinton in Nov. 1776, for the invasion of Rhode Island, but they do not appear as units on subsequent returns of troops at that post.

(36) Musgrave wounded 10.18.76 and replaced by Abercromby.

(37) In England there were three regiments of Horse Guards and three battalions of Foot Guards. The 1st foot was the Grenadier Guards, the 2nd foot was the Cold Stream Guards and the 3rd foot was the Scot Guards. Only Foot Guards were sent to America, some men from each of the three battalions. In America they were organized as the 1st and 2nd battalion of Guards. The 1st Guards consisted of four regiments, one of which was a grenadier regiment. Attached to the 1st Guards was one brigade company. The 2nd Guards consisted of five regiments, one of which was a light infantry regiment. All regiments and the brigade company were commanded by lieutenant colonels. Each regiment consisted of about 100 men.

Ens. Thomas Glyn of the 1st battalion of Guards listed all lieutenant colonels of the Guards as of approximately 8.16.76, as follows: 1st battalion, Lt. Col. Sir George Osborne (grenadier regiment), Lt. Col. Howard, Lt. Col. Hyde, Lt. Col. Sir John Westerley, Lt. Col. Cox (brigade company); 2nd battalion, Lt. Col. Twisterton, Lt. Col. Ogilvie, Lt. Col. Trelawny, Lt. Col. Grenville, Lt. Col. Martin (light infantry regiment). Glyn further showed Brig. Gen. Mathew as commander of the Guards with Lt. Col. Trelawny commander of the 1st battalion and Lt. Col. Ogilvie commander of the 2nd battalion.

(38) In 1776 light dragoons were augmented by the addition of 34 dismounted dragoons to each of 6 troops of a regiment of mounted light dragoons. *(KP 1:382)*

(39) It was the 4th battalion of Royal Artillery that came to America. The date given for Cleaveland's commission is when it became official as noted in the *Kemble Papers*.

(40) The marines were at Boston in 1776 but upon going to Halifax with the British army, the marines remained there.

(41) Ferguson's rifles were men detached from light infantry companies and trained in the use of a breech loading rifle developed by Ferguson. There were 130 men in the unit when they departed for Philadelphia in July 1777, with Gen. Howe. After the Battle of Brandywine they were so depleted in number that the unit was dissolved, and the men returned to their former units.

(42) This tabulation does not include the two pre-1776 regiments that went from Boston to Halifax with the British army and remained there. Nor does it include the one regiment that was recruited at Halifax and remained there. Further, it does not include the numerous regiments of Provincials formed after Gen. Howe's departure from America on May 23, 1778 nor changes in command and name after that date. Regimental totals are from British returns 1.1.78, and 3.24.78. *(PRO-CO 5:7:504 & 447)*

(43) Raised in New York 1776; mustered at Halifax 1776; returned with army; referred to in early reports as "Grant's Companies" or "New York Companies;" became New York Volunteers in 1777; in 1782-83 designated 3rd American Regiment.

(44) Campbell killed 3.16.1777.

(45) Grant killed at Ft. Montgomery 10.77.

(46) Turnbull from Loyal American Regiment.

(47) Brigade of three regiments ordered raised under De Lancey 7.4.76.

(48) De Lancey acted as brigade commander.

(49) Raised by Brown, former governor of the Bahamas; regiment also known as Prince of Wales American Volunteers.

(50) Regiment also known as Fanning's Associated Refugees; in 1782-83 regiment designated 4th American Regiment.

(51) Fanning was former secretary to Royal Governor Tryon of New York.

(52) Mounted rifle corps organized at New York by John Coffin who fought for the British at Bunker Hill.

(53) Also known as Robinson's Corps.

(54) Turnbull transferred to New York Volunteers 1777.

(55) Brigade of six regiments ordered raised 7.4.76 under Brig. Gen. Cortland Skinner, attorney general of New Jersey in 1754 and speaker of the House of Assembly from 1765. Brigade also known as Skinner's Greens.

(56) Lawrence taken prisoner on Staten Island 8.22.77 and regiment consolidated with the 5th, as the 5th, in the fall of 1778.

(57) Dongan wounded on Staten Island 8.22.77 and died within three days. Maj. Robert Drummond commanded the regiment until the fall of 1778 when the 3rd was consolidated with the 6th, as the 3rd, with Col. Isaac Allen of the 6th taking command.

(58) Allen moved to the command of the 3rd in the fall of 1778.

(59) Raised by Daniel Coxe, Trenton, New Jersey lawyer, in the winter of 1777. The regiment was first commanded by Capt. Daniel Gozens, and was incorporated into the New Jersey Volunteers in 1778.

(60) Earlier known as Rogers Rangers for Robert Rogers who raised the corps mainly in New York and Connecticut. Next it became Wemys' Corps for its then commander James Wemys, then Simcoe's Corps for John Graves Simcoe, and finally in 1782-83 it was designated the 1st American Regiment.

(61) Rogers is said to have been replaced in October 1776 after being "mauled by an American surprise attack at Mamaroneck in October 1776." This same authority says that French commanded the unit until May 1777 when James Wemys was given command. *(MC&H XXIV #1,20)*

(62) Wemys was replaced by Simcoe 10.15.77, with Wemys returning to his post as aide de camp to Maj. Gen. Robertson.

(63) Raised in 1777; known also as Allen's Provincials or Pennsylvania Volunteers.

(64) Raised in 1777; known also as Chalmers' Provincials; named for George Chalmers, prominent Loyalist of Baltimore, Md.

(65) Raised in 1777; in 1778 incorporated into Volunteers of Ireland.

(66) The name of this unit accurately describes its makeup: surveyors, woodsmen and the like. Capt. Samuel Holland, who commanded the unit from 1776 to some time in 1778, had previously been British Surveyor General of the Northern District. Capt. Robert Campbell, New Jersey Surveyor, also served in this unit.

(67) Consisted of two companies raised in 1777; in 1782 absorbed into the Nova Scotia Volunteers.

(68) The three troops organized into a squadron under Lt. Col. Watson in May 1778. Became a part of British (or Cathcart's)

Legion in 1778.

(69) Hovenden commissioned 11.7.77; troop raised in November and December 1777; mustered into service 1.8.78.

(70) Raised in Chester County, Pa. in January 1778; mustered at Philadelphia 2.5.78.

(71) Mustered at Philadelphia 4.24.78.

(72) This is only a partial list. Deputies, assistants, chaplains, etc. are also given. The staff of Gen. von Heister, who was replaced by Gen. von Knyphausen 6.21.77, may or may not have been precisely the same. (StAM 12.2.8659 b)

(73) Kospoth was referred to as a colonel in Hessian records as late as April 18, 1778 and as a major general as early as May 14, 1779. (Baur. 274)

(74) Faucitt is identified as of the British Guards. (Baur. 367)

(75) Beckwith is identified as of the 37th British regiment. (KP 1:564)

(76) Phipps is identified as of the British Guards. (Baur. 232 note)

(77) The Hessians had a somewhat different system from the British. Each regiment had a "commander" and a "colonel." The commander was an honorary rank, and the colonel was actually the field commander. In some cases, one man held both posts, but usually the commander was a major general, and, if he was in America, he was serving as a division commander or on the German general staff. However, because there was no brigadier general rank in the German army, most of the colonels were drawn off from their regiments to serve as brigade commanders or on headquarters staff duty. Thus, the end result turned out to be much like British service where lieutenant colonels, in most cases, actually were the field commanders of regiments. And still similar to British service, lieutenant colonels who were drawn off for other service, sometimes were not replaced, in which cases actual field command of regiments fell to ranking majors.

(78) After the capture of the Rall, Knyphausen and Lossberg regiments at Trenton on 12.26.76, Capt. Wilmowsky of the Prince Carl regiment took over temporary command of the few men who were able to escape. As new recruits came to America from Germany in 1777, this regiment was rebuilt and renamed Woellwarth.

(79) Brethauer of the Rall regiment had been one of the captured prisoners at Trenton and had been exchanged in 1777. Brethauer died of wounds received at the Battle of Red Bank, as noted by Capt. von Muenchhausen on 10.26.77.

(80) Bose was replaced as colonel commander effective 5.7.77.

(81) Heymell's ship captured and towed into Egg Harbor, N.J. in October 1777. He was paroled in August 78.

(82) Von Schieck was killed at the Battle of Red Bank 10.22.77.

(83) Porbeck replaced September 1777.

(84) Grenadier battalions were formed from grenadier companies of the other regiments before coming to America.

(85) The artillery was divided among the various regiments and had no regimental structure of its own. One regiment showed in a return the following: 1 lieutenant, 2 fireworkers, 1 drummer, 15 gunners, 2 drivers, 7 loading personnel. Another 1777 return showed a special artillery company composed of the following: 5 officers, 12 non-coms., 1 surgeon, 3 drummers, 129 men, total 150 men.

(86) Unit integrated with Hessian Jaegers 6.12.77.

(87) This total does not include garrisons at East and West Florida, Georgia, Bermuda, Providence and Nova Scotia, all under Howe's command. Nor does the total include Canadian troops under Maj. Gen. Guy Carleton and Lt. Gen. John Burgoyne who held commands that were not under Gen. Howe.

(88) This was Lt. Col. Henry Trelawny serving in a brigade command capacity.

(89) This was Lt. Col. Enoch Markham serving in a brigade command capacity.

(90) This was Lt. Col. Charles Mawhood serving in a brigade command capacity.

(91) This was Lt. Col. Thomas Stirling serving in a brigade command capacity.

(92) This was Lt. Col. Henry Calder serving in a brigade command capacity.

(93) This was Col. Carl Emil Ulrich von Donop serving in a brigade command capacity.

(94) This was Col. Ernst von Bischhausen serving in a brigade command capacity.

(95) This was Col. Johann August von Loos serving in a brigade command capacity. Baurmeister mentions "Stirn's and Woellwarth's brigades" in January 1778, suggesting that Col. von Woellwarth, by this date colonel of the Old Combined regiment but now bearing his name, was commanding the brigade that was earlier commanded by von Loos. (Baur. 148)

Editorial note. There is no known surviving likeness of Captain Friedrich von Muenchhausen, and there is some question as to whether there is a surviving likeness of General William Howe. The widely reproduced portrait of an officer said to be General William Howe, standing by a battery, one hand on hip, and leaning an elbow on a masonry wall, appears to be fictitious. The mezzotint engraving dated "November 10, 1777," and signed "Corbutt," a pseudonym used by an 18th century engraver named Richard Purcell, is one of a series of 13 portraits of generals and admirals popular at the time. These 13 mezzotints are listed in John Chalomer Smith's catalogue of British mezzotint portraits under the title "Officers of the War of Independence in America."

While the uniforms and decorations of all 13 officers in the series are probably correct for the period of the Revolution, their faces seem to have a look-alike appearance, suggesting that, for the most part, they were not done from life, nor copied from authentic portraits. Further, Richard Purcell died in 1765, thus, he could not have been the engraver during the period of the Revolution, of the subject mezzotint, despite the fact that it is marked "Corbutt delinit et fecit." General Howe, at the time of Richard Purcell's death, had attained only the army rank of colonel, and was serving in Ireland.

Another frequently reproduced engraving said to be that of General William Howe is signed "J. Chapman." Miss Elizabeth Roth, Keeper of Prints, New York Public Library, suggests that it might be the work of John Chapman, British engraver, active 1792-1823. William Howe did not die until 1814 so there is the possibility that the engraving could have been made from life, although Howe would have been 63 years old when Chapman's earliest known engraving appears. Other unsigned engravings purporting to be likenesses of General William Howe have been examined, but each of them, including the signed ones discussed above, have the appearance of being a different person.

There is another slight hope that a likeness of General William Howe has survived. Jonathan Trumbull, painting in London under Benjamin West, completed a work in 1786 titled the "Battle of Bunker's Hill," which shows General Howe in the center background, among numerous other figures. As to whether Trumbull sought out Howe for a sitting when he produced his Bunker's Hill painting, there is no information available. Theodore Sizer in his book *The Works of Colonel Jonathan Trumbull,* New Haven, 1967, has only this to say about its being a possible Howe likeness "if from life before 1786..."

INDEX

Note: Both diary and annotations are indexed. The introduction and appendix material are not indexed.